THE W.T. GRANT COMPANY

THE W.T. GRANT COMPANY

KNOWN FOR VALUES

ERIC A. JOHNSON

Published by The History Press
An imprint of Arcadia Publishing
Charleston, SC
www.historypress.com

Copyright © 2025 by Eric A. Johnson

All rights reserved

First published 2025

Manufactured in the United States

ISBN 9781467170086
Hardcover ISBN 9781540299833

Library of Congress Control Number: 2025943939

Notice: The information in this book is true and complete to the best of our knowledge. It is offered without guarantee on the part of the author or The History Press. The author and The History Press disclaim all liability in connection with the use of this book.

All rights reserved. No part of this book may be reproduced or transmitted in any form whatsoever without prior written permission from the publisher except in the case of brief quotations embodied in critical articles and reviews.

CONTENTS

FOREWORD

What sort of a man creates an international company that covers much of the continent and lasts for most of a century and also creates a charitable foundation that spans the globe and bears a perpetual legacy to support scientific discoveries to help people live happy and successful lives? William T. Grant was that sort of man. In this book, readers will learn about the man, the company and the foundation.

In 2025, we commemorate fifty-three years since the death of William T. Grant in 1972 at the age of ninety-six. The early years after his death were not kind to his legacy, as the company that bore his name entered into what was at the time the second-largest bankruptcy in the history of the United States. But the decades since have burnished Grant's legacy, both as an innovative businessman and as a visionary who saw a role for social science research in answering the pressing questions of the day. As the eighth president of the William T. Grant Foundation, I help ensure that we continue to fulfill our mission of supporting research to improve the lives of young people.

Dr. Adam Gamoran, president, William T. Grant Foundation. *Author's photo.*

In this unique volume, Eric A. Johnson has captured the spirit of the man, the ethos of the company and the aims of the foundation. Decade by decade, Johnson explores the story of the company, from its founding and expansion to its distinctive developments (for example, did you

William T. Grant Foundation president Dr. Adam Gamoran in June 2024 with the three board of trustees chairs under which he has served. Pictured from left are Russell Pennoyer (chair, 2015–21), Gamoran (president, 2013–), Scott Evans (chair, 2021–present) and Henry Gooss (chair, 2009–15). *William T. Grant Foundation.*

know that W.T. Grant stores were not five-and-dimes, but pitched their stock to customers who would pay a quarter?) and its eventual demise. In parallel, Johnson tells the story of William T. Grant the man, whose vaunted leadership drove the company for six decades. Through that story, we learn of Grant's motivation to start a charitable foundation for supporting research that, he believed, would be transformative in illuminating ways for ordinary people to achieve their potential. Tellingly, that belief—that research can be a valuable input to policies and practices that shape our lives—continues to guide the foundation today.

At one level, this book is a work of nostalgia. Most large dry goods stores, like Grants, have long since closed, replaced by a 24/7 online marketplace accessible from anywhere. Johnson looks back fondly at an era when a trip to a store would be an outing, and those who remember the W.T. Grant stores largely look back on them with affection. At another level, however, this book is oriented to the future. Not only does it offer lessons from the career of a successful businessman, but it also concludes with insights about how great wealth can be deployed to advance science and better the human condition. In this sense, a nostalgic look back can still help guide us for the future.

—DR. ADAM GAMORAN, President,
William T. Grant Foundation

ACKNOWLEDGEMENTS

Having written three local history books with Arcadia Publishing and thousands of magazine and newspaper articles and columns over more than three decades as a professional wordsmith, I've found that while it is true that crafting a story at the keyboard is largely a solitary endeavor, the larger creative process surrounding that writing is anything but, requiring the supporting contributions of many people in myriad ways, both large and small.

The creation of *The W.T. Grant Company: Known for Values* was no exception. Like most worthwhile endeavors, moving the book from a conceptual idea to a bound, printed and published reality was accomplished with the assistance, support and encouragement of many individuals and organizations.

I am extremely grateful to The History Press acquisitions editors J. Banks Smither and his successor, Mike Kinsella, for their enthusiastic belief in, and support of, bringing the rich legacy of retailer-philanthropist William Thomas Grant (1876–1972), the W.T. Grant Company department store chain (1906–76) and the enduring charitable William T. Grant Foundation (1936–) into a single, comprehensive volume from many disparate, often obscure and widely scattered historical resources. My thanks also to The History Press senior editor Ryan Finn for his work editing the final manuscript.

My appreciation also extends to the staff of the New York–based William T. Grant Foundation for its generous support and home-away-from-home hospitality in making the foundation's resources and historical archives available to me during my weeklong August 2018 research visit, as well as making numerous images available for inclusion in this book.

In particular, I offer my sincere thanks to the following William T. Grant Foundation staff members for their gracious assistance in support of my research efforts: Dr. Adam Gamoran, president; Ruth G. Nolan, assistant to the president and board of trustees; Lenore Neier, communications manager; and Rosanna Aybar, finance and administration vice-president.

My research trip to New York City also afforded me the opportunity to visit and conduct photo shoots at enduring Midtown Manhattan sites indelibly linked to the history of the W.T. Grant Company and the William T. Grant Foundation.

I am also indebted to the staff of the Rockefeller Archive Center in North Tarrytown, New York, for their support and gracious hospitality during my weeklong March 2019 research trip to the RAC archives at historic Hillcrest. In particular, I offer my deepest gratitude to RAC senior archivist Tom Rosenbaum and the Research Room staff for their generous accommodation of my voluminous requests for materials from their extensive William T. Grant Foundation archive and subsequently making numerous images available for inclusion in this book.

I am pleased that my book research provided the Rockefeller Archive Center with the first major use of its extensive William T. Grant Foundation archive of early foundation records and William T. Grant's personal papers, many of the latter put to paper, now yellowed and brittle, in Mr. Grant's own distinctive Spencerian cursive handwriting. Thanks to the Rockefeller Archive Center's William T. Grant Foundation archive, Mr. Grant's ebullient, visionary and common-sense "voice" is a welcome and unique first-person addition to the book's narrative on both institutions that would come to bear his name—the W.T. Grant Company and the William T. Grant Foundation.

My thanks are also offered to the Northwestern University Library in Evanston, Illinois, for making its bound collection of W.T. Grant Company annual reports spanning the years 1928–74 available to me during my four-day August 2018 research trip. The information and images gleaned from the annual reports offered comprehensive and invaluable insights into the operation of the W.T. Grant Company for much of its seventy-year run and are a key addition to the book's chapters on the development of Grants into one of the nation's leading retailers.

I offer my thanks to retired former *Milwaukee Magazine* colleague Jim Romenesko for his review of the evolving book manuscript, as well as his encouragement and helpful insights during the writing process.

I also want to acknowledge the invaluable contributions of Grants veteran Wes Smith, administrator of the "W.T. Grant Co." Facebook page, for his generous and invaluable donation of archival W.T. Grant Company materials, including those of late Grants veteran Connie L. Hunt, in support of this book. For decades after Grants' demise, Hunt coordinated the *Grants Memories* newsletter linking W.T. Grant alumni across the United States.

I also express a debt of gratitude to the many private individuals, businesses, historical organizations, magazines and newspapers that provided permitted use of archival photographs for the book.

Last, but certainly not least, I offer a substantial debt of gratitude to my family—wife Barbara, daughter Evelyn and son Andrew—for their support of, belief in and encouragement for this book project. I am deeply indebted to them for their many sacrifices during the researching and writing of this book, including their accommodation of my extended out-of-state research trips.

INTRODUCTION

Out of all the department stores that my family frequented in my first ten formative childhood years of life from 1965 to 1975 in hometown Milwaukee—locals like Gimbels, Boston Store, T.A. Chapman's, Moreway and Drews and nationals like Sears, JCPenney, Arlan's, Spartan-Atlantic, Target, G.C. Murphy, F.W. Woolworth, Kmart and Treasure Island—the W.T. Grant Company reigns supreme in my memories as my *favorite* store.

In my mind, I can still vividly remember the large Grant City department store that anchored the Mill Road Shopping Center in our urban neighborhood on Milwaukee's far northwest side, as well as the smaller variety store–styled Grants anchoring the Ruby Isle Shopping Center in suburban Brookfield that my "Nana" frequented, with me happily in tow during my periodic weekend visits.

Over the span of my sixty years, I've enjoyed an enduring love for Grants, even now nearly fifty years after its sad April 1976 bankruptcy liquidation passing into U.S. retailing history. Why this love—dare I say obsession—for a long-defunct retail chain, as exemplified by the large collection of W.T. Grant Company memorabilia filling my basement "Man Cave" haven? That's much harder to explain.

Why do we fall in love—with our spouse for example or, for that matter, with a favorite car, a favorite food, a favorite tree or flower, a favorite hobby, a favorite author or book series, a career profession that sparks an interest and passion and perhaps maybe dozens of additional "loves" unique to each of our lives? While we may have specific head-centered qualities or reasons that we can point to for our love of person, place or thing, there's a much deeper heart-centered aspect to love that's harder to put into words. We just *know* that "love" feeling.

And I love Grants. As it was our neighborhood store, we frequented the large Grant City anchoring the northern end of the Mill Road Shopping Center almost as much as we frequented the National Tea Company supermarket that anchored the southern end and, for that matter, the Minnesota Fabrics, Walgreens, Hallmark stores and the Mill Road Theaters triplex that lay in between the two—which means we shopped at Grants *a lot*, as in several times a week *a lot*.

At nearly 120,000 square feet, Grants' full-line Grant City department store at the Mill Road Shopping Center offered a vast array of merchandise and services under its expansive roof, and although it was large in size, I knew the store well. Televisions, home electronics and cameras in the far left corner. Apparel in the front left and center of the store. Pet supplies and a boisterous menagerie of hamsters, gerbils and parakeets along the left wall of the store by the eight-bay auto center, automotive department and hardware. Toys, seasonal and the outdoor garden center in the bump-out section behind pets and the auto center. Sewing goods and fabrics, draperies, lamps and vacuum cleaners by the side entrance in the far right back corner of the store, just off the promenade linking Grants to the rest of the strip mall. Home décor, crafts and housewares in the center rear, just off furniture and appliances. Jewelry at the front right of the store on the way to the culinary delights being served up at Grants' Bradford House Restaurant, itself just off the nut and candy counter, greeting cards, clocks, notions and the records department, where we picked up the latest edition of Grants' annual *A Very Merry Christmas* holiday album every December. And in the expansive, orange-bricked main entryway was Grants' snack bar, which served up freshly popped popcorn and the simple culinary delights of Hire's Root Beer and "roller dog" frankfurters.

In fact, I remember my Nana coming along once with my mom and me on a shopping trip to *our* Grants store, much larger than the variety-styled Grants that Nana frequented at Ruby Isle, and I led her right to what she was looking for in the sizable notions area with all the efficiency of a Grants sales clerk. I knew our Grants store that well.

As a child, naturally my favorite destinations at Grants were the snack bar, nut and candy counter and toy and pet departments, as well as Grants' popular full-service Bradford House restaurant, where my parents and I

Grants' Bradford House restaurants offered youngsters age twelve and under a hand puppet menu bearing the visage of Pilgrim mascot Bucky Bradford. Entrée selections on the back of this August 1972 menu, inclusive of fries and a beverage, were a quarter-pound hamburger, fish sandwich or chicken drumstick for ninety-nine cents or a seventy-nine-cent grilled cheese sandwich. A kiddie nut sundae dessert was thirty-three cents. *Author's collection.*

regularly dined on the bargain-priced featured nightly specials, our tasty meals served up on white Pyrex dishes bearing the Bradford House logo and a Greek key border in Grants' signature navy blue.

For all the visits we made to Grants over the years, it stood to reason that a lot of merchandise came home from Grants, including my pet hamster "Cinnamon." Looking at old Grants ads and annual reports while researching this book, I was awestruck by just how much in our home came from Grants. The photos in the ads and annual reports were like a photo album of my childhood, and decades later, my folks still have some retro-nostalgic relics that once bore a Grants price sticker.

And every Christmas, I still enjoy playing Grants' eight-volume series of vinyl *A Very Merry Christmas* albums issued between 1967 and 1974, so much so that I find myself humming the New Christy Minstrels' "Here We Come A-Caroling" before the album finishes tracking the silent space after Mahalia Jackson's incomparable rendition of "O Little Town of Bethlehem" or humming Leslie Uggams's "It's Beginning to Look a Lot Like Christmas" before the album finishes tracking the quiet gap after Robert Goulet's baritone-rich "Do You Hear What I Hear?"

As a child, I never imagined the possibility that Grants would cease to exist. Like our sprawling neighborhood Grant City store, Grants itself seemed larger than life, solid as the Rock of Gibraltar. But one fateful day in 1975, my paradigms got shifted and I learned an important life lesson—that nothing is forever.

It was a profoundly sad day for me when Grants closed its doors. For months prior, our neighborhood Grants had been known as "ANTS," the burned-out neon of the "GR" never having been repaired as the W.T. Grant Company desperately fought for its corporate life.

Being ten at the time, I knew nothing of all the financial drama playing out for Grants with its bankruptcy reorganization filing in New York, or at our local store for that matter, where employees waited warily for the proverbial shoe to drop on their store—and their livelihoods. At the time, all I knew was that Grants was, well, Grants—the *best store ever*. That the GRANTS sign said ANTS, what can I say? It appealed to the humor of the typical pre-adolescent.

But with the demise of Grants, I got a sobering dose of reality and the periodic vicissitudes of the grown-up world—and grew up a little in the process.

I vividly remember the sights and sounds of walking through our Grants during its store closing sale, a good-sized chunk of the store darkened and cordoned off as dwindling stocks of merchandise were consolidated to the front of the store. As it was my first going-out-of-business sale, the scene at Grants was a jarring experience—the usual bright and cheery, tidy orderliness of our Grants supplanted by the disarray generated by teeming hordes of bargain-hunters jostling for the thinning supply of merchandise on disheveled displays and the usual cheery Muzak background music replaced by the cacophony of the crowds and the overhead PA system blaring announcements like a carnival barker about the percentage-off values created by the bankruptcy-spurred store closing sale. It was profoundly sad.

Naturally, our final shopping trip to Grants also brought my last trip to the Bradford House. After dinner, I tucked away the blue Bradford House sandwich pick as a holy relic remembrance of Grants and handed over a ceremonial final nickel at the restaurant's check stand for my last foil-wrapped Grants Melrose peppermint patty.

The Mill Road Grants, soon darkened, quickly became a looming, vandalism-plagued eyesore, its busted-out display windows eventually replaced by sheets of plywood and the GRANTS signs ultimately removed,

October 1965 aerial view of the twenty-three-thousand-square-foot variety-styled Grants store that anchored Rapids Plaza in 89,144-resident Racine, Wisconsin, from 1963 to 1975. Other Rapids Plaza anchors included Waukesha, Wisconsin–based Sentry Foods and the first Wisconsin location of Framingham, Massachusetts–based department store chain Zayre. *Racine County Historical Society.*

leaving behind a tell-tale label-scar reminder of what once had been an integral anchor of our neighborhood. After sitting vacant for six years, the massive Mill Road Grants was eventually subdivided for multiple tenants. While the building physically still looms large on the north end of the enduring Mill Road Shopping Center, it's never regained the vibrancy offered by Grants back in the day.

For me, shopping has never been the same since Grants' demise. Perhaps the closest I've come to truly loving a store since Grants has been Green Bay, Wisconsin–based Shopko, a worthy Grants successor for my hard-earned money. Like Grants, I mourned the sad passing of Shopko (1962–2019), one of the pioneering big-box discounters. Again, nothing is forever.

A few years after Grants' demise, my family moved south from Milwaukee to Racine, where I attended William Horlick High School, which was serendipitously, at least for me, located across the street from the bankruptcy-shuttered variety-style Grants that anchored Rapids Plaza

Working with downtown Rockford, Illinois businessmen Jerry Kortman and Doc Slafkoski in 1993, author Eric A. Johnson (pictured) successfully persuaded the Rockford Historic Preservation Commission to award landmark status to the Art Deco–styled circa 1931 W.T. Grant Company Building, 203–209 West State Street, saving it from imminent demolition and paving the way for its preservation and subsequent $1 million redevelopment. First home to Kinko's Copies and then Paragon Restaurant, since June 2012 the historic Grants site has been home to District Bar & Grill. *Author's collection.*

from 1963 to 1975. The store rekindled my fascination with—and love of—Grants.

I spent many happy hours in the school library over the course of three years leafing through Horlick's voluminous archive of *The Readers' Guide to Periodical Literature*, searching for magazine articles on William T. Grant and the W.T. Grant Company and then filing innumerable requests with genial school librarian Marilyn Christensen for bound volumes of *TIME*, *Newsweek*, *Fortune*, *Forbes* and *Business Week* to fill my insatiable appetite to learn more about the history of Grants and try to understand its demise. A lot of allowance and milk money went into the coin slot of the library copy machine over those three years. I still have the photocopies from 1980 to 1983 to prove it.

What I learned about William T. Grant, the W.T. Grant Company and the William T. Grant Foundation fascinated me then—and still does. It's definitely a story worth telling. In a very real way, my research for *The W.T. Grant Company: Known for Values* got underway in the Horlick High School library forty-five years ago, thanks in part to the kind encouragement and support provided by Mrs. Christensen.

I invite you to remember anew, or maybe experience for the first time, the wonders of the W.T. Grant Company, long "Known for Values" and, as you'll find, much, much more.

THE MAKING OF A MERCHANT

"I Always Wanted a Store"

If one didn't know better, one might think that the story of American retailer-philanthropist William T. Grant Jr. was lifted from the pages of a rags-to-riches young adult novel penned by prolific nineteenth-century Massachusetts novelist Horatio Alger.

Indeed, Grant's life story makes for an interesting and compelling read worthy of Alger at his best in his 1868 novel *Ragged Dick*, the story of a poor bootblack's rise to middle-class respectability.

In Grant's case, the story is all the more amazing because it's true, as high school dropout Grant—possessed of an unquenchable, ebullient optimism and employing his innate traits of hard work, thrift, shrewdness, ingenuity, courage, self-reliance, honesty and individual enterprise—rose from a humble background to success, fame and wealth beyond his wildest youthful dreams as one of the nation's most respected retailers and philanthropists. "W.T. Grant" was emblazoned on more than 1,200 department stores from coast to coast, his cursive signature towered fifty-four stories above New York's Times Square in twenty-foot-high neon letters and his philanthropic legacy lives on through the enduring William T. Grant Foundation (1936–).

William T. Grant Jr. was born to William Thomas Grant Sr. (1851–1928) and Amanda Lewis Bird (1854–1945) on June 27, 1876, in Stevensville, Bradford County, Pennsylvania, although he spent most of his youth growing up in Massachusetts at Fall River and Malden.

Grant's grandfather Elihu was a Methodist minister and a West Point graduate whose roommate was a distant relative by the name of Ulysses S. Grant, later a famed Civil War general and U.S. president.

Though testing the waters as a house furnishing goods retailer in collaboration with L. Nichols & Company in hometown Fall River, Massachusetts, Grant's older brother, Dr. Elihu Grant (1873–1942), eventually followed in their grandfather's footsteps and was ordained as a Methodist minister in 1901. He later earned fame as a noted scholar and author, most notably for his 1907 book *The Peasantry of Palestine: The Life, Manners, and Customs of the Village*, feted as "a vividly accurate portrait of rural life in Palestine." Professor of biblical literature for thirty-one years between 1907 and 1938, first at Smith College and later at Haverford College, Elihu Grant served as superintendent of the American Friends Schools in Ramallah and Jerusalem from 1901 to 1904 and directed four archaeological expeditions at Beit Shemesh between 1928 and 1933.

Inspired by his father, William T. Grant Jr., meanwhile, seemed destined for life as a merchant. Recalled Grant in his authorized 1954 autobiography, "as told to his longtime neighbor and friend G. Lynn Sumner" in *The Story of W.T. Grant and the Early Days of the Business He Founded*, published in celebration of the opening of the W.T. Grant Company's landmark 500th store, "Looking back to the earliest days that I can remember, it seems to be that I always wanted a store. As it turned out, I did not get it until my thirtieth year. But all through my boyhood and youth the idea and the dream were there, even though I wasn't always clearly aware of it." In his autobiography, Grant recalled how he had "clung doggedly to…my dream of having a store of my own."

Known to his parents as "Willie," Grant came by his love of retailing naturally, with some of his earliest, formative memories being the Fall River, Massachusetts retail tea store operated by his "childhood hero" namesake father. "Some of my clearest childhood recollections are of the tea store my father had in Fall River, Massachusetts, when I was five," Grant recalled. "I can still smell the spicy aroma that met you as you opened the door. I can still see the big, colorful stenciled red and black canisters arranged along the walls. It meant nothing to me then that my father's store failed, or rather it meant only that we moved from Fall River to Malden, Massachusetts, where my father got a job as a furniture salesman in a Boston furniture store, and where he had adventures in selling that were both fabulous and exciting to me. When he would come home nights and relate these adventures in elaborate detail, I was convinced that a store must be the most romantic of places."

Left: From the 1870s to the 1930s, the Houghton & Dutton department store at Tremont and Beacon Streets in Boston was among the city's leading retailers. From 1895 to 1899, future retailer William T. Grant got his inspiring first taste of general merchandise retailing managing the store's bargain basement shoe department. *Author's collection.*

Below: Circa 1908 postcard showing the Almy, Bigelow & Washburn department store in downtown Salem, Massachusetts. It was while working at the store that William T. Grant conceived "The Idea" for a new kind of store—a low mark-up, high-volume twenty-five-cent store trailblazing the untapped middle ground between the five-and-dime variety stores and the fifty-cent and up traditional department stores. *Author's collection.*

In addition to kindling a fascination for and love of the retail business, Grant's father also passed along several other traits that served his son well:

> *The Grants had come to America from Scotland in the 1620s and the old Scottish traits of industry, thrift and piety had come to full bloom in my paternal grandfather, Elihu Grant. After graduating from West Point, where he had been a classmate and roommate of U.S. Grant—a coincidence, for the relationship was remote—he served in the Civil War and reached the rank of Captain. But when the war was over, although General Grant offered him any appointment he might be qualified for, he resigned from the Army to enter the Methodist ministry.*
>
> *Methodist ministers in those days were lucky to keep body and soul together, for Methodists were notoriously rich in spirit and poor in purse. But my grandfather had guarded jealously his modest inheritance, which he drew upon to educate his six children and set them on the road to independence. For my father, he acquired a small flour mill in Stevensville, Pennsylvania. In that village I was born June 27, 1876.*
>
> *Always the optimist, my father saw in this flour mill the opportunity for a great business success. But it soon became apparent that when those Scottish family qualities of thrift and industry had reached my father, they had hesitated, wavered and taken a short leap, skipping him completely. He failed with the flour mill just as he was to fail in the tea store in Fall River, just as he was to fail again and again in positions he could always get but never hold in later years. However, nature had endowed my father with something else…imagination, a sense of dramatic showmanship, and a love of people.*

Grant recalled that his mother, of Dutch and French ancestry, was "endowed with qualities of thrift and conservation, without which a home could not have been kept over our heads and her three children never could have been kept in school….There was never a time when the family income was sufficient to give my mother any sense of security. My father's earnings continued to be small, and uncertain and…frequently interrupted. Yet when he would lose one job and go searching for another, he was always the radiant optimist. Shining success was always just around the corner."

By the time he was nine, Grant's family encompassed his parents; his elder brother, Elihu, three years his senior; and a newborn baby sister, Olive L. Grant. A younger brother, George Bird Grant, born when Grant was five, died at nine months old in July 1882.

Young "Willie" learned well from both parents, combining his innate fascination for retailing with his father's indefatigable optimism, imagination, sense of dramatic showmanship and love of people and his mother's dedication to the virtues of thrift and conservation in the 1906 launch of his life's dream: the W.T. Grant Company. Both his parents would live to see their "merchant prince" son's success as one of the nation's most dynamic up-and-coming retailers.

Another youthful influence on Grant's retailing aspirations was his Aunt Elsie, who worked in a general store in Somerville, New Jersey, where the Grants would vacation every two years to see his maternal grandparents, remembered as being "prosperous farmers."

Said Grant of watching his Aunt Elsie handling merchandise and waiting on customers, "It seemed to me that she had the most interesting job in the world. What heaven it would be to work in a store!"

Something of a free spirit, hardworking young Willie Grant was always on the move. In order to help with family finances, Grant entered the workforce at age seven, "earning pennies running errands for people." By age eight, he was assisting a butter-and-egg wagon operator known as Johnny Yiyi, a "quaint character, only a little over four feet tall, with round red cheeks and shining eyes, a bald head and fluffy mutton-chop whiskers."

"Many times we had to move to a home where rent was lower," Grant recalled of his childhood. "To my mother, every penny that came to her hands was to be hoarded and used with care. It is no wonder that under such circumstances I started when very young to earn a little money as a help to my mother. It proved to be a great spur to my initiative and ingenuity. I soon found that I loved to sell things."

Unlike his brother, Elihu, Grant was not a scholar, happier to learn by doing, by experience, rather than learning in a typical classroom setting. Recalled Grant, "I was never a good student. My record was in sharp contrast to that of my brother Elihu, who was a brilliant student, the valedictorian of his class, and who went on to become a minister and, in later years, a distinguished archaeologist and a professor at both Smith and Haverford College. From my first years in school I found it easier to learn by experience.…I managed to get as far as the second year in the Malden high school, but only because for some reason my teachers seemed to like me in spite of my lagging interest in my lessons. Above all, I learned by doing.…Perhaps the experiences that meant more to me…than all I learned from books were gained in selling. After school, on Saturdays, and during vacations I sold everything I could get hold of that could be sold by a boy in our Malden neighborhood."

William T. Grant Jr. at fifteen or sixteen. Not much for academics, Grant dropped out of high school his sophomore year to pursue a career in retailing. After learning the ropes of the retail business with various employers, Grant by age thirty had hung out his own shingle with the opening of the first W.T Grant Company "quarter store" in Lynn, Massachusetts. *From* The Story of W.T. Grant and the Early Days of the Business He Founded, *by G. Lynn Sumner, author's collection.*

Among other things, Grant worked a route "as soon as I was big enough to carry newspapers," delivering the *Boston Globe*, *Herald*, *Post* and *Transcript*, as well as the *Malden Evening Mail*, earning a half cent per penny paper sold.

Grant also sold bluing and flower seeds from house to house and hustled sidewalk shoveling gigs in the winter months. Annually at Decoration Day (Memorial Day), Grant did a brisk trade selling flowers and potted plants outside the local cemetery. One summer, Grant worked as a soda jerk at the marble soda fountain at Morgan's Drug Store in Malden, earning two dollars per week. Another summer Grant worked at Billing Shoe Store in Malden, running errands, repairing shoes and, on occasion, working the sales floor.

"Selling always had a fascination for me," Grant recalled. "Much as I liked to play baseball, no ball game was important enough to interfere with the chance to sell something. And the need for money at home was urgent. So I seized upon every opportunity to sell, and was able to make a contribution to the family purse and to help buy my clothes."

Still later, Grant found summer work as an errand boy for Boston lawyers Chester M. Perry, Arthur J. Selfridge and George R. Jones. At age fifteen, Grant dropped out of high school midway through his sophomore year to work exclusively for Selfridge. But the siren call of mercantile salesmanship tugged at his heart, and Grant soon found a job running errands for Parker, Holmes & Company, a Boston wholesale shoe house, which was followed by a position with whetstone manufacturer Pike Manufacturing Company in Pike's Station, New Hampshire. Soon after, Grant found himself working the sales floor in two Boston shoe stores.

It was the policy of one of his employers, the Massachusetts Boot and Shoe Company, a Boston-area chain, to give its salesmen bonuses above their regular weekly wage for any extra money they could get out of the customer over and above the regular retail price, offering Grant $0.05 for every $0.50

earned over the store's "legitimate profit," with company salesmen regularly charging customers as much as $3.50 on a $1.50 pair of shoes. Grant was incensed and quickly moved on.

"That was my first experience—and my last—with a firm so completely unscrupulous in its treatment of customers," Grant recalled. "Needless to say, the Massachusetts Boot and Shoe Company has long since been out of business. But during my own brief period of employment there I could not help thinking what an opportunity that store had to build a sound business, one in which everybody would be given the best values and the best service to be found in all of Boston. Such a policy could be the means of attracting customers in ever-increasing numbers, and prompt them to come back again and again. That, I said to myself, was what I would do—if I ever had a store."

And Grant made good on his word with the 1906 launch of the W.T. Grant Company, which would be widely feted over its seventy-year run as the store "Known for Values."

William T. Grant Jr. as seen in his twenties. Grant worked for a variety of retailers early in his career, including leading Massachusetts department stores Houghton & Dutton in Boston and Almy, Bigelow & Washburn in Salem. *From* The Story of W.T. Grant and the Early Days of the Business He Founded, *by G. Lynn Sumner, author's collection.*

At age nineteen, Grant began his journey toward fulfilling his retailing dream in earnest when his working career crossed paths with Ed Dutton of Houghton & Dutton, remembered by Grant as "one of Boston's big, substantial department stores." Starting as a salesman in the store's bargain basement shoe department, Grant was soon department manager. "For the first time I had, with certain limitations, the responsibility for a department in a store," Grant recalled. "Though 'Bargain Basement—Shoes' may have been a lowly division of the firm's operations, I was happy because it was all mine. I thought of it, not as a department, but as a store—my store—and immediately began to figure out ways to increase its sales."

Establishing a bargain table one day to promote forty-nine-cent slippers, Grant sold as many slippers in a day as the department had in a whole week previously, earning well-deserved praise from Dutton for a job well done.

Noted Grant of the power of the positive affirmation provided to him by Dutton:

> *Through all the years of my boyhood in which I had worked at dozens of different jobs, I had always been bullied, until it seemed impossible that I would ever do anything that could win recognition for work well done. In fact, it seemed to be the custom of the time for employers to drive and criticize and browbeat their employees with the deliberate purpose of striking fear into their hearts. I guess they did this to discourage asking for a raise. Yet here was Ed Dutton actually giving me encouragement! Suddenly I said to myself, "Maybe I can amount to something after all." We hear a lot these days about the importance of human relationships, and we try to establish good will and good feelings between employer and employee, between salesman and customer. This was one of my first experiences with the importance of good human relationships in business. Those two words—"Good boy"—spoken to me by Ed Dutton, gave me a new confidence in myself, a new incentive to do my best. And they did something more. Right then and there I resolved that no hours could be too long, no work too hard, no sacrifice too great on my part to help Ed Dutton make a success of that basement shoe department. After that I was constantly on the lookout for more chances to win approval. I studied our customers to see what merchandise they wanted, and searched our stocks to see what merchandise represented the greatest values. Whenever I found something exceptional, I would ask for the bargain counter and get it. Ed Dutton continued to observe my enterprise and to give his approval.*

Grant learned several important lessons at Houghton & Dutton's, including "the power of a few kind words," and was a firm "stickler" in the belief in the power of "bargain tables at the front of the store." And when he finally owned his own store with the W.T. Grant Company, Grant prioritized carefully cultivating positive human relationships with his employees and customers, while also giving his store managers freedom and creative leeway to essentially operate as entrepreneurs within a chain store setting.

"Up to this time I had been learning largely from my mistakes," Grant recalled. "Here was a lesson in the importance of recognition for work well done, which was to be more valuable to me when I got my first store."

But for a season while working at Houghton & Dutton, Grant made an admittedly "wide detour on a strange road before that day arrived," working on the side as a fight promoter for his friend Timmy Kearns, an aspiring lightweight boxer—despite the fact that professional boxing was illegal in Massachusetts at the time. Grant arranged for boxing matches in Boston, soon expanding the match schedule to several nights a week in a rented loft atop a former candy factory. After a match got busted one evening by the police, Grant moved Kearns's matches to Lynn, Lowell and Lawrence, Massachusetts, as well as Manchester, New Hampshire, and as far afield as Cleveland, Ohio, where Kearns took on English lightweight boxing champion Eddie Connolly on February 15, 1898, in a twenty-round draw.

The sideline gig, Grant said, "might have had more serious consequences but for the restraining counsel of my mother, who cautioned me that I was bringing embarrassment to the family and also endangering my advancement in business, but it also taught me some important lessons that would one day serve me well when I got my first store."

Grant used seventy-five dollars of his fight promotion earnings to put a down payment on a home for his long-struggling parents, making small additional payments out of his monthly salary from Houghton & Dutton. "My father and mother had moved repeatedly during the past few years from one rented house to another," Grant noted. "Now it appeared that they were going to have to move again. I arranged to purchase a house for them....My father and mother lived in that house for more than 25 years."

Grant exited the fight promotion business not long after the Cleveland exhibition, following a "disappointing" match, both in terms of box office take and ring performance, at the Opera House in Lawrence, Massachusetts, when Grant and Kearns mutually decided to end their nascent careers in the boxing world.

Recalled Grant, "My older brother, Elihu, had entered the ministry, my mother was becoming a religious person, and my activities were becoming embarrassing to both of them. They told me that I had better devote all my time to business, and by this time I was ready to agree. But I had learned a lot about promoting which was to be useful to me all the rest of my life. I had discovered that to be successful in dealing with the public you had to manage to get people really excited about what you are offering them, whether it be entertainment or merchandise."

After four years with Houghton & Dutton, Grant took a position selling shoes in Boston for Jason S. Bailey. Grant was later transferred to Bailey stores in Amesbury, Massachusetts, and Biddeford and Lewiston, Maine. While in Bailey's employ, Grant experienced both failure and success, lessons he would also put to good work later at the W.T. Grant Company.

"Looking back now on my experience in working for Jason S. Bailey, I can understand both why I failed in the first job he gave me, and why the success I eventually achieved was won at such cost in trial and error," Grant noted. "No one ever attempted to teach me even the simplest rudiments of successful store management. I was sent out absolutely on my own to sink or swim. Years later when I opened my first store I decided that I would profit by this lesson. I tried my best to give each sales-person the benefit of what I knew of display, of keeping stock, of handling merchandise and serving customers. And then I tried to create a spirit of teamwork."

Grant would then move to "one of the best medium-sized department stores in all New England," the "fine, well-managed" firm of Almy, Bigelow & Washburn in Salem, Massachusetts, where Grant would conceive what he called "The Idea."

It would be Grant's brother, Elihu, who had married the niece of namesake Almy, Bigelow & Washburn founder James F. Almy, who got him a serendipitous position with the retailer. "Certainly I had never dreamed that my brother's marriage might have any bearing on my future," Grant recalled. "But it just goes to show you how the long arm of coincidence can reach out and tap you on the shoulder….Hearing that this store was looking for a shoe buyer, Elihu told Mr. Almy that he knew just the man for the job."

"Billie" Grant managed the shoe department at Almy, Bigelow & Washburn for three years, quickly rising to a position as one of the store's four managers. Under Grant, "amazing sales increases" were realized as Grant's signature bargain tables were placed front and center and a new merchandising policy was instituted—"clearing out the things that didn't sell and…seeing that we kept complete stocks of what did sell."

"Customers stopped by to look—and to buy," Grant noted. "Immediately in front of the store entrance we put a bargain counter with an ever-fresh and changing display of special items. That bargain table frequently sold more units of a single item than were sold in a whole department in the regular way….Women found it hard to pass a store where they could see a crowd around a bargain counter. It drew customers in from the sidewalk."

It was Grant's signature bargain counter at Almy, Bigelow & Washburn that would be the genesis for "The Idea" that would make his childhood dreams come true with a groundbreaking "new kind of store"—the industry-disrupting W.T. Grant Company twenty-five-cent department store or "quarter store."

Recalled Grant:

> *I could not resist watching the speed with which merchandise moved off those counters, especially items selling at 25 cents....No problem. No sizes. No fitting. No selling effort. Every purchase was an impulse purchase. The salesgirl only had to answer questions and make change. Suddenly I realized that this was the kind of selling I had been looking for! This was merchandise in motion! Seeing items move off a counter almost as fast as a girl could lay them out...was a chance for resourcefulness in buying—finding items that would sell on sight. Here was a chance for dramatic display and promotion.... Turnover was the magic that made more money, and turnover was made possible by featuring low-priced fast-selling items, well chosen, well displayed. My mind was on fire with a new idea! For days I watched the sales in other accessories departments. Twenty-five cent neckwear was a favorite—collars, jabots, fichus and berthas. At the hair goods counter, we had 25-cent switches, rolls and combs....All sold fast. Gradually the idea dawned on me that twenty-five cents was a magic price.... What a business we could do if we could only seek twenty-five cent items and we kept a complete supply on hand all the time.... You know, that might be an idea for a new kind of store—a store where everything would sell for 25 cents or less.... This was the chance I had been waiting for and I was burning with the desire to put the plan into effect.*

THE W.T. GRANT COMPANY

"A New Kind of Store"

Perennially a keen and perceptive observer, the entrepreneurial Grant decided to stake out a unique claim and blaze a new retailing trail in the as-yet-untapped middle-ground pricing niche between the fifty cent and up trade of the traditional department stores and the five-and-dime trade of the burgeoning ranks of variety stores operated by the likes of F.W. Woolworth, S.S. Kresge, G.C. Murphy, H.L. Green, J.G. McCrory, S.H. Kress, S.H. Knox and J.J. Newberry, among others.

Investing $1,000 of his own funds that he'd painstakingly saved over the years, coupled with the investment backing of three silent Almy, Bigelow & Washburn partners whom he would buy out in 1915—store president W.E. Bigelow, store general manager Louis Roskoff and the widowed Mrs. James Almy—the thirty-year-old Grant leased 5,400 square feet of ground floor and basement space in the new YMCA building on Market Street in 69,513-resident Lynn, Massachusetts, an oceanside industrial city just 3.7 miles north of the Boston city limits.

The intrepid Grant, boldly striking off on his own, quickly got to work creating the store of his dreams. "I knew the city of Lynn very well, for I had gone there frequently to buy shoes," Grant noted. "With its thousands of factory workers, it should have the kind of customers we wanted. And the location was fair, for Woolworth and Kresge stores had been operating for some time directly across the street, and there was a department store in the same block....Now the die was cast! I had a store! A barren, empty store to be sure, but in my mind's eye I could see shelves and counters loaded with a great variety of colorful merchandise. I could see the customers crowding the aisles! I could even hear the sweet sound of the cash registers ringing. But it was now September and Christmas was only a few weeks away. If we were going to get the benefit of the Christmas trade, I had to get busy!"

With each party having a quarter partnership in the new venture, the question arose as to what to name the new enterprise:

> *With that in mind, Mr. Roskoff discussed the subject with Mrs. Almy and Mr. Bigelow. I am not sure, but possibly out of that discussion came the thought that as this was a new and untried venture it might not be successful and therefore it might be unwise for any of their names—Almy, Bigelow or Roskoff—to be associated with it. Also I was the one who was to have the responsibility of management. On my ingenuity and industry its success or failure would depend. Also, I think they knew that if my own name was on that store I might work all the harder to make it succeed. Mr. Roskoff came back from that meeting with the suggestion that the name be the W.T. Grant Co. I welcomed the idea because to me it was a challenge. Not only would the opening of this new kind of store give me the opportunity I had long been waiting for, it would also give me the chance, if I succeeded, to make my name stand for something in the merchandising world. With such an opportunity and such an incentive, no work could be too hard, no sacrifice on my part too great to make this exciting new venture the success that I firmly believed it would be.*

Grant worked feverishly over the next two-plus months to ready the W.T. Grant Company for its historic December 6, 1906 debut. With layout plans in hand, Grant met with carpenters to construct counters, shelving, backs for the storefront display windows and "a big sign for the store front." The design of the sign was a huge consideration for Grant, who wanted his trailblazing twenty-five-cent store to stand out in the crowded and competitive retail marketplace, flanked by traditional flagship local department stores on one end of the retail spectrum and the plethora of copycat red-and-gold-fronted five-and-dimes on the other. In short, the visionary Grant needed to develop a fresh and distinctive signature look for his "new kind of store."

"Into it had gone many hours of careful thought," Grant recalled. "From the day the name was chosen I had studied styles of lettering on other signs, in magazines and newspapers, and on billboards and street-car cars, until I finally had chosen the easiest one to read—a simple block letter. Everywhere I went, walking along the streets of Lynn, Boston and New York, riding on trains, I looked for the color that could be seen the farthest. Finally I became convinced that a medium chrome orange was it. The orange fire plugs clinched my decision. Surely if that color had been chosen to make fire plugs stand out so no one would miss them, why wasn't it just the thing for a store sign that would catch the eye. I understand that scientific studies have since proved that this color can be seen at the greatest distance."

Thus it was that "W.T. GRANT CO." and later simply "GRANTS," rendered in orange outlined in dark navy blue, became the familiar signature look for the company's exterior signage, with Grant recalling in 1954 that the look "became the pattern for the sign that went up over our first store—and it is still the familiar design marking Grant stores from coast to coast. We have not been able to improve upon it."

The design lasted until 1974, two years after founder Grant's death, when a cursive orange Grant City logo became Grants' new, if short-lived, signage standard-bearer.

Once the sign design was squared away, Grant was off to Boston and New York "on the great adventure of buying merchandise for the first 25-cent store in America." Grant also received assistance from the experienced and well-connected buyers at Almy, Bigelow & Washburn.

Recalled Grant, "With the Christmas season uppermost in mind, I concentrated on items appropriate for gifts—handkerchiefs, women's neckwear, men's ties, toiletries, boxed stationery, raffia whiskbroom holders, satin pin-cushions, jewelry, toys. In New York I literally ran from one place to another, looking for special gift merchandise to buy for 16 to 18 cents so that I could sell it at not more than 25 cents."

Once goods began to arrive in Lynn, the store was stocked, and Grant "painted the signs for window advertisements, wrote the first [newspaper] advertisement for the *Lynn Item*, and hired about fifteen girls to do the selling."

W.T. Grant Company ads in the *Lynn Item* leading up to the store's December 6, 1906 unveiling outlined Grant's unique merchandising philosophy: "The mission of this store will be to show what can be done with 25 cents. Those who get in the habit of coming to the store at every opportunity will get the biggest bargains. We have two experienced buyers living in New York city who do nothing else but search for these big values and new things of which you will see samples if you attend the opening."

Even forty-eight years later in 1954, Grant's memories of his first "Grant Girls" at Store No. 1 in Lynn, the chain's "Mother Store," were still fresh in his memory—Miss Leutbecker on the ribbon counter, Miss Norris on the notions counter and Winnie Bond in charge of laces, embroideries and handkerchiefs. "I can picture some of those girls in my mind now as clearly as though it were only yesterday," Grant recalled, adding that Norris was "so good at selling and stock-keeping that eventually I put every new girl with her for the first week or ten days so she would get the right idea of how to make a success of whatever she was assigned to do."

Looking back, Grant had a special fondness for his charter roster of "Grant Girls" who staffed the sales counters at Store No. 1 in Lynn. "Most wonderful of all for me, in that first store, were the salesgirls," Grant recalled. "They caught the spirit and worked with me to make the store successful. They gave me continuous help and advice about the merchandise, rushing up to tell me that some certain item was making a hit, or telling me why certain items would not sell. I give the salesgirls a lion's share of the credit for helping me make that first store a success. If it had not been for them there wouldn't be any W.T. Grant Company as we know it today. That is why I am everlastingly boosting for the sales people."

Looking to economize where he could as he readied his first store for its grand opening debut, Grant bought secondhand cash registers for about half the price of new and sold emptied wood merchandise crates for twenty-five or fifty cents each.

In the days immediately leading up to the W.T. Grant Company's debut, Grant turned his attention to trimming the display windows arrayed across the store's forty-foot storefront, flanking the store's central entrance. "It called for everything I knew of showmanship," Grant said of his display windows, recalling that he credited his showmanship know-how to his father, whom he feted as a "master" of the art. "Into the windows went all the outstanding values I could find to draw people into the store."

Selling items priced up to a cap of twenty-five cents across twenty-one departments—notions, ribbons, handkerchiefs, millinery, jewelry, women's neckwear, hosiery, knit underwear, muslin underwear, corsets, petticoats, infants and children's wear, slippers, men's neckties, art goods, stationery, sheet music, piece goods, kitchen utensils, framed pictures and toiletries—Grant threw open the doors of his W.T. Grant Company twenty-five-cent store for the first time on Thursday, December 6, 1906. Looking to make a splashy debut, Grant brought in Boston's famed Handel and Haydn Society to perform musical programs throughout the afternoon and evening between periodic intermissions.

Although the weather in Lynn was not promising, with Grant recalling the city being "battered and drenched by a wild mixture of wind, snow and

The success of the W.T. Grant Company's 1906 debut of Store No. 1 (pictured) in Lynn, Massachusetts, spurred the beginnings of a chain with the opening of Store No. 2 at Waterbury, Connecticut, in 1908. By the company's 1972 height, Grants operated 1,238 stores in forty-six states coast-to-coast as the nation's seventh-largest general merchandise retailer. *Author's collection.*

rain" that "made walking hazardous," the store's 2:30 p.m. opening was met with "a great crowd" that "had been waiting, eager for the tempting values that filled the windows."

"We were swamped," Grant noted. "As the storm subsided, more and more people came, to look and to buy. All afternoon and evening the store was crowded. When we closed at eleven o'clock that night and checked the cash registers, I found that receipts for the first day totaled $1,500—a fabulous sum to me. The foreboding dark dawn had changed to a day of glorious success."

Grant, who had no safe and feared a possible theft of such a huge sum, divided up the first day's receipts three ways, giving part to a friend to take home, hiding part in the store's basement coal bin and taking part home with himself.

Purveying quality goods at a target twenty-five-cent price point, Grants from its opening day developed a well-deserved reputation as being "Known for Values," a longtime company slogan. A believer in volume selling and high merchandise turnover rates as the key for successful retailing, Grant immediately found a lucrative niche in the fast-selling twenty-five-cent trade.

With sixteen selling days to Christmas, excluding three "Blue Law" Sundays when the store was closed, Grant set to working a "mad rush":

> *I bought more goods, kept the books, paid the bills, carried the money to the bank, wrote the ads, set up displays, painted the signs, and all the while set a pace that kept the salesgirls going at top speed. I was my own porter and handyman, sweeping the floors and washing the windows. Another of my duties each day was to replace the carbons in the electric arc lights in front of the store at the risk of getting electrocuted. Pausing only for a bite to eat after the store closed, I was back setting up new displays, arranging goods on the counters, bringing up more stock from the basement for the next day. Some nights I slept on a counter because it was too late to catch a train or trolley to East Saugus where I was getting free board and lodging at my brother's home. My own enthusiasm, the fever of activity in which I worked, seemed to inspire everyone to pitch in to make the store a success. The people at the bank and at the newspaper office gave me invaluable assistance. The customers told their friends about the bargains we offered and urged them to come and see for themselves. Many customers took such a personal interest that they would have been offended if anyone had criticized the store in any way.*

A quintessential businessman, the canny Grant deftly catered to Lynn's lower-middle-class population, combining cost-saving spartan décor with an emphasis on offering a wide array of quality products at bargain prices. Despite all the flash and flourish merchandising spectacle of the company's trailblazing retail operations, the back office at Grant's newly opened Lynn "Store of Wonder Values" was a modest, homespun operation.

Recalled one of the original "Grant Girls" of working in Store No. 1 in the October 1946 fortieth-anniversary issue of *The Grant Game*, the W.T. Grant Company's corporate monthly newsmagazine: "We had a peculiar office. It was made up of a desk, a table and two chairs. The pattern stock boxes hid the office force from the shoppers. Several months later our office was moved to the balcony over the notion counter. When change of $5 or $10 was needed, the bill was stuck in a broom and handed up to the office girls. Then the single bills were handed down in the same manner."

The store's successful Christmas season debut created a new challenge for Grant heading into 1907. "The novelty of a 25-cent store had caught the public's fancy, but now I had practically to start all over to build a business that would attract customers throughout the year," Grant recalled. "That meant finding merchandise in a wide enough variety to justify calling ours a department store. The honeymoon was over. Now I had to find goods that would sell during the dreary days of January, February and March—which is still one of our big problems."

Grant met with scores of wholesalers and manufacturers in New York, on the prowl for "sensational bargains" to stock his fledgling twenty-five-cent store and give his customers "values such as they have never seen before."

In 1954, Grants was still doing business with some of its charter suppliers, including firms like I.E. Kleinert Rubber Company, Thomas Long, J.B. Williams, Century Ribbon Company, Lamport Manufacturing Company and A. Wilhelm.

As time went on, the W.T. Grant Company expanded its product offerings at Lynn to encompass thirty-one departments in a bid to give the store "increasingly a semblance of the department store we had planned," adding imported Japanese china, Nottingham lace curtains, hardware and home furnishing items, among other lines.

The fledgling Grant store ran a profit from day one thanks to Grant's operating strategy of "selling as many goods as possible at a mark-up 10 percent higher than my cost of doing business and…keeping our expenses as low as possible…by economizing in every possible way." Recalled Grant:

> *I did not spend a dollar or even a dime for anything that could be improvised with what we had. For example, instead of buying window display fixtures we would make them out of boxes and pails covered with scarves. Two sticks tacked together made T-stands. They served the purpose—and cost practically nothing. I never hired anybody to do what I could possibly do myself. For 15 to 18 hours a day I was on the job, never for a moment letting down in my effort to make the store a success. Said a neighboring businessman, "Nobody has a right to work as hard as that fellow Grant. He'll kill himself if he keeps this up." But…this was my one great chance.…After all, this was my store—the store I had dreamed about. Never in all the years since have I had more excitement or more satisfaction than in those early days of the Grant Company.… This new kind of store had won a place of distinction among the retail establishments of Lynn, Massachusetts.*

Early interior view of the W.T. Grant Company's "Mother Store" in Lynn, Massachusetts. *From* The Grant Game, *author's collection.*

In the company's early years, reflecting general retail trends at the time, almost half of Grants' weekly sales were conducted on Saturday afternoons.

First year gross sales for the W.T. Grant Company came in at $99,478, with a profit of $5,000 for Grant and his investors. The financials were surprisingly good considering the financial crisis sweeping the nation at the time, with the "Silent Crash" of September 1906–March 1907 followed by the Panic of 1907 that began in October.

The hardworking and gregarious Grant, busy working fifteen-to-eighteen-hour days to launch the W.T. Grant Company and then oversee all the buying and merchandising operations of his fledgling Lynn "quarter store," was oblivious to the financial crisis sweeping the nation. Recalled Grant, "I was too busy working hard to make my first store succeed to realize that business conditions were so bad."

The observant Grant credited much of his retailing success with Grants to the power of learning from mistakes—his and those made by others. Recalled Grant, "The fact is that mistakes can be a powerful lesson if one recognizes them for what they are and draws the right conclusions, particularly so if this is done while working for someone else."

Grant's sweat equity, innate knack for retailing and ebullient optimism, coupled with his dynamic, charismatic ability to win the enthusiastic loyalty of those who worked with him, made the flagship W.T. Grant Company "Mother Store" at Lynn a success. "Follow me and you'll wear diamonds," Grant is said to have famously told his charter "Grant Girls" at Lynn.

For those who followed Grant in the coming years and decades, they did just that, hitching their future to what would soon become the nation's fastest-growing retailer as "The Idea" grew from a singular store in Lynn into a regional and then national chain of Grants stores.

FORGING LINKS

A Chain Is Born

With the opening of his trailblazing W.T. Grant Company twenty-five-cent store, Grant had fulfilled his lifelong dream—and successfully so beyond his wildest dreams.

While admittedly he would have, at least initially, been content to stay within the friendly confines of the Lynn store working alongside his newfound "family" of assistants, floor men and "Grant Girls," word about the newfangled "quarter store" pioneered by the canny, balding, spectacled, ebullient and spritely merchant in Lynn quickly spread across New England. Requests for more W.T. Grant Company stores rolled in to Grant in short order, and soon enough, the first links of a chain were forged.

One day, a salesman traveling New England visited the W.T. Grant store in Lynn and changed Grant's paradigms with his chance encounter suggestion: "There's a wonderful opportunity for a store like this Waterbury, Connecticut. Why don't you open one there?" With that suggestion, the W.T. Grant Company quickly became a chain store with the opening of a second—and much larger—fifteen-thousand-square-foot store in Waterbury.

Taking an inferior location to save on start-up costs given the fledgling company's limited capital, Grant again turned to showmanship to build excitement for the store's October 17, 1908 opening:

> *For many days before the opening, our front windows had been completely covered with paper and on each window was painted a gigantic question mark. This aroused curiosity and stimulated speculation, as no one could*

> *get a look into the store to see what was going on. As opening day drew near we changed the signs to read: "A New Kind of Store—A Department Store With Nothing Over 25 Cents." A few days before the opening we started advertising in the newspapers, announcing the day and hour the doors would swing wide. Just before the all-important day arrived we took down the paper from the windows, revealing an array of tempting merchandise. A band, hired for the occasion, could be heard for blocks around. The crowd was so great that we had to call on the police for help, and when at last we opened the doors the people poured in, filling every aisle. The excitement was terrific.*

Opening-day sales at Waterbury totaled $1,885.

Building on the solid foundation laid by the pioneering "Mother Store" at Lynn, the Waterbury Grants offered customers several new features that would become Grants staples, including in-store candy manufacturing and a soda fountain dispensing sweet drinks. An immediate hit with Grants customers, candy and nut counters and in-store food service operations—soda fountains, snack bars, luncheonettes and full-service restaurants—would be a popular hallmark of W.T. Grant Company stores until the company's 1976 demise.

Grant continued his flair for showmanship at Waterbury beyond opening day, hiring a pianist to play popular tunes of the day in the store's sheet music department on Saturday afternoons and evenings. Recalled Grant, "It added gaiety to the store atmosphere. Also, it helped to sell great quantities of sheet music at 10 cents a copy."

First-year sales at Waterbury reached $146,551. Buoyed by the success of his Lynn and Waterbury stores, Grant soon expanded his horizons across New England. Recalled Grant, "Though I did not realize it at the time, our first store in that city [Waterbury] marked the beginning of the Grant chain. When, after a few months, it turned out to be such a substantial success, it gave me the courage to open a third store, and my attention centered on a larger city through which I had passed so many times on my way to New York—Bridgeport, Connecticut."

Grant opened additional W.T. Grant Company stores in quick succession. Grant's Store No. 3 at Bridgeport opened on April 10, 1909, with the same sense of spectacle that had worked so well in Waterbury—display windows covered with large sheets of paper festooned with six-foot question marks and the enticement of "A New Kind of Store—21 Departments—Nothing Over 25 Cents—Watch for Sensational Opening."

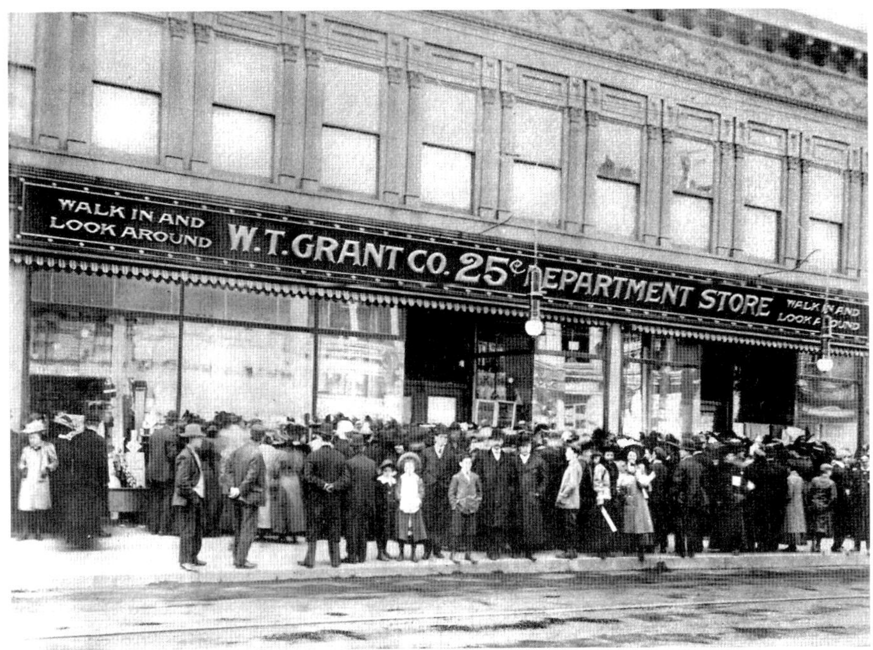

As word about the W.T. Grant Company's newfangled "quarter store" in Lynn, Massachusetts, spread, requests for more Grants stores rolled in to William T. Grant in short order. Soon enough, the first links of a chain were forged with the opening of additional stores, first regionally and then nationally. Pictured is an early W.T. Grant Company department store, location unknown. *Author's collection.*

Said Grant of the store's opening day reception, "The store opened with a fanfare of excitement. The crowd was so great that traffic was blocked and we had to barricade the front entrance for the protection of our windows."

With Bridgeport being only eighty minutes from New York City by train, Grant moved the company's corporate "General Office" from Lynn to Bridgeport, taking occupancy of a small six-by-eighteen-foot office space suspended from the store's low thirteen-foot ceiling by iron rods, a logistical challenge that required the office staff "to crouch to move about the office."

Overseeing the fledgling three-store chain was Maggie Walsh, who had come on board with Grant at Lynn during the store's first year at a salary of ten dollars per week. "She proved to be a wonder," Grant recalled. "She knew every phase and problem of the business. With her on the job, I felt that nothing could go wrong when I was away…with the eagle eye of Maggie Walsh surveying the entire three-store chain."

Grant soon opened a fourth store at Lewiston, Maine, on November 27, 1909, and a fifth store at New Bedford, Massachusetts, on April 22, 1910.

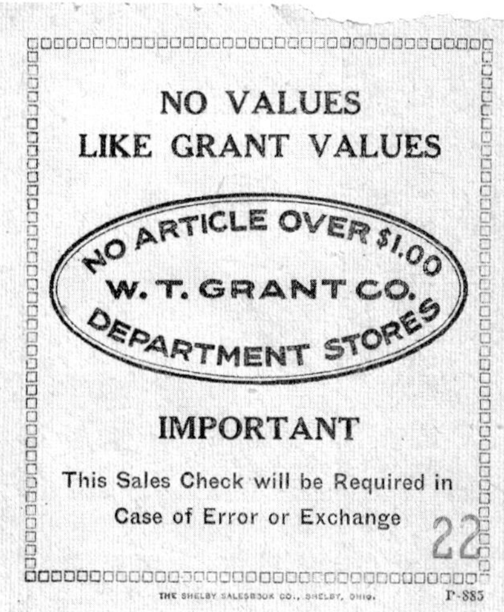

Circa 1910s sales check receipts. Starting as the W.T. Grant Company System of twenty-five-cent department stores, inflation around World War I saw Grants' price ceiling first raised to fifty cents and then one dollar. By the late 1930s, price limits were raised above the one-dollar mark and eliminated altogether by 1940. *Author's collection.*

"We now had five stores, all in Maine, Massachusetts and Connecticut," Grant recalled. "Up to this time we had never considered going outside the New England states, but repeated success prompted us to look toward wider horizons, even to dare to something undreamed of a few years before. And this took us into a venture where we were to learn some new lessons for which we were scarcely prepared—our first store in New York City."

Grant had long been in awe of New York City and, once established with his own successful company, desired to have an office in the "Big Apple":

> *From the earliest days of my buying trips to New York, I felt the awe that a country boy had for the big city. Even though I had lived and worked in Boston, New York was to me the city of glamour, excitement and achievement….I remember, too, one of the greatest thrills of my first year in our Lynn store. Coming to New York so frequently, I decided that I should have an office in the metropolis. It would make an impression of our importance on all with whom we did business. So I arranged for an "office." It consisted of a desk rented for $5 a month in a wholesale millinery house over Young's hat store at the corner of Houston Street and Broadway. But it was an office and the thrill I got was when I first looked at the letterhead that came from our printer: W.T. Grant Company, Lynn, Massachusetts—New York Office, 395 Broadway.*

An early undated ad for the Grants store on Lisbon Street in Lewiston, Maine, opened in November 1909. Famed as the "Originators of the 25 Cent Department Store," Grants stores visually stood apart from the competition as the "Store with the Orange Front." Orange would be Grants' signature color across its entire 1906–76 run. *Author's collection.*

Five years after founding the company, Grant was embarking on a new "stimulating adventure"—opening a W.T. Grant Company store in the throbbing heart of New York's bustling retailing district. "The location we had chosen was on Sixth Avenue at 18th Street, then one of the busiest shopping sections in America," Grant recalled. "Practically all of the city's large department stores were then concentrated on Sixth Avenue between 14th Street and 34th Street. Altman's on 18th Street, Siegel-Cooper, Simpson-Crawford, McCreery's, Stern Brothers—all were in our neighborhoods. Nearby, too, were many specialty shops, including Cammeyer's, the largest shoe store in the world, and most of the important 5-and-10-cent stores of that day. Not only were the sidewalks covered with shoppers all day long, but the streets were filled with street cars, carriages and cabs. These, with the roaring elevated trains above, filled the air with a continuous racket."

But where Grants' early history in New England was a rocket-like upward trajectory, the opening of the company's New York City store sorely tested its founder's mettle—and creativity.

On March 14, 1911, Grants made its splashy New York City debut at Store No. 6, where an extra two hundred sales clerks had been hired to help serve the anticipated large opening day crowds. But the twenty-five-cent store trade that had worked so well for Grants in the smaller and mid-size manufacturing cities of Maine, Massachusetts and Connecticut fell flat and drew a yawn in New York, the nation's largest city. The "Big Apple" was a whole different market than the ones that Grant—and Grants—was used to serving:

> *Into the midst of this activity we came, with all we knew of the merchandise we had sold so successfully in five small New England cities. We soon found that what we knew was not enough. Here in New York were a different kind of people, with different wants, different tastes and a different sense of values—a strange, skeptical type of people with whom we had no experience. To them the idea of a 25-cent department store was not sensational. Ours was just another store. We decided that there was one sure way to attract them—a value such as they had never seen anywhere. One of the best-known items of the day was the Ingersoll dollar watch. So we bought those watches at fifty cents each and offered them at 25 cents, figuring that such bargains, even though representing a heavy loss to us, would crowd the store with buyers. In Lynn or Waterbury or Bridgeport such an offer would have presented a stampede to buy. In New York it didn't cause a ripple of interest. Some people came in and looked at the watches, handled them and put them down again. Apparently they decided that no watch offered at 25 cents could possibly keep time.*

Eventually, Grants found its niche in New York City, but the store was never what Grant considered a true success. "We tried many other specials with little or no success, until finally we hit upon one combination of items that drew customers in gratifying numbers—wire hat frames and straw braid with which to cover them, a great fad at the time—when women made their own hats," Grant recalled. "Our prices were about one-fourth what milliners in the neighborhood were charging for the same materials. From this beginning we gradually built up a business in ribbons, artificial flowers, jewelry and other fashion merchandise. But in spite of all of our efforts the store was no great success."

With the establishment of the New York store, the W.T. Grant Company "Home Office" relocated from Bridgeport to a mezzanine overlooking the sales floor in the 6th Avenue store. Eventually outgrowing quarters there, the Home Office was moved to larger quarters on West 23rd Street in December

A massive total-loss April 1916 blaze brought the curtain down on W.T. Grant Company's struggling fledgling Manhattan Store No. 7 in the heart of New York City. Grants would eventually return to the Big Apple, opening stores across the city's five boroughs of Manhattan, Brooklyn, Queens, The Bronx and Staten Island. *Author's collection.*

1915. It turned out to be a fortuitous move, as a massive blaze destroyed Grants' New York City store in April 1916.

"One noontime my secretary rushed into my office to tell me that the Sixth Avenue store was on fire," Grant recalled. "While a fire is always serious, that fire solved a difficult problem. Our stock, which was fully covered by fire insurance, was almost a total loss. In addition, we had a use-and-occupancy insurance policy on the store. As I recall it paid us $99 a day for the first time during which we were unable to do business. That was more than our daily profits had been while running the store! We were quite content to ring down the curtain on our first New York try-out. We never re-opened a store in downtown Manhattan, although we afterward established successful Grant stores in other sections of the city."

Grant's later decision to open a store in Brooklyn, on Fulton Street next to popular iconic department store Abraham & Straus, also fell flat, albeit to a "tragic mistake" in store location. Recalled Grant, "What was the trouble? We were on the wrong side of Abraham & Straus. All around us were men's shops; on the other side of the store were women's shops. It was as simple as that. Women simply did not come over to our side to buy. No fire saved us in Brooklyn, but our location proved an advantage when we decided to retire from our second big-town investment. We recovered all our investment by disposing of our lease and improvements to a firm that opened a men's clothing store where men came to buy!"

Important lessons were learned from the company's early New York City retailing experiences. "Out of those first few years in New York came several important conclusions," Grant noted. "The opportunity for our type of store did not necessarily lay in the big cities, but in the many industrial cities throughout the country. That field was unlimited, and we had learned to succeed there."

The opening of W.T. Grant Store No. 7 at hometown Fall River, Massachusetts, later in 1911 saw Grants surpass the $1 million mark in annual sales, while the subsequent opening of Store No. 8 saw the addition of a second store on Union Street to serve Lynn.

Given William T. Grant's sobering experience with his ill-fated New York City store and the competitive retail market there, Grant thereafter opted to make his initial store developments in new state markets in the smaller second-tier industrial cities where the competitive pressures were lower and the showy grand opening extravaganza of a "new kind of store" Grants outlet would be keenly noticed.

Following the development of its initial Pennsylvania store in Johnstown, other W.T. Grant Company stores popped up in quick succession at Scranton, Lancaster, Erie, Philadelphia, York, Reading and Pittsburgh. Following the establishment of early Massachusetts stores in Lynn, New Bedford and Fall River, other Grants stores were quickly opened, including units in Holyoke, Haverhill, Brockton, Pittsfield, Hyde Park, Rockland and Norwood.

Grants' accelerated pace of expansion and the need for effective corporate communications across the growing breadth of the company spurred the early 1910s creation of the W.T. Grant Company's inaugural monthly house organ, *The Very Idea!*, refreshed and reimaged in July 1920 as *The Grant Game*, which published continuously until its final edition in September 1975.

Following the chain's star-crossed venture into New York City, New York State Grants stores would subsequently be developed in smaller manufacturing cities including Schenectady, Syracuse, Albany and Binghamton.

The W.T. Grant Company's fast-growing chain of twenty-five-cent stores, known colloquially as "Grants" beginning in 1915, quickly expanded beyond the company's northeastern U.S. footprint. Grants stores were soon established in the Mid-Atlantic, Midwest and South at New Jersey, Pennsylvania, Michigan, Virginia, Ohio, Indiana, Kentucky, Illinois, Virginia, Missouri, West Virginia, South Carolina, Tennessee, Florida, Arkansas, Georgia, North Carolina, Alabama, Rhode Island, Texas, Maryland, Louisiana, Wisconsin, Iowa and Minnesota.

Finding a welcome home in the nation's heartland, Grants' initial "Land of Lincoln" outlet, Store No. 31, was opened on November 15, 1917, in 45,401-resident Rockford, then Illinois' third-largest city, in the city's bustling downtown "Loop" retailing district. Located at 107–109 South Main Street in the Dow Block, wedged between two high-traffic anchor draws—premier local department store D.J. Stewart & Company and leading city druggist John R. Porter—Grants' novel new twenty-five-cent store was an immediate success with "Forest City" residents.

With founder Grant's penchant for retailing showmanship and traffic-generating spectacle, the W.T. Grant Company's opening of its "New Idea" Rockford store made headlines in the afternoon *Rockford Republic*. "As the doors were thrown open this noon, a great crowed was massed in front of both entrances, and three policemen were at the doors to maintain one door as entrance and the other as exit," the *Republic* reported, noting that Grants' general superintendent and future president Benjamin A. Rowe was in town for the grand opening. "The store is something new and novel….It is the only store of its kind in the state....The company carries no charge accounts and makes no deliveries. The store deals in miscellaneous merchandise. Dry goods, hardware, jewelry, toilet requisites, phonograph records and many other articles...are to be had. The store is attractively decorated and presents an inviting appearance."

Given Grants' popular reception in Rockford, additional Illinois stores soon followed at Peoria (Store No. 33) and Mississippi River port city East St. Louis (Store No. 45).

W.T. Grant Company stores in U.S. "Second City" Chicago, including the company's Windy City downtown flagship at State and Madison Streets, came online in later years after Grant stores were well established in numerous other Illinois communities. On State Street, that "Great Street" feted in song by Frank Sinatra, Grants successfully competed alongside Chicago's hometown favorites including Marshall Field & Company; Wieboldt's; Sears, Roebuck & Company; Montgomery Ward; Carson, Pirie, Scott & Company; The Fair Store; and Goldblatt Brothers, among others.

Mirroring the experience in Illinois, pioneering Grant stores in new states were soon followed by additional stores, also in second-tier industrial cities, with Grants' pioneering Ohio store at Dayton followed by stores at Toledo, Canton, Portsmouth, Mansfield, Marion and Elyria; Indiana's pioneering Fort Wayne store was followed by northwest Indiana stores at Gary and Hammond. In Wisconsin, Grants' pioneering store at Oshkosh was quickly followed by stores at Fond du Lac, Sheboygan, Green Bay, Madison and Milwaukee.

But despite its retailing forays into the Mid-Atlantic, Midwest, South and, eventually, the West Coast, growing into a coast-to-coast national retailer by 1932, states seeing the most widespread development of Grants stores were, not surprisingly, the company's early core northeastern markets in population-dense Massachusetts, New York, Pennsylvania and New Jersey.

By the end of World War I, Grants operated nearly forty stores, although due to World War I price inflation, the company's foundational quarter price ceiling was raised to fifty cents and then one dollar, with Grants' "Known for Values" stores of the late 1910s, 1920s and 1930s rebranded as "25 cent, 50 cent and $1.00 department stores." By the late 1930s, as important items were added in Grants' millinery and ready-to-wear departments, price limits were raised above the one-dollar mark and eliminated altogether by 1940 as Grants continued to focus on its successful middle-of-the-road pricing strategy between the five-and-dime variety stores and traditional department stores.

As the W.T. Grant Company continued to expand its store footprint across the East, Mid-Atlantic Midwest and South, Grants quickly grew into one of the nation's leading and fastest-growing retail chains, merchandised by a Home Office staff of ten company buyers in New York City.

To better serve its growing fleet of stores and begin to standardize its increasingly geographically dispersed operations, Grants in 1919 installed a "central display section" at its New York City Home Office, where Grants set up model window trimming displays and model department and counter merchandise displays to showcase best practices merchandising within the Grants chain. Not long after, Grants' first standard store displays were rolled out at Store No. 43 in Pittsfield, Massachusetts—and soon chain-wide.

"As the number of our stores increased…we reached a point where we had to put in a standardized system of window and store displays," Grant

As the W.T. Grant Company expanded its increasingly far-flung store operations into the Midwest and South, Grants' New York City Home Office in 1919 began to standardize display window and in-store merchandise presentations, showcasing "best practices" across the fast-growing chain. *From* The Grant Game, *author's collection.*

recalled. "We set up, at our headquarters office, model windows and model department and counter displays, photographed them, and sent them out."

And as the W.T. Grant Company added more and more stores, Grant learned additional "valuable lessons in running a department store chain—the necessity of choosing men for store management with great care as to all their qualifications, and the corresponding need for a method of compensation that would serve as a continuous incentive to success."

"The method of selecting men was worked out gradually over a long period.…Eventually we were to develop sound methods of selection and training, methods so well conceived and directed that they were to pay a part of vast importance in the growth of our company," explained Grant. "The method of compensation was put into effect at once. This provided that the manager should have a bonus of 20 percent of the profits of the store, with a $30-a-week drawing account. Thus he would be virtually in business for himself without making an investment. All his energies and resourcefulness would be concentrated on increasing sales and holding down expenses, for only in that way could he make a profit for the store and himself. That plan has remained the basis of compensation for our store managers to this day, and the years have demonstrated its fundamental soundness."

During the W.T. Grant Company's first decade, Grant himself oversaw the new store development responsibilities that would later fall to the new corporate Home Office Real Estate Department in New York City. Recalled Grant in 1945:

> *Today we have an efficient Real Estate Department, but for many years the choosing of locations for Grant stores and the making of leases were my personal responsibility. Picking a city in which to establish a store may be relatively easy. Finding a suitable location for the store in that city is a far more difficult task. Through the first ten years of our history, during which we opened 36 stores, I traveled not only throughout New England and down the Atlantic Coast, but also through the Central States and as far West as Texas, visiting cities again and again, searching for sites, talking to property owners, and working out the details of our leases.… Most of our early stores were located in something less than the best business districts, where we had to draw customers with our usual values and ingenious promotions. We refused to burden a store from the beginning with a rental which might handicap us in showing a profit. Rather, we worked on the basis then that a Grant store had to make a profit in its first*

year. Of course we were also somewhat timid in those early days because we had not yet developed what we considered a sure format for success, but gradually as we got more and more courage and confidence, we went into better and better locations.

And as Grants grew, so did the size and scope of the company's New York Home Office—from Houston Street to 6th Avenue to West 23rd Street, the latter running through to 22nd Street and serving as Grants' office, stockroom and shipping department. Eventually, Grants' Home Office was moved to a location on 7th Avenue, now part of R.H. Macy Company's flagship Herald Square store, and then in 1929 to its longtime home at 1441 Broadway, where Grants originally filled five floors as the major anchor tenant, in addition to later also leasing satellite office space in three nearby Midtown Manhattan office towers—the Bush, Longacre and Wurlitzer Buildings.

Recalled Grant of the company's growing Home Office operations, "As we grew we were going to need men—and more men—men to develop as store managers, men as buyers, men to look after accounting, real estate and all the many departments into which our company was now dividing itself. When I had one store it was a one-man business. When we had two, three, even four or five stores, it was still largely a matter of one man buying and one man management, and I had been that one. But now I realized that I had to both divide and multiply myself, I had to have help—men and women I could depend on, men and women with the talents, capacity and dependability to help our company grow, and to grow with it."

Grant—and his successors—were keen observers and quick to discern the proper strategies needed to further "The Idea," building the W.T. Grant Company into a leading retail powerhouse "Known for Values from Coast to Coast."

By the 1954 publication of Grant's autobiography, the W.T. Grant Company had grown to encompass more than twenty-five thousand employees and 521 stores nationwide serving more than 1 million customers every business day. And by its height in the early 1970s, $1.8 billion Grants would rank as the nation's seventh-largest retailer, with 1,238 stores and more than eighty thousand employees.

Noted Grant in 1954, "Today we are all working together to build an even finer Grant business, profiting by our mistakes and building on our successes—as we have from the beginning. I can't begin to tell you how proud I am of all of you who make up this wonderful organization, and how deeply I appreciate the help you have given me over the years in making my youthful dream of becoming a merchant come true. As the weeks and months roll by, we are adding new chapters to the story—all of them interesting, some of them exciting. It will not be finished in the lifetime of us, but I take it that we are having fun writing it. I know I am!"

THE ROARING TWENTIES

"Mr. Magic Buyer"

As Grants grew into a retail chain encompassing thirty-nine stores in a dozen states and thousands of employees by the dawn of what came to be ebulliently known as the "Roaring Twenties," the W.T. Grant Company was no longer a retail fledgling but coming of age.

The 1920s ushered in an unprecedented era of growth for Grants, which totaled 281 stores ringing up $75 million in sales across thirty-three states by decade's end.

Helping employees keep track of the company's exponential growth across an increasingly large geographic footprint was Grants' new monthly company magazine, *The Grant Game*, launched in July 1920 as the retooled and rebranded successor to Grants' inaugural house organ, *The Very Idea!*

Charged with a mission to "present a record of the company's steady, rapid growth" and encourage "each member of the company" to "work with greater enthusiasm, proud that his work is contributing to the general success" of the W.T. Grant Company, *The Grant Game* sought to bring together the fast-growing Grants family by educating employees about the latest in retailing best practices; spreading word about various company developments, including promotions and new store openings; and maintaining Grants' foundational close-knit family atmosphere with homespun coverage of business and social activities gathered by volunteer correspondents in Grants' local stores, warehouses, regional district offices and New York City corporate Home Office.

Left: Helping employees keep track of the W.T. Grant Company's exponential growth across an increasingly large geographic footprint was Grants' new monthly company magazine, *The Grant Game*, launched in July 1920 as the retooled and rebranded successor to Grants' inaugural house organ, *The Very Idea! From* The Grant Game, *author's collection.*

Below: *The Grant Game* welcomed freelance art and literary contributions from W.T. Grant Company employees, who creatively celebrated life working at Grants through cartoons, art sketches, photography and a wide range of literary styles, including poetry and limericks. *From* The Grant Game, *author's collection.*

This page: Proprietary house label 78 RPM Bell Records (*left*) and Diva Records (*right*) were produced exclusively for sale by the W.T. Grant Company by Orange, New Jersey–based Arto Company (1920–27) and New York–based Columbia Records (1927–31), respectively. *Author's collection.*

The Grant Game also welcomed freelance art and literary contributions from its employees, who creatively celebrated the W.T. Grant Company through cartoons, art sketches, photography and a wide range of literary styles, including poetry and limericks.

In the early 1920s, the W.T. Grant Company rolled out its first exclusive proprietary house brand under the "Grants" label in conjunction with the company's popular "Mr. Magic Buyer" logo, a cartoon mascot likeness of Grants' bespectacled "Magic Buyer" namesake, William T. Grant.

Created in 1914 and instantly popular with the public, Grants' Mr. Magic Buyer character, bowing with a dramatic flourish and tipping his bowler hat, quickly became a widely recognized trademark ambassador of the W.T. Grant Company, initially serving as Grants' spritely spokesman in local newspaper ads, promotional circulars, store merchandising and window displays.

Sales promotion director E.L. Dow had the Mr. Magic Buyer trademark—emblazoned on proprietary Grants-branded products beginning in the early 1920s as part of the rollout of the Grants label—registered with the U.S. Patent Office in 1923. Dow also figured prominently in Grants' history as the early 1920s creator of the company's famous and longstanding "Known for Values" slogan, which was trademarked in 1927.

In short order, the Grants name and the visage of Mr. Magic Buyer were being paired to identify a variety of proprietary Grants-branded products ranging from men's hosiery and safety pins to Grant's Golden Glow Mop Polish, the latter billed as "The Kind with the Strong Back-Bone." Contracted from third-party vendors and manufacturers, proprietary Grants-branded house label products were made to Grants' stringent specifications of offering quality equal to or better than name brand products at a cost savings.

Ambassador of "Service-Success-Happiness" to the burgeoning ranks of the Grants family, Mr. Magic Buyer also became the longtime cheerleading cartoon face of *The Grant Game*, beginning with the cover of the inaugural issue in July 1920.

And as the decade drew to a close and Grants dabbled in the new advertising medium of commercial network radio, Grants' Mr. Magic Buyer inspired the creation of the 1929 instrumental march "The March of the Magic Buyers," composed especially for the W.T. Grant Company by Edward "Eddie" Fitzgerald. Announced by Jane Day and performed by musical director Ricardo Sodero and his studio musicians, "The March of the Magic Buyers" made its world debut on Boston businessman John Shepard III's charter CBS Radio Network stations—WNAC-AM 1230 (today's WRKO-AM 680) in Boston and WEAN-AM 790 (today's WPRV-AM) in Providence, Rhode Island.

As the company grew exponentially in the 1920s, the need rose to present a standardized store image to the public. In their early years, Grants stores lacked a unified look, save for the distinctive orange and navy blue W.T. Grant Company signs that separated Grants from its red-and-gold-fronted look-alike five-and-dime competitors like F.W. Woolworth, S.S. Kresge and G.C. Murphy, among others.

From its 1906 founding in leased street-level and basement quarters in the YMCA Building in downtown Lynn, Massachusetts, Grants as a rule generally leased its store locations, the end result being an architecturally diverse array of stores by the 1920s.

Looking to bring a bit more architectural order to its fast-growing roster of stores as a burgeoning national player, Grants hired P.A. Cunnius to serve as its New York–based Home Office chief architect. Over the course of twenty-five years between 1926 and 1951, Cunnius worked with local developers and an array of high-profile collaborating architects and designers like Alfred S. Alschuler and Raymond Loewy on the design of scores of downtown flagship Grants stores across the country. Among Cunnius's most distinctive works were Streamline Moderne–styled Grants stores developed at Kalamazoo, Michigan; Syracuse and Buffalo, New York; Bangor, Maine;

As seen in this tribute collage, between 1926 and 1951 W.T. Grant Company chief architect P.A. Cunnius oversaw the design of scores of Grants stores in a variety of architectural styles reflecting both the changing times and the diversity of local architectural styles and sensitivities across the United States. *Author's collection.*

and Davenport, Iowa, as well as a localized nautical-themed Grants on Congress Street in downtown Portland, Maine.

Early orange-fronted Grants stores generally targeted medium-sized cities from 25,000 to 150,000 in population, although the company did make early forays into larger working-class industrial cities like Buffalo, Rochester, Newark, Boston, Chicago and Milwaukee, among others. The W.T. Grant Company's standard practice was to lease its store locations, with leases running no less than ten years, preferably with a renewal clause, and typically running twenty years and even up to thirty years.

Among the Grants stores of the 1920s was the flagship W.T. Grant Company store on busy West Wisconsin Avenue in 457,147-resident Milwaukee, Wisconsin's largest city. From 1924 to 1974, under twenty- and thirty-year leases, Grants occupied leased street-level and basement quarters in the western half of the Italian Gothic–styled Plankinton Arcade, whose high-traffic nearby neighbors included Gimbel Brothers, Boston Store,

Espenhain and JCPenney department stores, as well as F.W. Woolworth and S.S. Kresge five-and-dime variety stores.

Looking to broaden its horizons, Grants in 1927 launched its "Division D" roster of orange-and-navy-fronted Grants stores serving smaller communities. By January 1930, there were 86 Division D Grants stores serving a diverse array of smaller manufacturing communities, including Store No. 586 in 9,691-resident Conneaut, Ohio; Store No. 537 in 6,433-resident Skowhegan, Maine; Store No. 532 in 10,628-resident Bennington, Vermont; and Store No. 582 in 6,839-resident Clifton Forge, Virginia.

Those guidelines would remain mainstays of Grants' new store development program until after World War II, when the push was on by the W.T. Grant Company for new, larger, architecturally ambitious and futuristic "Store of Tomorrow" multi-level signature downtown flagship department stores in cities like Syracuse, Buffalo, Pittsburgh, Philadelphia and St. Paul, in addition to trailblazing new-style outlying urban and suburban greenfield strip shopping center "park and shop" locations.

The 1920s were also a pivotal turning point decade for the W.T. Grant Company in other significant ways. Since its 1906 establishment, the W.T. Grant Company had been very much a one-man company, synonymous with ebullient founding namesake William T. Grant and his paradigm-shifting "New Idea" in retailing. Following eighteen years of hard work as the "zestful, jaunty" and ever-optimistic namesake head of the Grants department store chain, high school dropout turned multimillionaire Grant, successful and wealthy beyond his wildest dreams with a net worth pegged at more than $40 million, retired as company president in late 1924 at age forty-eight to take up new pursuits as a globe-trotting world traveler, philosopher, speaker, writer, artist, photographer and philanthropist, engaging in the latter with his 1936 establishment of the nonprofit William T. Grant Foundation, then known as The Grant Foundation.

But busy all the time, focused on building the W.T. Grant Company into a national retailing powerhouse, Grant's preoccupation with business matters would take a deleterious toll on his October 5, 1907 marriage to onetime school teacher Lena Blanche Brownell (1875–1967), to whom Grant had been introduced by his brother, Elihu, while still in the employ of Almy, Bigelow and Washburn in Salem, Massachusetts. The Grants, who adopted two daughters, Marion and Helen, divorced in 1920.

On September 3, 1930, Grant married his "Grant Girl" personal secretary, Beth Bradshaw (1901–1954), with whom he adopted a daughter, Shirley. Both fans of gregariously entertaining Grants executives and

Top: Shoppers stroll past the W.T. Grant Company store in Newark, New Jersey, in the "Roaring Twenties," a decade of economic growth and widespread prosperity that saw Grants grow from 39 stores in a dozen states to 281 stores across thirty-three states by decade's end. *Author's collection.*

Bottom: Interior of W.T. Grant Company store, unknown location, circa 1920s. *Author's collection.*

On September 3, 1930, William T. Grant (1876–1972) married his "Grant Girl" personal secretary Beth Bradshaw (1901–1954). Both gregarious, the Grants enjoyed entertaining company executives and managers at their picturesque estates in West Falmouth, Massachusetts, and Miami, Florida. *From* The Grant Game, *author's collection.*

managers at their picturesque estates in West Falmouth, Massachusetts, and Miami, Florida, Grant enjoyed twenty-three years of marriage to Bradshaw, who passed away on February 9, 1954, in Manhattan following a cerebral hemorrhage.

With his "retirement," Grant turned over the day-to-day operations of his burgeoning W.T. Grant Company department store chain to a succession of trusted, capable career "Grant Men" who learned the business inside out from bottom to top, rising from humble starts as stockers and floor men in local Grants stores to, eventually, the company's highest Home Office executive ranks in Midtown Manhattan.

Looking for a like-minded successor to head the W.T. Grant Company's day-to-day operations as president, Grant found one in-house in Clayton E. Freeman, Grants' longtime treasurer and merchandise manager.

W.T. Grant Company president Clayton E. Freeman, 1924–29. *From* The Grant Game, *author's collection.*

But Grants still remained very much a one-man company even after its founder's so-called retirement. Retaining a keen interest in the success of Grants and its employees, Grant remained deeply engaged in the workings of the W.T. Grant Company—chairing board of directors meetings, serving as a vocal national spokesman against the rising tide of anti-chain store legislation in the 1930s and making personal appearances at major Grants store openings and corporate events.

A particular favorite pastime of Grant was popping in at Grant stores during his travels around the country. Noted one Grants employee, "Mr. Grant liked nothing better than to pop in at a store unannounced. He'd stroll about chatting with the girls, visit with the manager, and invariably include a stop for a Grant hot dog during his tour."

Grant would serve as chairman of the board of the W.T. Grant Company until his retirement at age ninety in 1966, although he drew no salary and increasingly withdrew from active management during his final decade as chairman, most notably after a serious 1953 illness at age seventy-six. In an unprecedented gesture of fondness, admiration and respect, Grant was unanimously elected as Grants' Honorary Chairman of the Board for Life, a title he held until his August 1972 death at age ninety-six at his home in Greenwich, Connecticut. Concurrently with his 1966 retirement from the W.T. Grant Company board, Grant also retired as board chairman of The Grant Foundation.

Another major development for Grants during the decade was the September 1928 listing of publicly traded W.T. Grant Company common and preferred shares under the "GTY" ticker symbol on the New York Stock Exchange by a syndicate composed of Lehman Brothers, Lazard Fréres, Redmond & Company and Blake Brothers & Company, a move spurred in part by the need to raise the increasingly large amounts of capital required to finance Grants' ambitious expansion into a truly national coast-to-coast retailer by the early 1930s.

Previously, common and preferred shares of Grants stock had been privately traded by company founder William T. Grant, the company's

Though retired from day-to-day operations in 1924, William T. Grant continued to keep tabs on W.T. Grant Company operations over the ensuing decades, making periodic impromptu visits during his travels to tour stores and talk with local store managers. Here Grant visits Store No. 205 in Utica, New York. *Author's collection.*

A favorite pastime of William T. Grant was visiting Grants stores during his travels around the country. Recalled one W.T. Grant Company employee, "Mr. Grant liked nothing better than to pop in at a store unannounced. He'd stroll about chatting with the girls, visit with the manager, and invariably include a stop for a Grant hot dog during his tour." *Author's collection.*

majority shareholder, for the benefit of loyal and capable Grants managers and longtime employees.

Grant retained a one-quarter interest in the now publicly traded firm. Combined with shares held by Grant, the W.T. Grant Company and Grants executives and employees, majority control of the company remained within the larger "Grant Family."

William T. Grant's personal 1936 donation of large blocks of Grants stock to establish the endowment for his newly created philanthropic legacy, The Grant Foundation, overseen by Grant and the W.T. Grant Company's sitting board chairman among others, further cemented control of the W.T. Grant Company within the expanding Grants circle.

NATIONAL AMBITIONS

"Known for Values Coast to Coast"

As the 1920s drew to a close with confetti, party hats, noise makers and the traditional midnight ball drop at One Times Square to the tune of "Auld Lang Syne," the W.T. Grant Company and the more than six thousand employees comprising the "Grant Family" could look back on the Roaring Twenties as a time of tremendous growth and transformation.

Entering the 1920s with 33 stores in twelve states doing $8 million in sales volume, Grants wrapped up the decade with the distinction of being the nation's fastest-growing retailer, its 281 stores ringing up $75 million in sales across thirty-three states.

The close of the decade also saw Grants' expanding Home Office operations relocated to take partial occupancy of the newly developed thirty-four-story Bricken Textile Building office tower at 1441 Broadway in Times Square in Midtown Manhattan, today's 10 Times Square.

Mirroring its growing stature in the U.S. general merchandise retailing industry, the W.T. Grant Company was among the notable firms to take charter occupancy in architect Ely Jacques Kahn's Art Deco–styled Bricken Textile Building, developed by namesake Abraham Bricken, Louis Adler and A.E. Lefcourt to satisfy the city's growing need for high-end office space. In addition to Grants and, beginning in 1936, company founder William T. Grant's charitable The Grant Foundation, other high-profile tenants at 1441 Broadway included the New York Telephone Company, several Wall Street firms and a number of specialized textile industry bankers serving the city's nearby Garment District.

In February 1930, the W.T. Grant Company took occupancy of the fifteenth to seventeenth floors of the thirty-four-story Bricken Textile Building at 1441 Broadway in Times Square in Midtown Manhattan, seen here in 2018 as 10 Times Square. As Grants grew into a nationwide chain, the retailer's Home Office operations expanded to eventually fill the renamed W.T. Grant Building before moving to the new W.T. Grant Building at 1515 Broadway in June 1972. *Eric A. Johnson photo.*

W.T. Grant Company president Benjamin A. Rowe, 1930–37. *From* The Grant Game, *author's collection.*

During the decade, the presidential torch at Grants had been passed by founder William T. Grant to two trusted early and longtime W.T. Grant Company associates—first to former treasurer and merchandise manager Clayton E. Freeman in late 1924 and then to Grants' Western District manager, Benjamin A. Rowe, in January 1930—exemplifying William T. Grant's foundational commitment to developing homegrown talent from within the company's ranks at all levels, from the store to the district to the New York City Home Office.

Rowe, who had joined Grants in 1910 at its fifth store in New Bedford, Massachusetts, later served as assistant manager and manager of Grants stores in New York and Pennsylvania before being tapped in 1924 to serve as company vice-president under Freeman.

W.T. Grant Company president Karl D. Gardner, 1937–40. *From* The Grant Game, *author's collection.*

Noted William T. Grant in the January–February 1930 issue of *The Grant Game*, "It is the culmination of a dream of mine—that…men who started, as practically all our men do start, at the very bottom, should come through sheer quality to the highest position in the Company."

Indeed, other longtime, loyal, ladder-climbing veteran "Grant Men" would eventually follow Grant, Freeman and Rowe at the helm of the rapidly expanding Grants empire, including Karl D. Gardner, Raymond H. Fogler, Edward Staley, Louis C. Lustenberger, Richard W. Mayer, Harry E. Pierson and James G. Kendrick, with homegrown talent heading the W.T. Grant Company for sixty-nine years from 1906 to 1975.

In 1937, the retiring Rowe was succeeded by Gardner, who had joined the fifteen-store W.T. Grant Company in 1913 upon graduating from Brown University. In typical Grants style, Gardner dutifully worked his way up through every level of the fast-growing company. Promoted to district manager in 1924, sales promotion manager in 1928, vice-president in 1933 and general manager in 1935, Gardner was elected to the presidency of the then 475-store, $100 million chain in January 1937.

While a much-changed company by the dawn of the 1930s, the core essence of the Grants remained little changed under the watchful eye of board president and company namesake William T. Grant and his trusted lieutenants. Observed Grants corporate personnel director and future president Raymond H. Fogler in the January–February 1930 issue of *The Grant Game*:

> *In ten short years every man in the Company has changed his job at least once and most of them several times, the business has been entirely remade, and there have been changes, more changes and then additional ones. During these ten years 248 stores have been opened, business has been extended into twenty-one additional states, district offices have been established in Atlanta, Boston, Chicago and New York, and the general offices have been twice moved into larger quarters. There have been changes of every possible kind. Some have proven beneficial, and some have not, but all have been evidence of a desire to improve and an attempt to eliminate the useless and the obsolete. Changes indeed, so many and at times so frequently that it has been difficult for any one person to know of all of them. But the W.T. Grant Company remains the same. Twenty-three years ago Mr. Grant established a retail business for the purpose of serving the public conveniently, economically, and pleasantly.... Today, the W.T. Grant Company is carrying on an ever new retail business for the purpose of serving the public conveniently, economically and pleasantly, and the purpose is fulfilled by following exactly the same principles as were followed twenty-three years ago, Yes, the W.T. Grant Company remains the same. Strange, isn't it, that a company can change so much, and still remain the same? In achieving this the W.T. Grant Company has achieved greatness.*

Despite its heady achievements and accolades of the decade just passed, the W.T. Grant Company, like its peer retail competitors and other U.S. firms, faced stiff economic headwinds during the 1930s Great Depression, which had been ushered in just months prior with the surprise stock market crash of October 1929.

With its enduring middle-market niche purveying high-quality goods in the twenty-five-cent to one-dollar trade, the W.T. Grant Company not only endured but also continued to prosper and even expanded its nationwide reach during the 1930s—no small feat when one considers the national unemployment rate skyrocketed from just under 5 percent to nearly 25 percent at the depths of the Great Depression.

The July 8, 1938 grand opening interior view of the W.T. Grant Company's new twenty-five-cent, fifty-cent and one-dollar department store at Green Bay, Wisconsin. *Author's collection.*

In addition to serving its foundational core workingman's middle-class market, Grants during the Great Depression also appealed to those on both ends of the economic spectrum, serving as the rich man's upscale five-and-dime and the poor man's upscale traditional department store.

Operating more than four hundred stores in thirty-eight states, Grants became a truly national chain with the summer 1932 opening of its first Pacific Coast outlet—a junior department store opened in leased quarters at 427–29 South Broadway in Los Angeles. Previous westward expansions had brought Grants as far west as Salt Lake City and Ogden, Utah, and El Paso, Texas. With the opening of its Los Angeles store turning the W.T. Grant Company into a true coast-to-coast retailer, "Golden State" California quickly became Grants' leading West Coast market.

Throughout the Depression-era 1930s, the W.T. Grant Company continued to add new stores to its steadily expanding chain, as well as expand, remodel and refresh its network of existing Grants stores.

In fast-growing blue-collar industrial city Rockford, Illinois, the W.T. Grant Company in 1931 expanded its previously relocated Store No. 31, the company's first Illinois store, unifying existing and new West State Street structures behind a stylish Art Deco cream-colored terra-cotta façade, an ambitious $100,000 Depression-era undertaking that earned praise as an "all Rockford" development that employed local workers and contractors. The state-of-the-art Grants store at 203–09 West State, anchored by a well-patronized quick-service luncheonette famous for homemade "good food" entrées, soups and chili and tempting twenty-cent double-thick malted milks,

Following customers west as they migrated to sunny California looking for jobs, opportunities and a new life during the Dust Bowl and Great Depression years of the 1930s, the W.T. Grant Company opened its first store west of the Rockies at Los Angeles in 1932. Here, Grants employees at 425–37 South Broadway in L.A. gather for a group photo on November 10, 1938. *Author's collection.*

was a popular downtown Rockford retailing mainstay for decades until its 1962 closure in favor of larger, newly opened outlying junior department store shopping center locations at North Towne (1957) and Colonial Village (1962).

The Great Depression–spurred 1933 creation of the $3.3 billion federal National Recovery Act (NRA) public works and economic revitalization program by the Franklin D. Roosevelt administration enjoyed early support from a variety of U.S. employers, including the W.T. Grant Company, which signed on to targeted industry-specific code agreements governing wage and hour standards and price controls, earning Grants the right to patriotically display the NRA Code's blue eagle emblem and "We Do Our Part" slogan in stores and company advertisements.

The NRA Industry Code Agreement was drawn up by representatives of government, labor and industry with a goal of setting minimum wage and maximum weekly hours standards, as well as establishing minimum prices at which products could be sold.

In fast-growing blue-collar manufacturing city Rockford, Illinois, W.T. Grant Company Store No. 31 anchored this $100,000 Art Deco Depression-era facility at 203–09 West State Street in Rockford's bustling downtown "Loop" shopping district from 1931 to 1962, when it was supplanted by outlying Grants junior department stores at the North Towne (1957) and Colonial Village (1962) shopping centers. *Bob Anderson photo.*

Additionally, Grants employees in some locales participated in community-wide torch-lit NRA drives, a popular venue in 1933 and 1934 for promoting NRA Code adoption by local employers. On October 25, 1934, W.T. Grant Company employees at Store No. 32 in Richmond, Virginia, were among the participants marching in support of NRA Code adoption at a citywide NRA parade at "River City" Richmond, home to the state NRA office.

In 1935, the U.S. Supreme Court unanimously ruled the NRA Code unconstitutional, saying that it infringed on the separation of powers, but many of the NRA's labor provisions would be incorporated later in the year into the Wagner Act, more commonly known as the National Labor Relations Act.

Always looking for new ways to further differentiate itself from the competition in the highly competitive general merchandise retailing industry, particularly in the depths of the Great Depression, the W.T. Grant Company was about three decades ahead of the times on March 3, 1934, when it experimented with the modern combination discount department

Window-shopping and the marketing art of window dressing were central to the make-or-break success of the nation's retailing industry in the Depression-era 1930s. Pictured is a fashion-themed circa 1933–35 Grants window display bearing the federal National Recovery Act (NRA) logo. The W.T. Grant Company was an early adherent to the NRA economic revitalization program. *Author's collection.*

store and supermarket "superstore" or "hypermarket" concept—successfully pioneered in 1962 by Grand Rapids, Michigan–based Meijer—with the debut of Grants' "Experimental Foods Department" in Store 282 at St. Nicholas Avenue and 163rd Street in the Washington Heights neighborhood of Upper Manhattan in New York City.

Going up against traditional grocers like New York–based supermarket industry giant A&P, Grants' experimental delicatessen and grocery department units offered packaged, canned and bottled groceries, fresh baked goods, delicatessen meats and cheeses and dairy items across hundreds of stock keeping units (SKUs)—purveying a mix of national household brand names like Armour, Del Monte, Kraft and Softasilk and proprietary house brand offerings including Grants salad dressings and Fra-Grant coffee and spices.

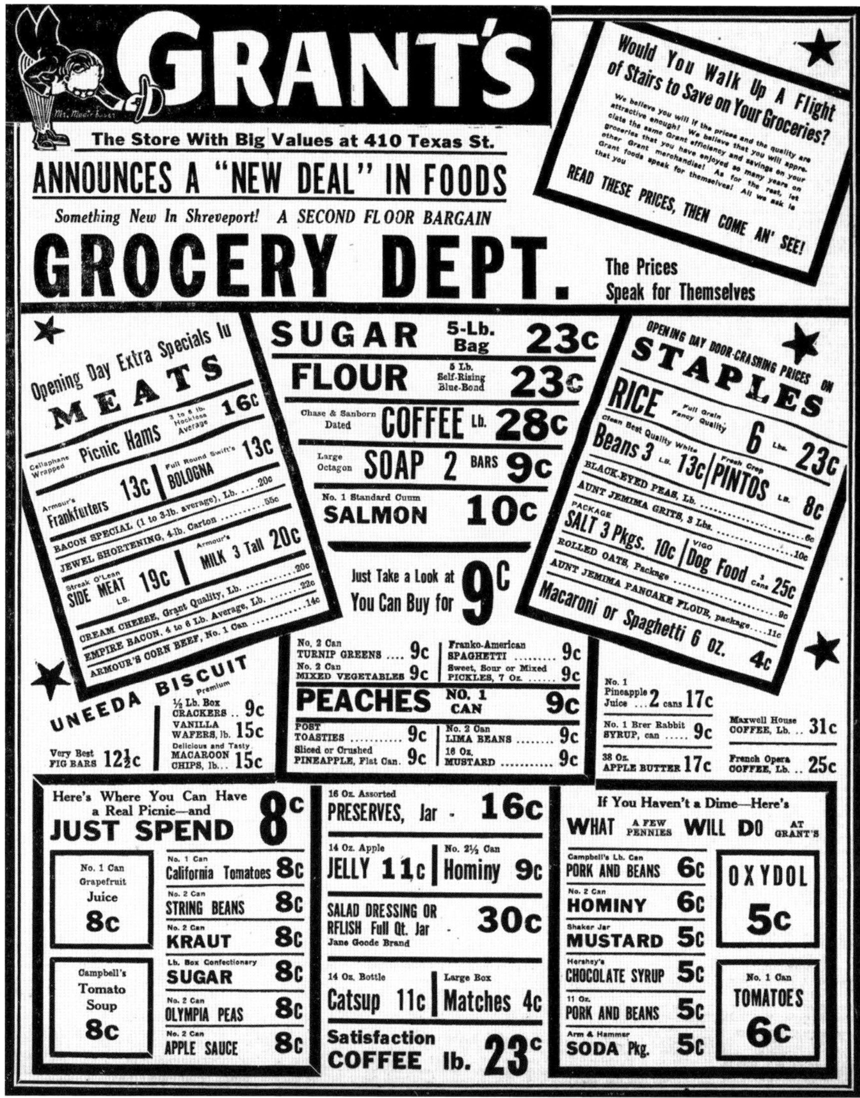

Offering customers "A 'New Deal' in Foods," the W.T. Grant Company's Shreveport, Louisiana store advertises its new second-floor Grocery Department. A pioneering concept in one-stop shopping that's now commonplace in today's discount SuperCenter era, Grants, beginning in 1934, trail-blazed the addition of groceries, including delicatessen and bakery operations, to many of its larger downtown general merchandise stores, catering to price-sensitive Depression-era shoppers. Among Grants' house grocery brands were its Fra-Grant line of coffees and spices. *Author's collection.*

On July 14, 1934, Grants held a celebratory grand opening gala for its delicatessen and grocery department at its downtown Paterson, New Jersey store at 146 Main Street, offering a variety of specials including one-pound cans of Grants' trademarked Fra-Grant coffee for twenty-one cents, quart jars of Checker brand dill pickles for fifteen cents, Swiss cheese at twenty-five cents per pound and frankfurters for seventeen cents per pound.

"Grant's Food Department will be your favorite shopping place," noted the grand opening ad for Grants' delicatessen and grocery department in Paterson. "Ready to serve you quickly and efficiently with wholesome fresh foods at the lowest prices consistent with good quality....Cut your grocery bills way down....Your family's health comes first—Buy at Grants where cleanliness is guaranteed!"

By November 1934, pilot delicatessen and grocery departments were in place at twenty-nine select Grants stores in New York, New Jersey, Massachusetts and Pennsylvania, including flagship Grants stores in New York City, Boston and Philadelphia, with interest expressed in also expanding the concept to select Grants stores in the Midwest and South.

Noted the November–December 1934 issue of *The Grant Game* of Grants' delicatessen and grocery pilot:

> *It was quite a new venture in the chain store field....The Department is of great service and convenience to our customers. Johnny's mother comes in to buy a pair of shoes and hose for Johnny and on her way out she can conveniently purchase from an attractive, clean-looking, perfectly kept display the items needed when the boy comes tearing home impatiently for his noontime meal. Customers can now purchase almost everything for the table from soup to nuts and it is a convenience to be able to shop for all their daily needs within a Grant store....It can truly be said, "Now Grant's carries darn near everything!" The retail business of today is very keen and competitive. Methods and ways of doing business are continually changing and new developments are constantly emerging which must be tried out if one wishes to grow. Because customer service is an important factor in retailing today and this department provides another step in our completing our service to the customer, we feel that our entering so definitely into the foods line will succeed and spread into the future into many more stores. Today the Foods Department is a new star among the old players on the stage.*

The forerunner to fast-food, quick-service lunch counters were the popular go-to restaurant of choice for shoppers and downtown workers from the 1930s to the 1970s. Seen here is the luncheonette at Grants' downtown St. Paul, Minnesota store on Cedar Street in the 1930s. *Author's collection.*

While Grants' experimental delicatessen and grocery department test pilot proved ultimately to be a noteworthy but short-lived footnote in Grants history, a handful of Grants' most popular delicatessens and bakeries—at Boston, Philadelphia, Cleveland and New Brunswick, New Jersey, among them—endured for years and sometimes decades.

With the exception of one-year sales downturns in 1932 and 1938, W.T. Grant Company sales continued their historic upward trajectory during the Great Depression, with Grants breaking the $100 million mark for the first time in 1939 at $103,761,686 as the company served more than 1 million customers each business day.

With air-conditioning becoming widely used commercially in luxury hotels, restaurants and movie theaters beginning in the 1930s, Grants was among the retailers at the forefront of adopting air-conditioning for customer comfort, with Grants stores featuring air-conditioning accounting for fully 20 percent of company sales as the decade drew to a close.

Entering the 1930s as a largely eastern regional chain with scattered market footholds in the Mid-Atlantic, Midwest and South, by decade's end Grants' steady westward expansion had built the chain into a truly coast-to-coast retailer, employing eighteen thousand year-round, with an additional twelve thousand employed on a seasonal basis. Additionally, Grants'

Famed for its cutting-edge Art Moderne styling by architect Alfred S. Alschuler and industrial designer Raymond Loewy, the W.T. Grant Company's new circa 1939 Buffalo, New York "Store of Tomorrow" at Main and Huron was billed as "the last word in modern design and construction." Offering a modern department store feel, Grants No. 50 was noted for its streamlined interior and exterior designs, open sightlines, wide aisles and artistic wall coverings. A crowd of seventy-five thousand visited the store at its November 1, 1939 grand opening. *Otto Ulrich Company Inc. postcards, Ezra Stoller photos, author's collection.*

operations were supported by a network of five thousand manufacturers and suppliers in forty-two states that provided the W.T. Grant Company with merchandise, store equipment and supplies.

Observed William T. Grant as the 1930s came to a close:

> *When I was a youngster working in a store I was instructed to get as much as I could from the customer. This experience gave me the germ of the idea that has been largely responsible for the success of the W.T. Grant Company. That idea was to see how much I could give the customer instead of how much I could get from her and to treat everyone as fairly as I knew how, customers, employees, manufacturers—everyone. Thirty-three years ago, with one thousand dollars capital, I started working along this line. Last year's sales ran over one hundred million dollars, thanks to the help of all of you in the Grant Company who have continued the policy of giving the best you can. As we work in the interests of our customers we will be making our contribution to better business throughout the United States and thereby to the happiness of millions of other people. I know you will do your part.*

THE '40S

Grants in War and Peace

Promotion from within was a longstanding tradition at the W.T. Grant Company for long-tenured career track "Grant Men" who had capably and diligently advanced their way up the many various rungs of Grants' corporate ladder, from humble beginnings as entry-level stockmen and floor men to store, district and regional manager postings, with some ultimately ascending to executive positions at the company's Midtown Manhattan Home Office at 1441 Broadway, all learning the breadth of the dynamic retail business along the way and, in particular, demonstrating their unflagging loyalty to the "Supremacy" of William T. Grant's middle-ground "New Idea" in general merchandise retailing.

W.T. Grant Company president Raymond H. Fogler, 1940–52. *From* The Grant Game, *author's collection.*

In May 1940, longtime Grants veteran president Karl D. Gardner was succeeded by A. Montgomery Ward & Company president Raymond H. Fogler, an experienced longtime 1919–32 Grants veteran who returned to the fold to head Grants as president, general manager and board director.

Always keen to spot new trends as a savvy, trailblazing retailer, the W.T. Grant Company, in a precursor to the massive retailing shift that would take the United States by storm in the post–World War II years, opened its first strip shopping center "park-and-shop" Grants store at Amherst (Buffalo), New York, in 1941.

With a goal of being the best employer in any community it operated, the W.T. Grant Company strived to build a fun-loving spirit of camaraderie among its employees through a variety of social gatherings, including parties, holiday dinners and annual outings, such as this circa 1940s employee outing at Knoxville, Tennessee. *William T. Grant Foundation.*

While war raged abroad in Europe in the early 1940s, Grants continued its steady, business-as-usual expansion course until the United States' December 8, 1941 entry into World War II following Imperial Japan's surprise December 7, 1941 military attack on the U.S. naval base at Pearl Harbor, Hawaii. Declarations of war against Germany and Italy followed on December 11, 1941.

Heading into World War II, Grants' store count stood at 495 stores in thirty-nine states. Company sales for fiscal 1941, ending on January 31, 1942, hit a record $130,55,901—a hefty 16.8 percent increase over 1940 sales of $111,774,965—while earnings for the year were $4,446,393 as the second highest in the company's history, just shy of Grants' record earnings of $4,594,000 in 1936.

With the United States suddenly conducting war on two fronts against the German, Italian and Japanese Axis powers in the European and Pacific Theaters, the W.T. Grant Company and its employees did their patriotic part in support of the Allied war effort.

With the country now on a war footing, business changed quickly and radically for Grants as scores of employees—including an initial cadre of 151 high-ranking company executives, store managers and store management men-in-training—left their civilian jobs to serve in the U.S. military, both domestically and overseas. Additionally, all available resources, including building materials, were funneled toward the war effort.

Among those tapped for active duty in the armed services was Grants board director and recently retired company president Karl D. Gardner, who accepted a commission as a lieutenant colonel and was placed in charge of purchasing for the Army Exchange Service, stocking post exchange (PX) units at home and abroad until his death on February 25, 1944.

For the duration of World War II and many months thereafter, large portions of Grants' monthly newsmagazine, *The Grant Game*, were filled with "Mail Call" news briefs from deployed Grants employees serving domestically and abroad, as well as correspondent reports of employee enlistments, draft registrations, deployments, discharges, war injury convalescence and the legacy of Grants' fallen war dead. At one point, nearly five hundred Grants employees received their copies of *The Grant Game* overseas.

Some expert W.T. Grant Company buyers mustered into the service were put to work by Uncle Sam using their procurement skills in support of wartime military operations. Captain V.J. Donnelly, an assistant buyer of women's wear, saw active service with a combat cargo outfit in the India-China-Burma Theater as a supply officer. Technical Sergeant W.S. Von Stein, assistant sportswear buyer, was assigned to civilian procurement in the Quartermaster Corps in England, France and Luxembourg. U.S. Navy Lieutenant R. Brighton, assistant buyer of domestics specializing in blankets, bedding and bedspreads, served in New York City and Washington, D.C., heading the Progress and Expediting section in the navy's clothing and textile procurement branch. Army Air Force Captain J.T. Reynolds, senior buyer of jewelry and leather goods, served domestically in Ohio, Kansas, Colorado and Nebraska as a contracting officer for B-29s. Major R.J. Wood, associate buyer of curtains and draperies, served the army as a production, planning and control officer charged with inspecting stock control procedures in posts, camps and stations. Later sent to Hollywood to write scripts for army films on stock control, after the war Wood was promoted by Grants to the position of assistant merchandise manager for soft lines. A.W. Scannell, a buyer of rugs and furniture before the war and a buyer of novelty cotton yard goods, woolens and heavy fabrics after, spent the war in a variety of procurement and quartermaster roles, including service as a buyer for overseas exchanges in the Army Post Exchange system.

Numerous Grant men served with honor during World War II, including three Bronze Star medal recipients—Major Duncan J. MacLennon, a floor man in Store No. 137 in Willimantic, Connecticut, for meritorious service on the Anzio Beachhead, with seven combat stars totaling 110 points to his credit; Second Lieutenant Robert A. Maloney, shoe man at Store No. 155 in Boston, who received a battlefield commission to second lieutenant and the Bronze Star while serving in Germany as a member of General Patton's Third Army; and Sergeant Norbert F. Mayer, floor man at Store No. 224 in Philadelphia, feted for "meritorious service in support of active combat operations…in Belgium and Germany. As interpreter of both French and German, Sergeant Mayer did much to further the health, comfort, morale and well-being of all personnel."

Among the Grant women in service were Private Helen V. Herngren of the treasurer's department at the Midtown Manhattan Home Office in New York and WAVE Sp. 5 3/c Anna J. O'Brien, neckwear department head at Store No. 155 in Boston.

Like "Rosie the Riveter" in the factories, a number of women in the employ of the W.T. Grant Company also filled the workplace roles of men who were enlisted and drafted into military service, including many buyers and those employed in the store manager ranks.

On the homefront, Grants actively played its own patriotic part in the war effort, selling U.S. Defense Bonds and stamps and conducting war bond drives in hundreds of Grant communities across the United States in support of the war effort against the Axis powers. Over the duration of World War II, W.T. Grant Company sales of war bonds and stamps totaled more than $38 million.

Grants' steady history of expansion since its 1906 founding came to a grinding halt during World War II, with the chain's store count dipping slightly from 495 to 484 between 1942 and 1945 as older, outdated and declining stores were closed. Governmental limitations on the use of construction materials precluded the opening of planned new stores for the duration of the war and quickly grew to also preclude the planned expansion and renovation of Grants' existing store fleet.

But thanks to the industrial activity generated by war effort ending the protracted Great Depression, Grants' sales soared to stratospheric new heights of $154,204,453 in 1942, an 18.1 percent increase.

The W.T. Grant Company was particularly challenged on the personnel front in 1942 as 746 employees entered the armed forces, including 87 store managers and approximately half the roster of Grants' managerial

With the U.S. entry into World War II, the W.T. Grant Company did its part in support of the war effort, including the sale of U.S. Defense Bonds ("war bonds"). Over the duration of World War II, Grants sold more than $38 million in war bonds and stamps in hundreds of communities nationwide. *Author's collection.*

development pipeline Men-in-Training Program. Additionally, many Grants saleswomen resigned their positions to accept employment in factories producing war materials.

Wrote Grant and Fogler, "Such changes in personnel, which will undoubtedly continue throughout the war period, place a great responsibility on those who remain for training many new people and at the same time carrying on reasonably satisfactory service to customers. They have met this challenge splendidly and we extend to them our sincere appreciation."

With much of U.S. factory production dedicated to the war effort, World War II also presented merchandising challenges as Grants continued to sell goods to millions of Americans on the homefront. While merchandise at the time was "being obtained in sufficient quantity" to stock W.T. Grant Company stores adequately, Grant and Fogler noted that "many items and lines of merchandise are, however, no longer available, and while new lines made of non-critical materials are constantly being developed, they do not as yet give promise of full replacement of those which can no longer be obtained." Cautioned Grant and Fogler as they turned their sights to 1943, "It is…becoming increasingly difficult to assure supplies of merchandise."

Continuing a longstanding history of advancement, sales were up 6.3 percent in 1943 and profits rose to a record $9,778,864.

Given ongoing wartime restrictions, Grant and Fogler noted to company shareholders in the 1943 annual report that investments in the company's stores were confined to "adequate" maintenance and repairs, while the company struggled with "merchandise shortages." "There is increasing difficulty in securing lines which normally contribute a large portion of our sales volume, particularly in lower priced textile and wearing apparel lines," they wrote. "Losses in sales in these lines are being overcome through aggressive merchandising of lines which are available, but sizable increases in sales cannot be anticipated until there is a more general availability of merchandise."

Personnel issues remained Grants' biggest wartime challenge, as the number of Grants employees in the armed services increased to 1,075, including 186 store managers "difficult to replace because of their years of training and experience." The situation was partially alleviated by "promoting women to managerial positions" according to Grant and Fogler, with 32 Grants stores being "managed competently by women."

"The greatest wartime problem…is in the maintenance of an adequate managerial and sales force," Grant and Fogler wrote. "Military service, shifts to defense industries, and family relocations account for the far greater than normal turnover of employees."

Faced with "the general shortage of experienced saleswomen to wait on customers," Grant and Fogler reported to shareholders that Grants had "converted a number of…stores to a 'self service' basis," a shift that continued after the war as staffed sales counters throughout the store gave way to consolidated checkouts at the doors. "Store layouts and displays have been modified to facilitate the selection of merchandise by the customer, permitting the store organization to devote the bulk of their time to merchandising and store up-keep," Grant and Fogler wrote, adding that "it is too early to predict the effect of this experiment on the post-war merchandising of the company."

In the end, the "self service" concept driven by wartime necessity would prove to be the future of retailing not just for Grants but also for the retail industry as a whole.

Looking ahead to 1944 as the tide began to turn in favor of the Allied forces, Grant and Fogler set their sights on the postwar era and renewed expansion of the W.T. Grant Company: "We look forward to the time when the war will end and the company can build for the future. The return of men now in military service will reestablish our managerial organization. The resumption of full manufacturing production of civilian goods will permit the normal merchandising of wide assortments of popular priced merchandise which make Grant stores interesting to customers. The elimination of restrictions on construction will enable the modernization of existing stores and expansion into new cities. Four locations for new stores have been acquired and in five cities where stores are now operated, new and larger locations have been purchased or are now under lease for post-war use."

Despite merchandising challenges, Grants sales increased 7 percent to a record $175,460,824 from 490 stores in thirty-nine states, with sales increases coming principally "in departments where merchandise shortages were least acute," and geographically in the company's Southern and Pacific Coast stores.

Thanks to World War II industrial production ending the protracted Great Depression, W.T. Grant Company sales soared to stratospheric new heights despite wartime merchandise shortages. Pictured is holiday season foot traffic outside Grants No. 255 at 21–23 South Pinckney Street on Capitol Square in Madison, Wisconsin. *Wisconsin Historical Society Image 34472.*

The number of Grants personnel serving in the armed forces reached 1,272 in 1944, including 166 store managers and 103 women. With ranks of male store managers continuing to thin, 47 stores were being managed by women in 1944.

Store inventories continued to be challenged in 1944, according to Grant and Fogler. "As long as the war lasts, the requirements of the armed forces will limit materially the manpower and materials available for production of civilian goods," they noted. "During the past year, shortages have grown increasingly more acute. Upon cessation of hostilities in Europe, some improvement in the amount of merchandise available for civilians is anticipated."

Looking for a fresh look, a new corporate logo was developed in 1944 for the W.T. Grant Company, adopting the company's longtime "Grants" sobriquet. Reading "Grants, Known for Values," with the "Grants" name styled after founder William T. Grant's distinctive Spencerian Script cursive signature, the logo, with various refreshing modifications, including a 1964 simplification of Grant's cursive signature, endured until the company's 1976 demise.

In addition to refreshing its image, the W.T. Grant Company also continued to lay plans for renewed postwar growth. Wrote Grant and Fogler, "The company continues to plan for the post war period. During the year a store location was acquired on Market Street, Philadelphia, which will be larger than any existing Grant store. A number of other locations have been purchased or leased for new stores or the enlargement of existing stores at the end of the war when merchandise becomes available and restrictions on new construction are removed."

Sales for 1945 rose 2.76 percent to a record $180,306,612 as growth was dampened in part by "the unavailability of moderately priced goods, principally in the textile lines."

As the war drew to a close in 1945, with V-E Day on May 8 and V-J Day on September 2, Grant and Fogler paid tribute in the W.T. Grant Company's 1945 annual report to the contributions of the 1,298 Grants employees who served in the armed forces during World War II. A total of 24 Grants employees made the ultimate sacrifice of their lives in defense of their country over the 1941–45 duration of the war.

With hostilities ended and the return of scores of Grant employees from military service at home and abroad, the W.T. Grant Company laid plans for expansion. Capital expenditure plans for 1946 alone were set at $11,770,000 for stores and fittings.

Noted the July 1946 issue of *The Grant Game*, "Postwar merchandising plans call for expanding our present lines of merchandise to meet the needs of 109,000,000 potential Grant customers who live in the trading areas of 489 cities and towns in which Grant stores are located. To that end, we are planning larger stores, and an expansion of all lines of merchandise. To supply the need of the Grant customer our postwar stores will be larger, well constructed and well equipped, but they will be simple, economical and in good taste. We are planning larger stores because we believe we can distribute merchandise more economically in larger units. Our principle of how much we can give necessitates economy."

In regard to merchandising and store development, Grant and Fogler were optimistic for the year ahead in 1946, the company's fortieth anniversary year, predicting "very satisfactory" sales and profits as factory production transitioned from a wartime footing to a civilian focus, as well as an embrace of an "extensive" postwar store program encompassing the modernization and expansion of existing stores and the "development of many properties acquired for post war expansion," including Grants' planned showcase store on Market Street in downtown Philadelphia.

Fowler and Grant, however, conceded that there would be an initial delay in fully realizing the company's postwar expansion plans due to prevailing "extremely high" commercial construction costs as four years of pent-up demand for new construction were unleashed with the end of the war. "It is

Birthday dinner held in honor of W.T. Grant Company founder William T. Grant as part of Grants' fortieth anniversary celebrations, held on June 27, 1946, at Hotel Astor, Times Square, New York City. *Empire Photographers photo, author's collection.*

hoped that the remainder of the program can be undertaken without undue delay," Grant and Fogler said.

With the nation on a solid postwar footing, W.T. Grant Company sales skyrocketed 17.75 percent to a record $212,324,212 in 1946, the company's fortieth anniversary year, posting record profits of $10,877,577 from its 484 stores in thirty-nine states—Alabama, Arkansas, California, Colorado, Connecticut, Delaware, Florida, Georgia, Illinois, Indiana, Iowa, Kansas, Kentucky, Louisiana, Maine, Maryland, Massachusetts, Michigan, Minnesota, Mississippi, Missouri, Nebraska, New Hampshire, New Jersey, New York, North Carolina, North Dakota, Ohio, Oklahoma, Pennsylvania, Rhode Island, South Carolina, Tennessee, Texas, Utah, Vermont, Virginia, West Virginia and Wisconsin.

As wartime hostilities ended, personnel challenges facing the company switched to integrating returning Grants veterans back into the company. Most Grant employees who entered the military service had returned by the end of fiscal 1946, with Grant and Fogler noting the returning Grants employees were "being retrained and reinstated in positions of equal opportunity with those held at the time of their entering military service."

At long last, the W.T. Grant Company returned to a growth-oriented footing, with expansion and modernization of existing stores and plans laid for the development of new stores in existing and new Grants trade markets, including the development of ambitious new "Store of the Future" flagships in Buffalo and Syracuse, New York, and Bangor, Maine.

Grants' headquarters "New York Office," which also shared quarters with founder William T. Grant's charitable Grant Foundation, had grown by 1946 well beyond its five floors in the thirty-four-story Bricken Textile Building at 1414 Broadway in Midtown Manhattan, spilling over into three other nearby Times Square area buildings—the since-razed Longacre and Wurlitzer Buildings and the enduring Bush Building on 42nd Street.

W.T. Grant Company advertising and promotion copywriter Alice Reichenbach reflected on the company's storied forty-year history in the October 1946 anniversary issue of *The Grant Game*:

> *Way back in 1906, when William T. Grant was his own Director of Sales Promotion, as well as proprietor, merchandise director, chief buyer, and head of stock, his little store in Lynn, Massachusetts, was known as "The Store of Wonder Values." Gradually the motto evolved into the now famous "Known for Values." The phrase symbolizes, better than any other, the type of store and operation in which W.T. Grant had firm*

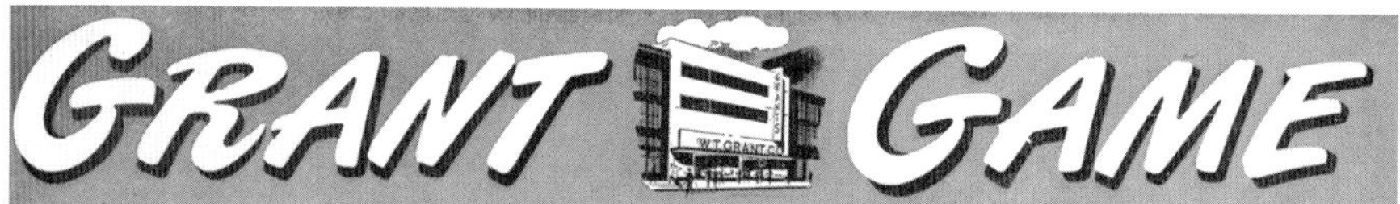

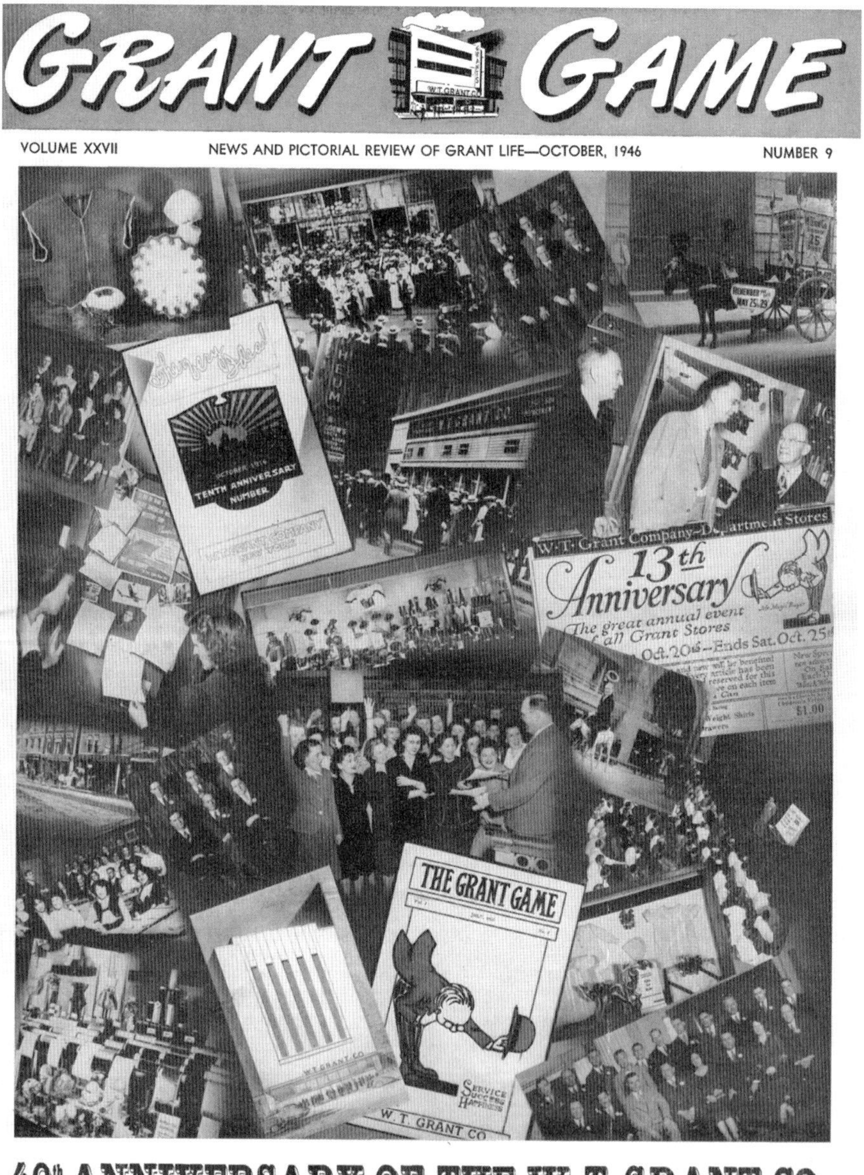
GRANT GAME
VOLUME XXVII
NEWS AND PICTORIAL REVIEW OF GRANT LIFE—OCTOBER, 1946
NUMBER 9
TENTH ANNIVERSARY NUMBER
13th Anniversary
The great annual event all Grant Stores
THE GRANT GAME
W. T. GRANT CO.
40th ANNIVERSARY OF THE W.T. GRANT CO.

The October 1946 issue of *The Grant Game* highlighted the forty-year history of the W.T. Grant Company, which had grown from the singular Lynn, Massachusetts "Mother Store" into a nationwide chain of 484 stores in thirty-nine states. *From* The Grant Game, *author's collection.*

> *faith—a store where the guiding principle was not to see how much he could get for his money, but how much value he could possibly give the customer. Many things have changed since 1906. One store has grown to 489 stores. Instead of a single town, the Grant market now comprises forty million people living in 39 states. The variety store, which sold items for no more than 25 cents, is now a giant chain of department stores, stretching from coast to coast. The Grant organization has expanded, too, from 12 employees to more than 20,000 store and office personnel.*

That month, Grants marked its milestone anniversary in grand style, holding a gala October 10–19 sale to "give Grant customers a collection of values that would outdo anything since the original store opened."

Planned by all sixty-four members of Grants' Buying Department, a full year of preparation went into Grants' 40th Anniversary Sale, which was promoted via the distribution of 5.5 million circulars and an intensive newspaper and radio advertising campaign. A June 1946 advance preview of Grants' 40th Anniversary Sale was held at Hotel St. George in Brooklyn for regional managers, district managers and store managers to view sale merchandise and specially designed Anniversary Sale window and interior displays trimmed in Grants' signature orange and navy blue.

In conjunction with its 40th Anniversary Sale, the W.T. Grant Company announced its trailblazing launch of installment credit sales, with Credit Departments rolled out in two of the company's largest stores—Store No. 70 in Atlanta, Georgia, and Store No. 69 in St. Paul, Minnesota, with Erie, Pennsylvania; Portland, Maine; and New Haven, Connecticut, slated to begin credit sales in November–December 1946. Fifteen more Grants stores were slated to go online with credit selling in 1947 in the largest-volume store in each of the company's remaining districts. Noted *The Grant Game*:

> *Then, as experience is gained, Credit Departments will be extended to other stores in the Company. This action was taken in order to facilitate the sale of higher priced items, both in hard and soft lines, which are necessary to round out assortments. Until now, customers buying higher priced items and unable to make a full cash payment have been confined to the layaway procedure. The Easy Payment Plan will supplement the layaway plan. Under Grants' Easy Payment Plan, credit will be extended under either an individual contract or a coupon book. The individual contract plan is used on most cases of a large unit sale. The coupon book plan is designed for the customer who may desire credit for a wide variety of merchandise in all departments....For convenience*

> *for customers, the Credit Department will be located on a selling floor, adjacent to merchandise frequently purchased through time payment. Here in one unit will be gathered the personnel necessary to interview and investigate credit applications and to handle all collections. Since credit customers will be frequent visitors to the store, Credit Department personnel will have a splendid opportunity for establishing good will as well as increasing sales.*

Developing Grants' installment credit program was former Sears, Roebuck & Company regional credit manager Warren G. Finnan, an experienced retailing veteran in both merchandising and credit who had established Sears' successful installment credit program. At Grants, Finnan was assisted by Margaret Vargo, a former office supervisor at Grants' Chicago Region headquarters.

Meanwhile, the success of Grants' initial early 1920s foray into proprietary private label branding saw Grants selling merchandise under no fewer than sixty Grants-exclusive house brand labels across a wide variety of product lines by 1946.

In addition to the enduring flagship Grants name, other propriety house brand labels marketed by Grants had grown to include I'sis hosiery, Lyncrest tissues, Excello razor blades, Busy Beaver children's shoes, Pennleigh men's shirts, WTG (Wear Tested Garments, later Wear Tested Guaranteed) work clothes, Gran-Tone paints, Hudson Forge tools, Gran-nit outerwear, Wearite fashions, Grantline radios and electric appliances, Robby Roller tailored felt hats, Marion Crane candies and Grants' Soft Tufties chenille rugs, among others.

Exclusively a retailing operation, the W.T. Grant Company contracted with numerous well-known and highly respected third-party manufacturers to supply the chain with proprietary Grants-branded merchandise specifically built to Grants' exacting specifications and stringent quality standards.

Over the years, well-known contract manufacturers supplying Grants included General Electric, RCA, Fedders, Norge, Dan River Mills, Briggs & Stratton, Franklin, Hardwick and Westinghouse, among others. And although not a household name, Newark, Ohio–based contract lawn mower manufacturer E.T. Rugg Company supplied a variety of well-known U.S. retail chains with proprietary house-branded lawn equipment, including Grants, JCPenney, Montgomery Ward and Western Auto.

The fortieth anniversary issue of *The Grant Game* noted that Grants' expansive roster of house brands had been "developed over a period of years to identify quality merchandise which has been manufactured to our specifications, and of which we are justly proud.…An honored trade name is one of the most valuable assets of a business.…When the public puts its trust in the integrity of our established trademarks, it puts a moral responsibility on our buyers and manufacturers to make sure that their merchandise measures up to our reputation for quality and economy, the 'Known for Values' upon which we have built our business."

The following year, Grant set another sales record, rising 7.68 percent to $228,636,024.

Among the company's showcase postwar crown jewel store developments was the high-rise "modern type" Streamline Moderne–styled replacement for Store No. 15 in downtown Syracuse, New York. Opened in August 1947 as "Four Stores in One"—a variety store, a dry goods store, a fashion store and a home furnishings and hardware store—Grants' Syracuse "Store of Tomorrow" instantly earned recognition as the company's highest volume store.

"The Company policy of making every Grant Store an important shopping center in its community requires constant growth…as populations grow and as modern living expands the needs of our customers," noted Grants' 1947 annual report.

The merchandising mix of Grants stores, meanwhile, was evolving in the postwar years, adapting to a changing—and more affluent—nation. "The objective of the Grant Company is to distribute the maximum quantities of reliable merchandise at reasonable prices," the 1947 W.T. Grant Company annual report explained. "With the higher wages and increasing standard of living of American customers, Grant stores in recent years have continued to widen the lines carried to serve its customers more completely with those items in popular demand in the mass market.…Public acceptance of new lines is being tested constantly in limited groups of stores and extended to additional stores as space permits. Merchandise carried is confined to the most popular price lines, and every effort made to offer exceptional values in those price lines."

With its personnel objective that "Grants shall be the best place in the community in which to work," another major factor in the company's continued growth according to the annual report was Grants' "good people well paid" emphasis on ensuring job satisfaction for its employees, "whose abilities and loyalties have made—and will continue to make—the Grant Company prosper." Known for its low employee turnover, Grants offered a wide array of generous benefits including retirement, group insurance, sick pay, Christmas bonuses, employee discounts and job security.

One of the W.T. Grant Company's postwar crown jewel store developments was this towering six-story Streamline Moderne–styled "4-Stores-in-1" flagship, Store No. 15, opened in August 1947 at 425–27 South Salina Street in downtown Syracuse, New York. Billed by Grants as the "fastest one-stop center in the nation," the facility was a variety store, dry goods store, fashion store and hardware and home furnishings store. *William Jubb Company Inc. postcard, author's collection.*

Sales at the W.T. Grant Company hit another record in 1948, rising 2.3 percent to $233,904,425 from 482 stores.

Grants' modernization and expansion program got into full swing as the 1940s began to draw to a close, with capital expenditures of $6.4 million in 1948 and nearly $7 million in 1949.

A replacement store that opened in Medford, Massachusetts, on August 18, 1949, was a sign of things to come as Grants became an early pioneer in the shift from traditional downtown retailing to cutting-edge outlying greenfield strip shopping center developments that offered extensive parking facilities. The company's capital expenditure investments in shopping center–based store developments would prove to be money well spent in the ensuing decades.

Sales for Grant dipped slightly in 1949 to $233,167,686 due to a deflationary "downward adjustment in retail prices," as also experienced in 1932 and 1938, the only other years the W.T. Grant Company marked a year-to-year decline since its 1906 founding. A bright spot for Grants, and a harbinger of better days to come, could be found in the underlying data, as unit sales exceeded those of 1948 and the number of customer transactions set a new record high.

Grants' continuing emphasis on its renewed and accelerated expansion program, meanwhile, laid the groundwork for truly building Grants into a leading national retailer in the 1950s and beyond. "Grants extensive store improvement and development program…should contribute much to enhance the Company's position in the years ahead," Grants' 1949 annual report noted, as Westerly, Rhode Island; Pasadena and Alhambra, California; and Marshalltown, Iowa, received their first W.T. Grant Company stores. Said the annual report of the new Grants stores, "Each of these new units was planned as an outstanding store of its kind in the shopping area, offering comprehensive assortments of all of the Company's basic lines of merchandise."

FROM THE CITY TO THE SUBURBS

Rise of the "Park-and-Shop"

Following the end of World War II and the return of active-duty soldiers from the European and Pacific Theaters, a societal shift quickly got underway in tandem with the postwar baby boom of the late 1940s and 1950s as Americans nationwide shifted en masse from the established, crowded urban city cores to the appealing and beckoning bucolic pastures offered by new greenfield residential and commercial developments—high-density urban neighborhoods giving way to low-density outlying subdivisions and established downtown and urban core shopping districts losing favor with shoppers as they flocked to convenient, user-friendly "park-and-shop" strip shopping centers offering acres of free parking.

The shift was spurred in part by the seemingly unlimited mobility afforded by the automobile and an increasingly car-centered American culture of drive-in restaurants and theaters, a growing nationwide network of high-speed highways and interstates and catchy, toe-tapping advertising jingles to "See the U.S.A. in Your Chevrolet."

Also bolstering the shift from downtown and the urban cores to the newly developing city fringes and burgeoning suburbs were the opportunities offered by the Serviceman's Readjustment Act of 1944, better known as the G.I. Bill, which provided a vast array of benefits to returning World War II veterans including low-cost mortgages, low-interest business or farm loans and dedicated tuition payments to attend college or vocational schools.

Long possessing a keen eye to spot emerging trends, retailing and otherwise, the W.T. Grant Company was among the first major U.S. retailers to greet

This direct-mail twenty-eight-page 1950 Christmas gift guide catalogue, the W.T. Grant Company's first such publication, was one of many published annually throughout the decade to showcase the increasing variety of merchandise available in Grants' growing roster of outlying greenfield strip mall variety and junior department store developments. *Author's collection.*

In the postwar urban flight of the 1950s, 1960s and 1970s, the W.T. Grant Company moved with its customers to outlying greenfield developments. Seen here is the new Grants- and Gimbels-anchored Southgate Shopping Center "park-and-shop" opened in 1951 along South 27th Street (U.S. Highway 41) on Milwaukee's then southern fringe. *L.L. Cook Co. postcard, author's collection.*

shoppers in the 1950s and 1960s as they arrived at the nation's coast-to-coast cadre of newly developed strip shopping centers.

Sales for the 480-store, twenty-thousand-employee Grants chain rebounded 7.5 percent to a record $250,573,987 in 1950, while capital expenditures for new stores and the modernization of existing units totaled a sizable $8,095,000.

While the bulk of Grants' capital expenditures for 1950 were still directed toward the headline-grabbing development of new state-of-the-art showcase flagship downtown stores and the enlargement and modernization of Grants' existing fleet of urban stores to allow "for more extensive presentation of Grants value assortments for the family and home," a closer look beyond the annual report headlines showed a subtle shift getting underway in Grants' new store development program, with the company's groundbreaking for a new-style park-and-shop Grants slated for completion in 1951 at the rising Southgate Shopping Center in Milwaukee.

Among the nation's leading early shopping centers, twenty-store Southgate was developed by Milwaukee brewery malt supplier Kurtis Froedtert on the city's then southern fringe on South 27th Street, which doubled as the busy Chicago-Milwaukee-Green Bay U.S. Highway 41 corridor in the pre-interstate days.

The first post–World War II suburban-style shopping center in the Milwaukee area, Grants was a charter anchor at Southgate, which would later come to include the first branch department store for Gimbel Brothers, five-and-dime rival F.W. Woolworth and supermarkets Krambo (later Kroger) and National Tea. The Southgate Grants was Milwaukee's third W.T. Grant Company store, joining long-established urban Grants stores on West Wisconsin Avenue in downtown Milwaukee and on "Upper Third" at North 3rd Street and West North Avenue.

Operating 492 variety stores in thirty-nine U.S. states on the strength of fiscal 1951 sales of more than $268 million, Grants kicked off its strategic shift toward shopping center stores in grand form with the September 20, 1951 ceremonial ribbon-cutting for its Milwaukee anchor store at Southgate, where an astounding sixty thousand Milwaukeeans turned out for the shopping center's grand opening.

Noted the *Milwaukee Journal* of Southgate's debut, "Most amazing of all was the way the crowd spent money. Milwaukee enjoys a national reputation as a place where almost everybody will go to anything that is free, but almost everybody will stay away if it costs a lot. Nonetheless, a good three-fourths of the persons on the grounds carried bundles, purchases they had made while exploring."

As Grants continued to grow in the postwar years, so did the need for employee development opportunities, including a "Men in Training" store manager training program launched in 1949, regional conventions launched in 1950 for store managers to learn about merchandising opportunities and company plans and policies and the 1951 debut of the William T. Grant Achievement Award, recognizing store and district managers with outstanding performance records.

With its longstanding reputation for values, Grants continued to strengthen and expand its "Grants Own Brands" private label merchandising program heading into the 1950s, with major laboratory-tested house labels including WTG work clothes, Wearite underwear, Bouncing Baby infant's wear, Flight Club boy's wear, Joyce Lane slips, Marion Crane candies, Carefree Casuals shoes, Lovelee gloves and blouses, Busy Beaver children's shoes, Pennleigh shirts, Lyncrest stationery, Charm-Crest home furnishings, Little General anklets, Wee Lassie children's dresses, I'sis hosiery, Paramount aluminum ware, Grantline scissors and Toy Town children's wear.

Noted Grants' 1952 annual report, "Grant Stores serve all the family and the home. Good quality and wide assortments—those are important

Made to our exacting specifications, by America's best-known manufacturers. Exhaustive lab-tests prove their serviceability. Continual tests guarantee constant high quality. Thrift low prices mean more savings for you every day.

First launched in the 1920s, the W.T. Grant Company continued to strengthen and expand its lines of proprietary private label merchandise lines in the 1950s under a wide assortment of brand names and private categories. *Author's collection.*

words at Grants. Add exceptional savings and our customers know why Grants is 'known for values' every day in the year. Millions of Americans depend upon the Grant stores to help them get the most for their dollars. Grants was a pioneer in designing stores for speedier shopping. Now more than ever, our customers can save time and steps as well as money when they shop in one of our stores."

With Grants continuing "an active program of opening stores in new communities and relocating, enlarging and modernizing existing stores," Grants committed $8.8 million to new construction and store equipment for 1952, including fourteen Grants stores in new communities. Grants' store development program continued its traditional mix of closing smaller, older, outdated stores; building ever-larger new store developments; and remodeling and expanding existing urban stores.

Building on the success of the Southgate Grants at Milwaukee, five of Grants' fourteen new store developments announced in 1951 for 1952 openings—at Arlington, Virginia (Parkington) outside Washington, D.C.; Cheektowaga (Buffalo), New York; North Sacramento, California; and Roselle and Youngstown, Ohio (Boardman Plaza)—were shopping center stores.

The year 1952 was noteworthy for the W.T. Grant Company, with Edward Staley becoming company president following the retirement of longtime

W.T. Grant Company president Edward Staley, 1952–59. *From* The Grant Game, *author's collection.*

Grants veteran Raymond H. Fogler (1892–1996), Grants' president and general manager since 1940.

In his "retirement," Fogler took on a new role as the final assistant secretary of the U.S. Navy in 1953–54. A University of Maine alumnus and Maine native, Fogler served on the university's board of directors from 1955 to 1962. Upon his board retirement, the University of Maine's main academic library was renamed the Raymond H. Fogler Library.

Staley, himself a longtime Grants veteran, joined the W.T. Grant Company as a trainee and floor man in 1926. A Grants store manager when he left in 1933 to join Chicago-based rival A. Montgomery Ward & Company as an assistant merchandising manager, Staley returned to Grants in 1940 as director of merchandising. Staley served as Grants' president from 1952 to 1959 and as vice-chairman of the board from 1959 to 1966, when he succeeded company founder William T. Grant as board president until his 1973 retirement.

With its family camaraderie atmosphere and myriad opportunities for advancement, the W.T. Grant Company historically enjoyed high levels of employee loyalty and low levels of employee turnover that would be the envy of any retailing company today.

Grants sales rose 5.8 percent in 1953 to hit a new record high of $299,767,741 across 502 stores in thirty-nine states, falling just short of the $300 million sales milestone. Of note, the W.T. Grant Company hit an all-time high in single-day sales, tallying $4,280,000 on Saturday, December 19, 1953.

Reflecting the company's growing and heightened stature as a major U.S. retailer, the W.T. Grant Company by 1953 was among the nation's largest distributors of infants' wear, nylon hosiery, children's wear, cotton house dresses, lamps and shades, cotton yard goods, birds and bird cages, slippers, women's slips and underwear and brassieres and girdles.

Accelerating the company's capital program in 1953, Staley invested $14.6 million into fifty-five major capital projects, including seven new shopping center stores at Arcadia and Whittier, California; Barberton, Cuyahoga Falls and Warren, Ohio; and Levittown and Philadelphia, Pennsylvania.

Among Grants' 1953 capital improvement remodeling projects was that of thirty-year-old Store No. 56 at 315–27 Summit Street in downtown Toledo, Ohio, where a $300,000 remodeling project had encompassed a full interior and exterior remake of the variety store into a junior department store.

A poster child for the company's store development crossroads, the downtown Toledo store was a precursor of things to come nationally as the W.T. Grant Company's focus increasingly turned in earnest from the urban marketplace toward outlying greenfield shopping center developments in the 1950s and 1960s, as Grant's newly refreshed downtown Toledo flagship store would quickly be supplanted—and later replaced altogether—by four new geographically located outlying strip mall junior department stores at Great Eastern, in Toledo's historic "Old West End" at Swayne Field, on the north end at Miracle Mile and on the south side near suburban Maumee and Perrysburg at Southland.

Of particular historic significance for the company in 1953, namesake company founder and longtime board chairman William T. Grant attended the September 24, 1953 opening of the company's milestone 500th store at Levittown, Pennsylvania, outside Philadelphia. The ribbon-cutting at the twenty-thousand-square-foot Levittown Shop-A-Rama Grants, the most modern to date in the Grants chain, would be one of final major public appearances for the seventy-seven-year-old Grant.

The largest shopping center east of the Mississippi River at the time, Levittown Shop-A-Rama offered parking for more than five thousand vehicles and featured more than ninety stores, including supermarkets Food Fair and Penn Fruit and general merchandise anchor retailers Grants, Woolworths, Kresge, McCrory, Sears, Pomeroys, N. Snellenburg and JCPenney.

As a planned community established on land purchased in 1951 by Levitt & Sons to serve as a model suburban community in Bucks County, Pennsylvania, construction of homes began in 1952; 17,311 homes built in six different styles were constructed by the completion of Levittown in 1958.

Fittingly, the milestone opening of the Levittown Shop-A-Rama Grants marked a major turning point in the company's expansion and store development program. Within a decade, Grants' expansion and store development program would pivot from the company's traditional downtown focus to a mix of downtown and shopping center projects to a near exclusive focus on the development of outlying greenfield urban and suburban shopping center and standalone stores, accompanied by an accelerated shutdown of the company's older, smaller and financially declining fleet of stores anchoring the nation's fading downtown retail districts.

As part of its accelerated store expansion program, Grants in February 1954 realigned its operations and increased the number of field operating offices from four to five with the establishment of a new Western Region office in Los Angeles to serve the Rocky Mountain and far western states. In 1953, Grants operated twenty-one stores in the West—seventeen in California, three in Utah and one in Colorado at Denver—with plans and leases in place to open Grants' first stores in Arizona, Oregon and Washington in the coming years.

Grants grew its store count to 520 stores in forty states with the 1954 opening of its first store in Washington State at downtown Spokane on September 30, 1954. Sales for the year rose 5.8 percent to crack the $300 million milestone at $317,157,138.

Increasingly for Grants, new and enlarged stores were becoming the company's primary growth driver, with the company's entire increase in sales coming from new and enlarged stores opened in 1953 and 1954, while same store sales decreased 2 percent over the same period as commerce nationwide began transitioning away from traditional downtown and urban shopping districts to outlying urban and suburban shopping center developments.

In 1954, Grants completed fifty-one major capital program projects totaling $14.6 million.

Noted the 1954 annual report of the trend toward shopping center developments by both Grants and the buying public, "Your Company is continuously alert to opportunities in Park-and-Shop developments which offer a wide variety of merchandise and service attractions for the public, as well as ample parking facilities."

Tellingly, the 1954 annual report would be the last to exclusively feature a downtown Grants outlet as a cover illustration.

Also noteworthy in 1954, Grants' longstanding warehouse in Jersey City, New Jersey, was closed as the company's new state-of-the-art warehouse and distribution center in Metuchen, New Jersey, came online, "designed to speed deliveries, reduce transportation costs, and improve the turnover rate in a wide variety of items."

Supporting its growing executive office and buying operations in Midtown Manhattan as the W.T. Grant Company continued its nationwide expansion, Grants signed a long-term lease agreement for the entire thirty-four-story Bricken Textile Building at 1441 Broadway, which was renamed the W.T. Grant Building in honor of its lead tenant. The lease agreement, slated to run through May 1, 1976, and inclusive of several renewal options, paved the way for Grants to consolidate its satellite offices in the nearby Bush, Longacre and Wurlitzer Buildings at the corporate headquarters office at 1441 Broadway and also provide "space for necessary expansion in the years ahead."

Grants' store count rose from 520 stores in forty states in 1954 to 574 stores in forty-two states in 1955, in part due to the realization of the company's plans to solidify and expand its store footprint in the fast-growing western United States, adding the first Grants store in Arizona, the company's first two stores in Oregon, an additional three stores in Washington State, a fourth Grants in Utah and eleven additional stores in California, bringing its total store count in the Rocky Mountain and Pacific Coast states to 41 from 21 just two years prior.

Sales for 1955 rose 10.9 percent to a record $351,848,626—the sizable increase coming entirely from new and enlarged stores opened in 1954 and 1955.

Grants' capital program for 1955 increased to a record $11.9 million as Grants' shopping center store openings outpaced downtown store openings for the first time, with thirty-four new stores in park-and-shops versus the twenty-seven opened in downtown locations. By the close of the year, Grants operated sixty-one shopping center locations coast-to-coast.

In addition to Grants' accelerating store development program, also of increasing importance to the company was the attention paid to the role of growing the company's installment credit sales program, which was launched in 1946 to help facilitate the sales of higher-priced, higher-margin merchandise. Customer installment account sales, available in most Grants stores by 1955, totaled 7.2 percent of sales or $25,182,125 in 1955. Noted Grant and Staley, "Our goal continues to be to sell more merchandise to more people, at a reasonable profit; and to maintain a steady expansion."

The turn of the calendar to 1956 marked the golden fiftieth anniversary of the 1906 founding of the W.T. Grant Company, which had grown from a single store in oceanside Lynn, Massachusetts, to a coast-to-coast national chain of 632 stores in forty-one states.

Among the company's major golden anniversary celebrations was a testimonial dinner held in William T. Grant's honor at the famed Hotel Astor in Times Square, with nearly one thousand store managers and Home Office and regional field office Grants executives in attendance.

Honoree and keynote speaker William T. Grant, said to be "often impromptu and always lively" in his public speaking engagements, reflected on his career in the retailing industry. "I know of no other business which

The crowded Grants Luncheonette at the April 28, 1955 grand opening of W.T. Grant Company Store No. 133 in downtown Santa Ana, California. *Author's collection.*

could give a man so much action, so much challenge, so much satisfaction and so rich a reward for good service to the community than this wonderful business of ours," he said. "I have enjoyed every minute of it....I deeply appreciate the help you have given me over the years in making my youthful dream of becoming a merchant come true."

Artist's conception of the W.T. Grant Company store slated for a November 1955 completion on Cedar between 7th and 8th Streets in downtown St. Paul, Minnesota. Featuring a design typical of Grants' final class of downtown stores, the 70,800-square-foot multi-level store was faced with glazed brick, marble trim and polished granite. *Author's collection.*

In addition to special sales and celebrations, Grants marked its golden anniversary with comprehensive interior and exterior remodeling projects at some of its larger, enduringly successful old-line downtown flagships, including Grants' popular downtown New Orleans flagship at 1019 Canal Street, opened in 1924. A reopening celebration for Store No. 60 was held in August 1956 for the complete "in-and-out" facelift, which had begun in April.

Store manager W.H. Walsh told the *New Orleans Times-Picayune* that the remodeling included new fluorescent lighting, expanded merchandise displays, a 25 percent expansion of the store's popular lunch counter, installation of new blond basswood counters, the enlargement of several departments and a completely new storefront on the three-story building.

Total sales for 1956 rose 8.3 percent over 1955 levels to $380,915,043. The sales increase for 1956, mirroring results posted in recent years, saw the entirety of the company's increases being driven by stores opened in the previous two years, with same store sales for the two-year period declining by 3.7 percent as American downtowns continued their decline. Total company employment rose to 28,900.

Grants' Customer Installment Plan credit operations continued to increase in importance, expanded to all 632 Grants stores in 1956. Credit sales for 1956 totaled $33,582,880 or 8.8 percent of total company sales, up from 7.7 percent in 1955.

Grants' capital outlays for 1956 encompassed ninety-six capital program projects, up from seventy-nine the previous year, including the opening of seventy-one new stores—sixty-four in park-and-shop centers and seven in downtown locations.

Continuing the streamlining of its store-level operations, a trailblazing, industry-disrupting move born of necessity during wartime labor shortages, Grants continued to open and convert stores to this model of operation, which numbered 108 self-service stores by the end of 1956, with more such stores planned in 1957.

Other major 1956 developments included the opening of a second Grants distribution center in Fort Wayne, Indiana, as a complement to the company's recently opened New Jersey warehouse and distribution center at Metuchen "to improve the Company's merchandising in its mid-west and southern stores."

Grants' sales for 1957 topped the $400 million milestone, rising 6.7 percent to $406,337,450 on a store base spanning 691 stores in a reduced forty-state footprint following the closure of its far-flung lone North Dakota store at Fargo. Again, Grants' entire sales increase was credited to new and enlarged stores opened in the previous two-year period, with same store sales in the same period declining 3.9 percent with the continued erosion of Grants' longtime market strongholds in the nation's increasingly struggling downtown business districts.

Wrote Grant and Staley in their 1957 letter to shareholders, "The Company continued to direct its expansion program to shopping centers. At the year end, 193 of the Company's 691 stores were in shopping centers, and these stores accounted for 26 percent of the Company's 1957 sales."

Following population migration from the nation's northeastern and midwestern Snow Belt to the Sun Belt, much of Grants' growth came in the western United States, where the company operated fifty-six stores—thirty-nine in California, five in Washington, four in Utah, three each in Oregon and Colorado and two in Arizona. Another large growth area for Grants was in the South, including major Grants markets in Texas, Oklahoma, Tennessee, Alabama, Georgia, Louisiana and Florida.

The W.T. Grant Company's capital program for 1957 spanned eighty-six projects, including sixty-seven new stores—sixty-five in shopping centers and two downtown stores at Knoxville, Tennessee, and Ensley, Alabama.

Grants continued its chain-wide conversion to the self-service and check-out model of retail operations, with 204 of the company's 691 stores operating on that basis at the end of 1957. Noted Grant and Staley, "We plan to open additional stores on this basis in 1958. This method of operation provides quick service to customers and is especially suitable and well accepted in

shopping centers, and it has the potential of doing business at a lower cost than does the conventional method of operation."

By 1958, Grants had grown to encompass 739 stores in forty states, although more than half of the W.T. Grant Company's general merchandise stores remained highly concentrated in the northeastern United States. Other major Grants markets were centered in California; the industrial Midwest; mid-Atlantic states including Virginia and North Carolina; and the Sun Belt Gulf Coast running from Texas to Florida.

Employing thirty thousand people coast to coast, Grants 1958 sales rose 6.4 percent to $432,240,571 as December 1958 sales of $81,481,277 set an all-time monthly record—a $7,894,800 increase over the previous record set in December 1957.

With its stores ranging from small, traditional variety stores to larger junior department stores, Grants' annual sales per store ranged from $100,000 to $3.9 million, averaging $585,000. Merchandise items generally were priced up to $5, although some items ranged up to $100. While most purchases were cash sales, credit service was available in all stores, with Customer Installment Plan credit sales contributing $39,588,950 of Grants' $432,240,571 in total 1958 sales.

Merchandise lines at "Friendly Family Store" Grants in 1958 were centered in women's, men's and children's apparel, as well as home goods. Noted the 1958 annual report of Grants' merchandising program, "Merchandise on sale in Grant stores is thoroughly screened by experienced buyers and merchandise review committees. This is a continuous process which insures top values to a customer at all times. Included in our lines are a number of Grant-developed brands of merchandise. Overwhelming customer acceptance over the years proves recognition of our 'built-in' unusual values. The constant sales growth of the Company is evidence that Grants is 'Known for Values' to its customers from coast to coast."

By 1958, the company's expansion program was largely targeted toward leased shopping center stores offering retailing opportunities in the nation's growing suburbs, with 259 of Grants' 739 stores located in newer shopping center developments in growing outlying urban fringe and suburban areas. Grants outlets in shopping centers provided an increasing portion of company sales—32 percent in 1958 as compared to 26 percent in 1957.

Opposite: Mid-1950s portrait photo of W.T. Grant Company founder and namesake William T. Grant, a prominent fixture in all Grants stores. *Author's collection.*

Above: Circa 1950s main floor view of new W.T. Grant Company Store junior department store, No. 589, located at 48–54 Main Street in 5,217-resident Newport, Vermont. *Author's collection.*

Grants' capital program for 1958 included sixty-four new stores, all in shopping centers across nineteen states—California, Florida, Georgia, Illinois, Indiana, Ohio, New Jersey, Michigan, Mississippi, Missouri, New York, North Carolina, Oklahoma, Pennsylvania, Rhode Island, Tennessee, Texas and Wisconsin. While fifteen existing Grants stores were relocated, enlarged or modernized, sixteen small downtown stores were permanently closed.

Among 1958's executive promotions that would loom large in Grants' company history was the election of Richard W. Mayer as assistant treasurer and credit manager and the election of Grants' Western Region manager, James G. Kendrick, as president and director of Grants' Canadian subsidiary, Zeller's Ltd., of which Grants held a controlling 51 percent ownership stake. Both would eventually ascend to the presidency of the W.T. Grant Company.

Capitalizing on America's population surge in the postwar baby boom, sales and net earnings both set records for Grants in 1959, with $479,997,477 in sales generated by 801 stores in forty-one states, as Grants reentered Arkansas after a multi-year absence with a new shopping center store in state capital Little Rock. Net profits of $12,257,940 for 1959 beat Grants' previous $10,877,577 profit record set in 1946. Company employment numbered a record thirty-two thousand employees.

December sales also continued to set new year-to-year records, with Grants' December 1959 sales of $87,894,876 topping the previous year's record. Grants' credit sales, which posted annual year-to-year increases since the inception of the company's credit program in 1946, reached a new high of $45,066,166 in 1959, an increase of 13.8 percent over 1958 figures.

By 1959, states with 10 or more Grants stores included New York, 105; Pennsylvania, 89; Massachusetts, 63; Ohio, 66; California, 55; New Jersey, 50; Florida, 35; Connecticut, 31; Texas, 28; Illinois, 26; Michigan, 21; Georgia, 19; Virginia, 16; Alabama, 15; Indiana, 17; Maine, 15; North Carolina, 15; and Wisconsin, 12.

As the 1950s drew to close, Grants' stores of the era included a mix of older urban variety stores and new, larger suburban junior department stores offering a wide variety of well-made, popularly priced general merchandise including men's, women's and children's apparel, housewares, hardware and garden supplies, toiletries, jewelry, notions, leather goods, books, stationery and toys, as well as luncheonette and lunch bar food service.

Changes in top company management in 1959 saw Edward Staley promoted to vice-chairman of the board under company founder and board chairman William T. Grant, with longtime executive vice-president and general manager Louis C. Lustenberger succeeding Staley as president of the W.T. Grant Company.

Lustenberger had joined Grants in August 1940 as vice-president and assistant to President Raymond H. Fogler after working as personnel vice-president for Chicago-based A. Montgomery Ward & Company. Along with Staley, Lustenberger was one of three other Montgomery Ward executives to transition from slow-growing Ward to fast-growing Grants over a several-month period in 1940.

Other notable changes in 1959 included the death of fifty-year W.T. Grant Company veteran Clayton E. Freeman, former company president and a board director since 1919. Freeman had been associated with Grants since 1910. Albert E. Kelly, financial advisor to William T. Grant, was elected to succeed Freeman on the board.

W.T. Grant Company president Louis C. Lustenberger, 1959–68. *From* The Grant Game, *author's collection.*

Grants' growing ranks of shopping center stores continued to garner an ever-increasing portion of the company's sales, contributing 38.8 percent of company sales in 1959, up from 32 percent in 1958. Shopping center stores totaled 340 or 42.4 percent of Grants' 801 stores in 1959. Ten years prior in 1949, by contrast, downtown stores comprised 99.6 percent of Grants' store base, when the company operated just two shopping center stores at Amherst (Buffalo), New York, opened in 1941, and Medford, Massachusetts, opened in 1949.

The company's $7,470,000 store expansion program for 1959 saw the opening of eighty-five new stores—eighty-one Grants units in shopping centers and four downtown locations. The shutdown of Grants' downtown locations increased in 1959 as twenty-three downtown stores were permanently closed as their leases expired, with Grants executives seeing little profit potential for the locations.

Wrote Grant, Staley and Lustenberger in their joint 1959 annual report to company shareholders, "In 1960, we anticipate shopping center stores to continue to contribute increasing portions of the Company's sales and earnings. We anticipate another good year for the Company, along with the continuation of our steady program of expansion."

As the 1950s drew to a close, merchandising vice-president J.L. Knies reported on changes in Grant's merchandising program: "Today, more than ever, we are able to supply virtually all of the everyday needs of more American families in the non-food lines. Our continuous program of improving merchandising presentation bore particular fruit in 1959….As we enter the decade of the 1960s, we are engaged in further preparations to capitalize on America's population surge and contribute to its rising standards of living."

Local advertising was Grants' main promotional driver, with an annual program encompassing more than 40 million lines of display advertising placed in local newspapers across the country, a lineage volume that made Grants "one of the nation's leading retail advertisers." Additionally, local newspaper display advertising was supplemented by circular, package stuffer, direct mail, radio and television advertising, as well as participation in various traffic-driving shopping center promotions running the gamut from center-wide sales and classic car shows to carnivals and Santa's Christmas season arrival by a variety of modern mechanized conveyances ranging from fire engines to helicopters.

Heading into the 1960s under Lustenberger, the 1959 annual report, featuring two of Grants' new cutting-edge shopping center stores on the cover, outlined the 1949–59 transformation of the company into "a NEW W.T. Grant Company—new in coverage of the country, new in its policy of locating stores in shopping centers, new in the type of stores, new in the size of stores, new in providing the convenience of consumer credit and new in a broadened line of merchandise."

Between 1950 and 1959, Grants' capital program fixed asset expenditures totaled $64,709,000 as the W.T. Grant Company opened 332 shopping center stores and 74 downtown stores and relocated or enlarged 223 existing stores. During that period, 80 percent of company stores had either been newly opened, relocated, enlarged or modernized in architectural design, décor, lighting, air-conditioning and fixtures. Grants headed toward 1960 with 801 stores, including 340 shopping center stores.

"We not only adjusted to meet the changing location preferences of the shopping public, but went far ahead of our industry in following customers to the suburbs," the 1959 annual report noted. "Since 1955, we have opened each year from 60 to 80 new modern stores, nearly all in shopping center locations. We expect this rapid growth to continue."

Additionally, the average size of Grants stores grew 55 percent between 1949 and 1959, providing counter and display space for greatly expanded lines of merchandise and improved facilities for an enhanced customer service experience.

Grants' larger stores and broadened lines of merchandise also spurred the meteoric growth of the company's consumer credit program, launched in 1946 as an industry pioneer in the variety store/junior department store segment. Indeed, between 1949 and 1959, Grants' annual credit sales grew 514 percent from $7,338,000 to $45,066,000.

The scope of the company had shifted massively over the decade, growing from largely a midwestern and eastern regional into a national retailing powerhouse. Where Grants had operated largely east of the Mississippi River, with a fourteen-store Pacific Coast presence in California, twelve southwestern stores in Texas, two western stores in Utah and a smattering of Great Plains stores in North Dakota, Missouri, Kansas, Oklahoma and Nebraska, Grants' presence had grown to include fifty-five stores in

California, twenty-eight stores in Texas and entry into several new markets including Washington, Oregon, Arizona and Colorado, as well as expanded store penetration in existing Great Plains markets in Oklahoma, Missouri, Kansas and Missouri.

"In 1949, the Company operated 480 stores, located chiefly in the eastern half of the United States," the 1959 annual report noted. "In 1959, Grants had grown to a truly national chain of 801 stores from coast to coast, an increase of 321 stores, or 67%. During this period the Company also acquired a 51 percent ownership in Zeller's, Ltd., an expanding Canadian chain operating 69 stores similar to Grant's."

Looking ahead to the 1960s, Grants' 1959 annual report predicted continued growth potential for the New York–based chain. "Because the Company's growth has been so steady, and because it has flowed so naturally from the carefully developed policies on which our expansion is based, we believe the momentum developed in the 1950s will continue through the 1960s at an accelerated rate, and that today Grants is actually a NEW general merchandise chain with virtually unlimited potential for growth."

RISE OF THE BIG-BOX

"Grants in Grant City"

The 1960s got off to an auspicious start on February 2, 1960, as William T. Grant, the W.T. Grant Company's eighty-four-year-old founder and longtime board president, was conferred his secondary honorary degree, a Doctor of Humane Letters, from the University of Miami, a private research university in Coral Gables, Florida. He had previously earned an honorary Doctor of Laws degree from Bates College in Maine in 1947.

Said University of Miami president Jay F. Pearson in conferring the degree:

> *William Thomas Grant: Imaginative merchant, philanthropist, enthusiast in art and archaeology. His New England forebears, dating back to the first years of the Massachusetts Bay Colony, followed for nearly three centuries the traditional ways of hard-working farm people. Son of a flour miller, he himself never finished high school. But his native energy and inventiveness came to maturity at a time when his country was ripe for new methods to meet vastly expanding needs. His contribution was the concept of store proprietor as being buyer for the public, permitting customers to make their own buying selections. Pioneer of this nowadays familiar and important trade practice, he built a nationwide mercantile structure in 18 strenuous years, placed it in the hands of his colleagues, and began an equally strenuous retirement. Because he has devoted his later years and his means in fruitful social service, particularly the promotion of mental health among children, and because he has balanced his marketplace pursuits with a creative part in oil painting, photography and archeology, I present William Thomas Grant for the Degree of Doctor of Humane Letters.*

Left: While focused on the development of anchor shopping center and standalone destination department stores in the 1960s and 1970s, the W.T. Grant Company still maintained a number of well-trafficked downtown flagship stores in major U.S. cities, including this store at 11th and Market Streets in downtown Philadelphia, which logged millions of sales transactions annually. *Author's collection.*

Below: Pivoting to full-fledged department stores in the 1960s, the W.T. Grant Company prioritized anchor store development in the nation's burgeoning ranks of greenfield urban and suburban strip mall shopping centers, including this eighty-thousand-square-foot "largest W.T. Grant store in the world," opened in August 1962 at Schwegmann-Grant Plaza at 1615 West Bank Expressway in New Orleans. *From the* New Orleans Times-Picayune.

The 1960s would also prove to be an auspicious decade for the venerable W.T. Grant Company, feted as a "grand old name" in American retailing, as it continued to evolve and transform in the face of an increasingly uphill battle to keep pace with the quickly changing face of the American retail industry.

No stranger to skirmishes on the retailing battlefield, Grants had been the department store sector's pace-setter in the game-changing 1950s transition from traditional old-line downtown business districts to the brave new retailing world of the outlying greenfield urban and suburban shopping center developments. Leading at the forefront of the strip mall shopping center craze that would sweep across the nation, Grants was a familiar anchor fixture in many of the nation's major shopping center developments of the 1950s, 1960s and early 1970s. Indicative of the shift, Grants opened its last downtown store in 1961.

Concurrent with its move to the nation's burgeoning ranks of new shopping center developments, Grants also began transitioning its new store developments in earnest from Grants' heritage niche of operating middle-range variety-styled stores into increasingly larger junior department stores encompassing a wider range of necessities, apparel and staple merchandise classified into thirty-five separate departments.

And as the U.S. population increasingly shifted to the warmer climate "Sun Belt" states in the years following World War II, Grants was quick to spot the trend and follow its loyal New England and midwestern customers south and west, investing heavily in the development of new southern and Gulf Coast stores in Florida, Georgia, Alabama, Louisiana and Texas and western stores in the desert southwest and along the Pacific Coast, particularly in California.

Over the course of the previous decade, Grants had invested a massive $69,604,000 in capital program expenditures for the development of 408 new shopping center stores, 74 new downtown stores and 218 relocated or enlarged existing stores, growing its store roster from 477 units in 1950 to 864 stores in 1960. Additionally, between 1952 and 1959, Grants had acquired a controlling 51 percent ownership stake in Montreal, Quebec–based Canadian general merchandise retailer Zeller's Ltd.

Grants' growing ranks of increasingly larger and more comprehensive shopping center stores exponentially increased their impact on the company's ledger, growing their contributions from a mere 1.5 percent of annual sales in 1950 to 45 percent of sales in 1960 as the contributions of Grants' aging roster of downtown stores slid from 98.5 percent of sales in 1950 to just 55 percent in 1960.

GRAND OPENING SALE

77,000 SQ. FT. MODERN DEPARTMENT STORE TO SERVE THE SHOPPING PUBLIC OF SASKATOON OPENS THURSDAY, JUNE 4th at 9 A.M.

WALTER P. ZELLER

1890-1957

Walter Phillip Zeller, born in Waterloo County, Ontario in October, 1890, began his retail career with the F. W. Woolworth Company in Chatham, Ontario as a stockroom boy.

By 1928, having gained further experience with S. S. Kresge Co. and Metropolitan Stores Ltd., he launched his own group of Ontario stores in London, St. Catherines, Ft. William and Guelph.

It was not long before his reputation, as a highly successful retailer, was noticed by the large U.S. retail chain, Schulte-United Ltd.

His Ontario stores were purchased by the American company, not because they wanted them, but primarily to obtain the services of Mr. Zeller as the company's Assistant General Manager in New York.

The Depression Years of 1929-30 brought bankruptcy to the Schulte United chain and in 1931, Walter P. Zeller formed the Company that purchased their 12 Canadian stores - thus launching Zeller's Limited, now a highly successful retail chain of 120 stores, coast-to-coast.

Between 1931 and 1956, Mr. Zeller lead the Company as President, General Manager and later Chairman of the Board. Looking forward to his retirement years, he prepared the way for the future of the Company and in 1952, an affiliation with the W.T. Grant Company, a large U.S. retail chain, was arranged. Grant's obtained 51% of Zeller's common shares, but Zeller's continued to operate as a separate Company with its own Board of Directors and Management. Mr. Zeller remained Chairman of the Board until his death in 1957.

The growth and aggressiveness of Zeller's as a young Company, is shown by its recent venture into Auto Centres, Drug Stores, Beauty Salons in Suburban Department Stores and often combining Food Service Outlets under the same roof.

The Company employs over 6,000 persons and close to 10,000 during the Christmas selling period. Employee benefit plans include Pension, Group Life and Health Insurance, Sick Benefit, Profit Sharing Bonus and paid Summer and Winter Vacations, depending on length of service. Employees also benefit from purchase discounts in any of Zeller's stores across Canada.

Zeller's Limited has continued to grow and maintain a highly competitive outlook in the highly competitive retail field. The Management of the Company foresees unlimited opportunity for future development of new retail outlets to meet the expanding needs of the Canadian consumers.

The present Executive of Zeller's Limited consists of 11 directors and 9 Officers. Mr. Peter Kilburn serves as Chairman of the Board of Directors. The remaining officers are J. G. Kendrick, President; J. G. Balfour, Sr. Vice-President, Merchandise; R. W. Marvell, Sr. Vice-President, Store Expansion W. H. Buggs, Vice-President, Store Operations; T. H. Burdon, Vice-President Personnel; A. V. Rowland, Vice-President Finance and Treasurer; E. G. Collard, Q.C., Secretary and General Counsel; and C. C. Ross, Comptroller. The executive Offices of Zeller's Limited are located in Montreal, Que.

ZELLER'S NEWEST STORE, OPENING THURSDAY, JUNE 4th, WILL OFFER SASKATOON SHOPPERS AN ALL-INCLUSIVE ONE-STOP SHOPPING CENTER FOR FAMILY NEEDS AND FOR THE HOME.

The Grand opening of Zeller's County Fair in Saskatoon, will take place on Thursday June 4th. This will add another Zeller store to the long list already serving the Canadian shopping public from coast to coast.

Designed as a self-service store for family fashions, soft goods and furnishings for the home, it will have a total selling area of over 58,000 sq. ft. and a parking lot to accomodate over 1200 cars. The modern, colourful decor and fixtures will incorporate the latest merchandising techniques, creating an inviting cheerful atmosphere for customers, who will shop in air conditioned comfort.

Customers will be offered an all-inclusive merchandise assortment, highlighting fashions for the family, with a smart "Salon Rendez Vous" fashion area for the ladies. The male shopper will also find a choice of smart year-round fashions, including suits and sportswear.

Other important departments to be found in the new Zeller's include Home Improvement; Camera, Home Furnishings, Home Entertainment Centre, "Four Seasons" Shop, "Smoke Shop", a Zeller Rexall Drug store with a Pharmacy to fill your prescriptions. A 78 seat Skillet Restaurant will provide full course meals or snacks for Zeller customers.

STORE HOURS

Mon. - Tues. - Fri. - Sat. -
9 A.M. - 6 P.M.

Wed. - 9 A.M. - Noon
Thurs. - 9 A.M. - 10 P.M.

ZELLER'S COUNTY FAIR STORE MANAGER

Mr. R. J. MacPherson, manager of Zeller's newest store in Saskatoon brings with him many years of experience in the retail field. Mr. MacPherson first joined Zeller's in 1958. Since then he has successfully managed Zeller stores Edmonton, Regina and Yorkton.

His past outstanding record with the Company has earned him his present promotion and he looks forward to meeting and welcoming the many new customers who will make a habit of shopping at Zeller's County Fair.

MR. R. J. MacPHERSON

WHEN SHOPPING AT ZELLER'S COUNTY FAIR BE SURE TO VISIT "THE SKILLETT" RESTAURANT

See for yourself what good eating is all about! Stop at our "Skillet" Restaurant for a meal or a snack. Bring the family for our "Daily Special" meals! Relax in the friendly atmosphere of the "Skillet"... to meet friends, for a refreshing snack or family-style dining! You'll approve of the service, the tasty food... and you'll love the generous portions!

Try our "Daily Feature" for hard-to-beat values in good eating!

WATCH FOR ZELLER'S EXCITING 10 PAGE FLYER FULL OF BIG SURPRISES!

SHOP THE EASY...CONVENIENT WAY AT ZELLER'S COUNTY FAIR!

Open a Zeller charge account, 3 easy-on-the-budget plans to suit your immediate needs! No down payment required!

UP TO 2 YEARS TO PAY!

Zeller's County Fair 3310 - 8th ST. EAST at HIGHWAY 11, SASKATOON

Following leading U.S. retailers A&P, Woolworth, Kresge and Sears north of the border, from 1952 to 1976 the W.T. Grant Company held an ownership stake in department store chain Zeller's Inc. (1931–2020), "The Store for Thrifty Canadians," taking a controlling 51 percent stake by 1959. Grants provided Zeller's with its merchandising, real estate, store development and general administration expertise, with the two firms making common buying trips to East Asia. *Author's collection.*

Grants' earnings increased 13.5 percent over the previous decade to $9,198,133 in 1960, while annual stock dividends rose from $0.75 to $1.20 per share and the number of common stockholders more than doubled from 5,690 in 1950 to 12,914 in 1960. Sales attributed to Grants' in-house credit program, established in 1946, spiked 532 percent between 1950 and 1960.

Buoyed by the news, company shareholders approved the board's recommendation for a two-for-one stock split in April 1960, with Grants financial vice-president and comptroller M.F. Ketz reporting that "the company remains in excellent financial position" with "no bank loans or long-term debt outstanding" and "no present plans for new financing."

Entering the 1960s, Grant, Staley and Lustenberger reported to Grants' 755 preferred and 12,914 common stockholders that the vast majority of Grants' resources were now being "directed almost entirely to leased shopping center stores that offer retailing opportunities in the suburbs," with 417 of Grants' 864 stores in 1960 located in neighborhood strip malls and early regional destination shopping centers where Grants served as a major or sole anchor tenant.

As part of its ambitious store development program, Grants closed increasing numbers of its fading legacy downtown stores where management-projected returns did not warrant lease renewals due to a variety of factors, including unprofitability, documented patterns of declining shopping traffic and inadequate square footage to adequately stock Grants' ever-broadening lines of merchandise.

Merchandise vice-president J. Luther Knies reported to shareholders that "1960 saw Grants forging ahead in its program of becoming the Complete Family Store in non-food lines in communities it serves" with "expanded assortments in many lines of merchandise…to better serve its customers."

In profitable and well-patronized smaller-format Grants stores unable to present all of the company's expanded merchandise lines because of space limitations, stores supplemented their assortments with use of the *Grants Order Catalog.*

During 1960, the number of outdoor sales areas adjacent to its shopping center stores were increased to offer expanded lines of horticulture, gardening supplies, outdoor furniture, outdoor cooking equipment, outdoor gyms, wading pools, lawn mowers and storage sheds, among other items.

Capitalizing on more than five decades of nearly uninterrupted growth, the turn of the calendar to 1960 saw Grants' sales surpass the $500 million milestone as 864 Grants stores coast-to-coast generated $512,686,823 in sales—an average of $593,000 per store—and $9,198,133 in profits.

While the majority of Grants' sales were still cash transactions, Grants' credit service, including charge accounts, had steadily grown since its 1946 inception to encompass all company stores and garner ever-increasing percentages of Grants' annual sales—12.1 percent of sales in 1960 versus 9.4 percent of sales in 1959. The sharp year-to-year increase was attributed to the addition of a thirty-day card account plan to Grants' existing budget plans and a rise in the number of Grants credit accounts from 535,000 in 1959 to 647,000 in 1960.

Grants' 1960 sales figures, while small by current corporate earnings report standards, were impressive at a time when most prices at Grants ranged up to $5, although some items were priced up to and beyond the $100 mark as Grants broadened its merchandising mix into bigger ticket items, including console televisions and stereos.

"Thanks to the steady growth of the company over the past decade…the Grants of today is actually a NEW general merchandise chain, with virtually unlimited potentials for service to American consumers, and for growth as one of the country's leading retailers," Grant, Staley and Lustenberger said. "The company is continuing to grow steadily and soundly, and is becoming an increasingly important factor in American retailing. The management aims to continue to expand, both in number of stores and in the breadth and diversity of lines of merchandise it offers to the public.…Today more than ever before, Grant stores are merchandised to supply most of the non-food needs of America's families at money-saving prices."

A part of Grants' merchandising mix since the W.T. Grant Company opened its first in-store soda fountain at Store No. 2 in Waterbury, Connecticut, in 1908, food service operations were in place in 340 of Grants' 864 stores by 1960. A popular amenity for shoppers and a hugely profitable department for Grants, by the company's 1973 peak fully 840 of Grants' 1,238 stores offered the Grants snack bar, The Skillet luncheonette and full-service Bradford House food service facilities collectively seating fifty-five thousand customers, with seventh-ranked Grants placing third in food service sales among all U.S. retail chains.

Said Grants store management vice-president Herbert T. Wilkinson of Grants' burgeoning food service operations, "A steady program of opening luncheonettes in selected stores will continue.…Grant luncheonettes pride themselves in top quality food, generous portions, fast friendly service and budget prices. In 1960, we served more than 67 million meals. Coffee, hamburgers and frankfurters continue to be the top volume items. In 1960, for example, we served over 25 million cups of coffee and served over 10

'SKILLET' RESTAURANT

NEW

TAKE HOME DEPARTMENT GET ACQUAINTED OFFER

CHICKEN BACHELOR PAC
- 3 PIECES GOLDEN FRIED CHICKEN
- TASTY FRENCH FRIES
- CREAMY COLE SLAW
- FRESH-BAKED DINNER ROLL

REGULARLY PRICED 98¢
THURSDAY, FRIDAY, SATURDAY

SALE 2 FOR 98¢

CHICKEN-IN-THE-BUCKET
DIRECT FROM GRANTS
'SKILLET' RESTAURANT

only **$2.69**

2½ LB. AVG.
FEEDS 3 TO 5 PEOPLE!
WHOLE CHICKEN—ROLLS
CREAMY COLESLAW
TASTY FRENCH FRIES

Lined and covered with heat-holding aluminum foil!

FISH-IN-THE-BUCKET
DIRECT FROM GRANTS
'SKILLET' RESTAURANT

only **$2.69**

8 SUMPTUOUS PIECES
CREAMY COLESLAW
FRENCH FRIES
FINE, SPICY TARTAR SAUCE

Lined and covered with heat-holding aluminum foil!

FISHERMAN BUCKET
- FISH FILLETS
- BREADED OYSTERS
- GOLDEN SHRIMP
- CRAB CAKES
- FRENCH FRIES
- CREAMY COLESLAW

ONLY $3.50

SHRIMP BUCKET
- 20 GOLDEN SHRIMP
- FRENCH FRIES
- CREAMY COLESLAW
- COCKTAIL SAUCE ..

ONLY $3.29

TAKE HOME SPECIALTIES

PURE GROUND
CHUCK HAMBURGERS .. 5 for $1
SOFT DRINKS ..... 10¢ & 20¢
MALTS AND SHAKES ... 35¢
SODAS .... 35¢

SKILLET RESTAURANT DAILY SPECIALS

THURSDAY
ALL YOU CAN EAT
BARBEQUED SHORT RIBS
MASHED POTATOES
BUTTERED VEGETABLE
ROLL & BUTTER ......
ONLY $1.29
SERVED EVERY THURSDAY

FRIDAY
ALL YOU CAN EAT
GOLDEN FISH FILLETS
FRENCH FRIES
CREAMY COLESLAW
ROLL & BUTTER ......
ONLY 99¢
SERVED EVERY FRIDAY

SATURDAY
ALL YOU CAN EAT!
FRIED CHICKEN
MASHED POTATOES
TOSSED SALAD
ROLL & BUTTER ......
ONLY 99¢
SERVED EVERY SATURDAY

"CHARGE IT"
NO MONEY DOWN
UP TO 2 YEARS TO PAY

W. T. GRANT CO
Your Friendly Family Store

NORTHTOWN
HU 7-1678

From 1959 into the 1960s, The Skillet was Grants' unifying national banner for in-store luncheonette operations. Explained Grants national food service manager Vaughn Alexander Jr., "The standardization is important. A customer should be able to walk into any Grants Food Service Department and immediately get the feeling this unit is part of the Grant family." Pictured are advertised September 1965 specials at The Skillet in the Northtown Shopping Center Grants at Spokane, Washington. *Author's collection.*

million customers with hamburgers and frankfurters. Modern equipment is used in Grant luncheonettes, with the emphasis on serving food to our customers in clean and pleasant surroundings."

Nationally, times were changing with the rise of the civil rights movement in the 1950s and 1960s. Operating "local custom" segregated lunch counters closed to African Americans in its southern stores, the W.T. Grant Company had been a targeted retailer since 1954, with occasional protest pickets outside southern stores and the corporate Home Office in Manhattan. Although overshadowed by the headline-grabbing February 1960 Greensboro, North Carolina lunch counter sit-ins at rival F.W. Woolworth Company, sit-ins were also staged at Grants' southern soda fountains, snack bars and luncheonettes in Norfolk, Virginia; Charlotte, North Carolina; Tampa, Florida; Charleston, South Carolina; Chattanooga, Tennessee; Fredericksburg, Virginia; Atlanta; and New Orleans, among other cities.

Bowing to intense local pressure, depressed store sales and the negative publicity associated with the ongoing picket and sit-in protests, by June 1964, when African American North Carolina business executive Asa T. Spaulding

Protesting the W.T. Grant Company's "local custom" segregated southern luncheonettes, stockholder James Peck, a member of the Congress of Racial Equality, speaks from the floor of the W.T. Grant Company's April 26, 1960 stockholders meeting at Grants' Midtown Manhattan headquarters. *William Eckenberg and the* New York Times *via Redux Pictures.*

(1902–1990) was named to the W.T. Grant Company's nineteen-member board of directors, all ninety-five of the W.T. Grant Company's segregated southern lunch counters had been desegregated.

Continuing the evolution and expansion of its longstanding private label merchandising program, Grants in February 1961 debuted its new trademarked Bradford brand, rolling out a full line of five-year parts-and-labor guaranteed Bradford refrigerators, freezers, washers and dryers in 138 select stores, an initiative subsequently expanded to encompass additional stores and appliance lines, including Bradford-branded televisions and stereo systems. By 1967, Grants' nationally advertised Bradford appliances would be available in 259 of the company's larger Grants and Grant City stores.

Capitalizing on the trading stamp craze that swept the nation from the 1930s into the 1970s, peaking in popularity in the mid-1960s, the W.T. Grant Company, the nation's third-largest variety retailer behind Woolworth and Kresge, made a head-turning retail industry splash in its fifty-fifth anniversary year with the April 1961 announcement of its landmark contract with trading stamp giant Sperry & Hutchinson Company to offer S&H Green Stamps in its coast-to-coast network of 878 stores spanning forty-four states.

In making the announcement, Grants joined a small, elite group of major national S&H retailing partners including U.S. service station operator Texaco, operator of more than thirty-five thousand gas stations across all fifty states, and Chicago-based National Tea Company, the nation's fifth-largest supermarket chain with more than nine hundred stores from Pittsburgh west to Denver and the Upper Midwest south to the Gulf.

The nation's leading trading stamp program provider, S&H Green Stamps were offered through more than ninety thousand businesses, with Sperry and Hutchinson operating seven hundred stamp redemption centers across the United States to serve the 33 million Americans—49 percent of U.S. families—saving S&H Green Stamps. Producing more stamps than the U.S. Postal Service, S&H's Green Stamps were pasted by customers into 1,200-stamp books, which were redeemable for more than 1,700 name-brand gifts available through S&H redemption centers and on a mail-order basis through S&H's thick, lavishly illustrated *Ideabook* catalogue.

While Sperry and Hutchinson had some partnerships with local department store chains like Chicago-based Wieboldt's, S&H's landmark contract with Grants was its first with a coast-to-coast general merchandise retailing chain.

Implementation of the S&H Green Stamp Service contract partnership was rolled out regionally in phases across the Grants chain during April

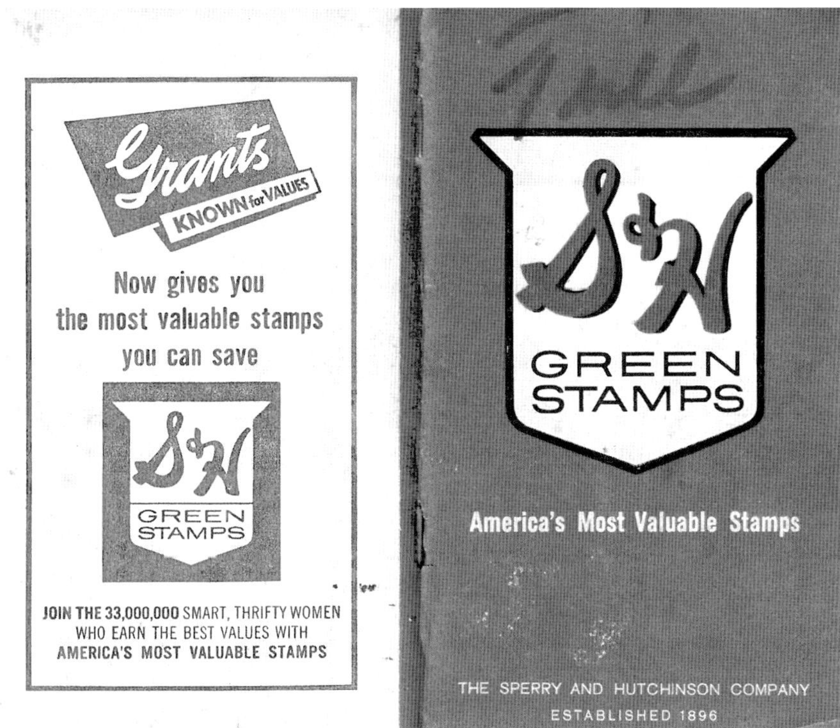

With great fanfare, 878-store W.T. Grant Company in April 1961 announced its trailblazing partnership with trading stamp giant Sperry & Hutchinson Company, Grants being the first coast-to-coast general merchandise retailer to offer customer loyalty program S&H Green Stamps. With little fanfare, the program was dropped in March 1963, as Grants' S&H-spurred sales boost was outpaced by the cost of the trading stamp program. *Author's collection.*

and May 1961 as stores were outfitted with S&H signage and Green Stamp dispensers, beginning with Grants' New England and Eastern Division stores. Following implementation of the S&H Green Stamps program in Grants' Central and Southern Division stores, the rollout wrapped up with the addition of the S&H trading stamps program in Grants' ninety-two-store Western Division.

Early results of Grants' S&H Green Stamps pilot were promising according to *The Grant Game*: "First word that we have received indicates that the program is a smash success and that enthusiastic customer response has created real excitement in stores offering the Green Stamp program."

But with little fanfare, Grants quietly dropped S&H Green Stamps in March 1963, with a company spokesman telling the Associated Press that while adoption of the S&H Green Stamps program had indeed provided

Grants with some sales increase, the rise in business had not been sufficient to offset the cost of Grants' participation in the program.

Other major developments for Grants in 1961 included the May opening of an eighty-thousand-square-foot distribution center in Buena Park, California, to better service its West Coast Grants stores, most of which were concentrated in California, with foothold scatterings of western stores in Arizona, Washington, Oregon, Utah, New Mexico, Colorado and Wyoming. A southern regional distribution center, Grants' fourth, would be added at Albany, Georgia, the following year.

From the day it opened its doors, the W.T. Grant Company had always been evolving, innovating and reinventing itself—creating the twenty-five-cent store retailing niche in 1906; introducing soda fountain "snack bars" and "luncheonette" lunch counters to the variety store business in 1908; developing a wide slate of exclusive proprietary private label store brands beginning in 1923; experimenting with the modern-day hybrid general merchandise and supermarket "superstore" concept with its "Experimental Food Departments" in 1934; pioneering the "self-service" concept out of short-staffed wartime necessity in 1943; blazing trails in 1946 as the first discount general merchandise chain to offer a credit program; and being at the forefront of the seismic 1950s retail shift to suburban shopping centers with its growing roster of ever-larger strip mall anchor department stores.

But aside from its historic 1961 plunge into trading stamps, Grants slipped from a historically proactive competitive position into an increasingly reactive stance as it began falling behind its competitors, most notably arch-rival S.S. Kresge Company.

The mid- to late 1950s and 1960s were a challenging time for traditional old-line variety store retailers like Grants, Woolworth, Kresge, Murphy, Kress and others, given the accelerating decline of the nation's heritage downtown and urban commercial districts at the hands of suburban flight and the plethora of newly developed outlying shopping centers. The competitive situation became even more challenging with the concurrent rise and popularization of early no-frills discount chains including Arlan's, Zayre, the Giant Store, Topps, Nichols Discount City, Spartan and Atlantic Mills, among others.

Presciently sensing the urgent need to dramatically change its longstanding business model, Kresge was reinvigorated under the leadership of new president Harry B. Cunningham, who among other innovations launched Kresge's fledgling Jupiter Discount Stores division in May 1960 with the conversion of three fading Detroit Kresge stores.

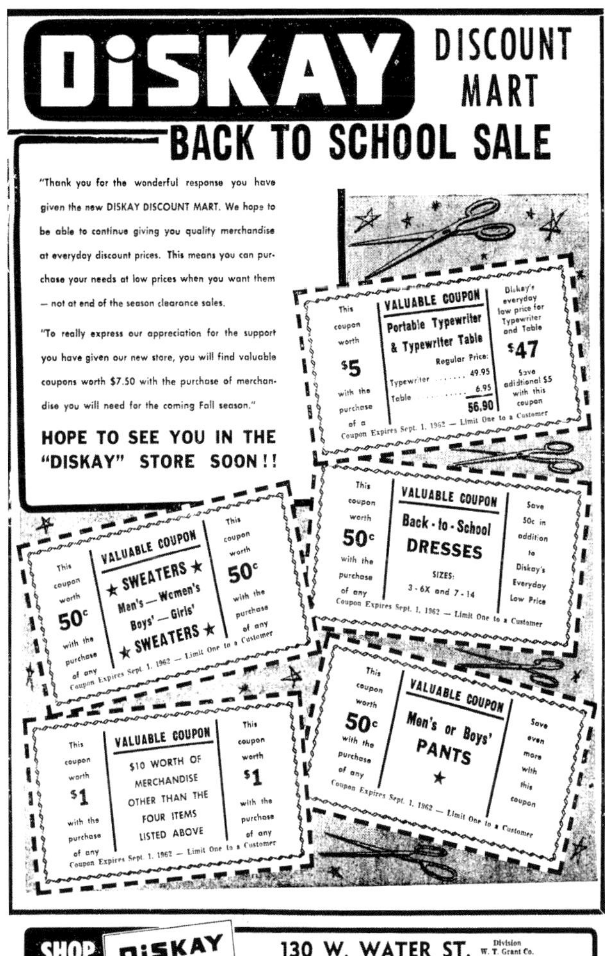

Beginning in 1962, fading but still marginally profitable urban and downtown legacy W.T. Grant Company variety stores were rebranded under Grants' new low-overhead and high-turnover Diskay Discount Mart division banner to ride out their leases. Pictured is an August 1962 back-to-school ad for the Diskay Discount Mart at 130 West Water Street in downtown Elmira, New York. *Author's collection.*

Charged by his board with increasing Kresge's profitability and strengthening its long-term viability, Cunningham created Jupiter as a separate retailing division to convert many of Kresge's older, smaller and outdated but still economically viable old school downtown and urban five-and-dimes into bare-bones, low-overhead Jupiter-branded outlets. The Jupiter format offered customers a limited line of high-demand basic goods at deep discounted prices while Kresge ran out the store leases. By 1967, Kresge was operating 117 Kresge turned Jupiter stores.

Taking a page from Kresge's successful rollout of Jupiter, Grants launched its similarly styled Diskay Discount Mart division with the May 1962 debut of rebranded and refreshed former downtown Grants stores in Jersey City,

New Jersey; Pittston, Pennsylvania; Milford, Connecticut; and Elmira, New York—marginally profitable fading legacy Grants stores said to be "ideally suited for the bargain-powered, fast turnover operation being developed for the new [Diskay] discount stores" as Grants ran out the balance of their twenty- and thirty-year leases. Grants filed for trademark status for Diskay in 1964.

Although run as deep-discount operations, Grants' remodeled, remerchandised, refixtured and rebranded Diskay stores typically retained several popular elements of the Grants stores that they replaced, including Grants' popular foodservice operations and Grant subsidiary Jones & Presnell Studios' traveling Lil' Darlin' Pin-Ups pop-up photo studios. Merchandise sold at Diskay included national name-brand cosmetics and toiletries, as well as staple goods sold under Grants' proprietary Diskay house label.

"You'll find no fancy frills or breathtaking appointments, but you will surely be impressed the sensational bargain buys on sale every day," charter Diskay director Harold Schwartz said of Grants' new Diskay Discount Mart division stores at the 1962 launch. "We are concentrating upon making… Diskay Discount Mart the most exciting family bargain bazaar."

Operating in large cities and small towns alike from Massachusetts, New York and Connecticut south to Florida and west to Texas, Missouri and Iowa, by December 1964, twenty-one former downtown and urban Grants stores in eleven states had been rebranded and converted to the Diskay Discount Mart banner, a number that rose to thirty-seven Diskay stores in fifteen states the following year. As existing Diskay stores were closed at the end of their leases, other older, outdated and fading downtown Grants stores were rebranded to Diskay in their place.

And following the industry-disrupting 1962 debut of the modern "big-box" discount department store concept by a cadre of general merchandise retailing rivals including S.S. Kresge (Kmart, March 1), Shopko (April 5), Dayton-Hudson (Target, May 1), F.W. Woolworth (Woolco, June 6) and former Arkansas Ben Franklin franchisee Sam Walton with his Wal-Mart Discount City (July 2), a behind-the-curve Grants belatedly reinvented itself with the August 6, 1963 unveiling of its own full-line big-box department store concept on White Horse Pike in Clementon, New Jersey: Grant City.

While partly a "me too" reactive response to the competitive debut of Woolco and Cunningham's wildly successful Kmart concept for Kresge, Grants' store-of-the-future "Grant City" concept was also reflective of its

Playing catch-up to the big-box discount department stores pioneered in 1962 by Woolworth (Woolco), Kresge (Kmart), Target, Shopko and Wal-Mart Discount City, the W.T. Grant Company on August 6, 1963, unveiled its massive 113,000-square-foot store-of-the-future "Grant City" concept on White Horse Pike in Clementon, New Jersey. Opening new Grant City stores at a breakneck pace, by October 1974 fully half of Grants' nationwide store fleet were full-line Grant City department stores ranging from 50,000 to 180,000 square feet—or larger. *Author's collection.*

organic decade-plus evolution from variety stores to junior department stores to full-service, full-line department stores.

But standing in competitive contrast with the discount-oriented Target, Kmart and Woolco stores, Grants' large-format full-line Grant City department stores were conceptually leaning toward the traditional department stores operated by Sears, JCPenney and Montgomery Ward, with Grants adding tire and auto service departments, L'il Darlin' Pin-Ups photo studios, furniture and major appliance departments, hair salons and full-service sit-down restaurants. And as the Grant City concept continued to evolve throughout the 1960s and into the 1970s, new test pilots included rollout smatterings of in-store pharmacies and, hearkening back to Grants' Depression-era foray into groceries, limited assortment "Family Chef" grab-and-go prepared food shops.

At a massive 113,000 square feet and staffed by 250 employees under store manager Robert H. "Bob" Drake, Clementon's "spectacular" Grant City store was feted in grand opening newspaper ads as "The Largest Grants Store in the World," offering a 1,500-vehicle parking lot and a massive, ornate masonry entryway façade.

Another trailblazing feature of the new Grant City in Clementon was Grants' inaugural full-line table service restaurant under its The Skillet banner, later rebranded under the company's new Grants Bradford House Town & Country Family Dining format.

Noted the *Camden Courier-Post*, "Complete meals at budget prices will be served in 'The Skillet' of the Clementon store of W.T. Grant Co. The restaurant, first of its kind in the Grant chain, is designed to seat 159 persons and give fast service with modern facilities and trained personnel. Other Grant installations are the luncheonette-type operation."

Beginning with the company's rollout of its new Grant City full-service department store concept in 1962, all new Grant City stores were equipped with full-service restaurants, many with quick-service front-end grab-and-go hot dog and root beer snack bars as well.

With Grants opening ever-larger Grant City stores throughout the 1960s and into the 1970s, the company's flagship Clementon Grant City was expanded to 175,000 square feet in 1971. The expansion provided larger quarters for various store departments and increased the size of Grants' auto center to twelve service bays. Parking facilities were expanded to accommodate two thousand cars, and the store's personnel roster expanded from 250 to 300 employees.

Illustrative of Grants' new store development emphasis, the company's 1963 annual report showcased the pioneering Grant City at Clementon. "The company plans to continue its aggressive growth program of new and larger stores," Grant, Staley and Lustenberger noted in their letter to shareholders, noting that 732 of the company's 1,092 stores were now located in shopping centers.

Looking to make a bold architectural and merchandising statement as part of its sixtieth anniversary celebrations in 1966, the W.T. Grant Company, in a move befitting its rising status as one of the nation's fastest-growing retailers, unveiled its distinctive, futuristic prototype "Showcase for Progress" Grant City stores.

Uniquely recognizable for their soaring, dramatic entrance towers bearing the Grants name in a new type font, a handful of "Showcase for Progress" Grants stores would be developed in the mid- to late 1960s, largely in select southern and western Grants markets, including Homewood, Alabama, and Santa Clara and Long Beach, California. Sales at the three-day grand opening of Grants' 92,969-square-foot "Showcase for Progress" store in the Bixby Knolls Shopping Center at Long Beach ran 66.88 percent over projections.

Founded in 1906, the first W.T. Grant Company department store operated in rented ground floor and basement quarters in the new YMCA building on Market Street in Lynn, Massachusetts, as pictured in this 1907 postcard, the earliest known view of the fledgling company and its No. 1 "Mother Store." *Author's collection.*

In 1916, the twenty-six-store W.T. Grant Company chain marked its tenth anniversary with an October 23–28 anniversary celebration, as advertised on this promotional stamp. By 1916, Grants twenty-five-cent department stores were located as far south as Norfolk, Virginia, and as far west as Erie, Pennsylvania; Dayton, Ohio; and Kalamazoo, Michigan. *Author's collection.*

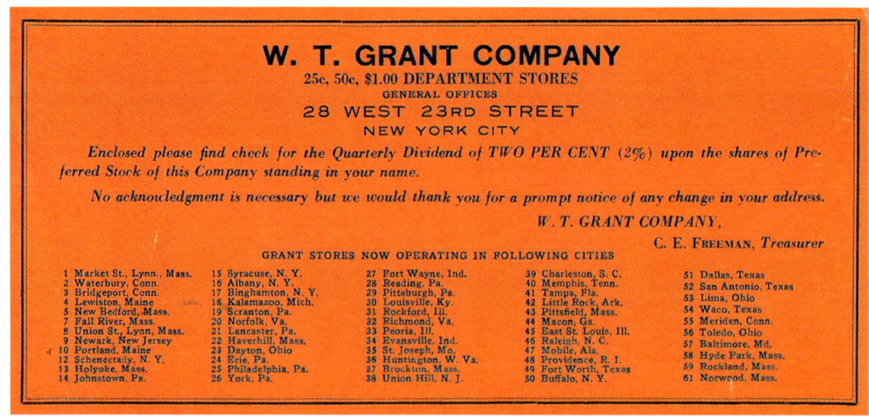

W. T. GRANT COMPANY

25c, 50c, $1.00 DEPARTMENT STORES

GENERAL OFFICES

28 WEST 23RD STREET

NEW YORK CITY

Enclosed please find check for the Quarterly Dividend of TWO PER CENT (2%) upon the shares of Preferred Stock of this Company standing in your name.

No acknowledgment is necessary but we would thank you for a prompt notice of any change in your address.

W. T. GRANT COMPANY,

C. E. FREEMAN, *Treasurer*

GRANT STORES NOW OPERATING IN FOLLOWING CITIES

1 Market St., Lynn., Mass.
2 Waterbury, Conn.
3 Bridgeport, Conn.
4 Lewiston, Maine
5 New Bedford, Mass.
7 Fall River, Mass.
8 Union St., Lynn, Mass.
9 Newark, New Jersey
10 Portland, Maine
12 Schenectady, N. Y.
13 Holyoke, Mass.
14 Johnstown, Pa.
15 Syracuse, N. Y.
16 Albany, N. Y.
17 Binghamton, N. Y.
18 Kalamazoo, Mich.
19 Scranton, Pa.
20 Norfolk, Va.
21 Lancaster, Pa.
22 Haverhill, Mass.
23 Dayton, Ohio
24 Erie, Pa.
25 Philadelphia, Pa.
26 York, Pa.
27 Fort Wayne, Ind.
28 Reading, Pa.
29 Pittsburgh, Pa.
30 Louisville, Ky.
31 Rockford, Ill.
32 Richmond, Va.
33 Peoria, Ill.
34 Evansville, Ind.
35 St. Joseph, Mo.
36 Huntington, W. Va.
37 Brockton, Mass.
38 Union Hill, N. J.
39 Charleston, S. C.
40 Memphis, Tenn.
41 Tampa, Fla.
42 Little Rock, Ark.
43 Pittsfield, Mass.
44 Macon, Ga.
45 East St. Louis, Ill.
46 Raleigh, N. C.
47 Mobile, Ala.
48 Providence, R. I.
49 Fort Worth, Texas
50 Buffalo, N. Y.
51 Dallas, Texas
52 San Antonio, Texas
53 Lima, Ohio
54 Waco, Texas
55 Meriden, Conn.
56 Toledo, Ohio
57 Baltimore, Md.
58 Hyde Park, Mass.
59 Rockland, Mass.
61 Norwood, Mass.

NC 8 697

20

COMMON STOCK

COMMON STOCK

(INCORPORATED UNDER THE LAWS OF THE STATE OF DELAWARE)

W. T. GRANT COMPANY

This Certifies that PAUL L BAXLEY 178 GLACIER AVE YOUNGSTOWN OHIO is the owner of

TWENTY

FULL-PAID AND NON-ASSESSABLE SHARES OF THE COMMON STOCK

of W.T. Grant Company (hereinafter called the "Company") transferable on the books of the Company by the holder hereof in person or by duly authorized attorney upon surrender of this certificate properly endorsed. This certificate and the shares represented hereby are issued and shall be held subject to all the terms and provisions of the Certificate of Incorporation, as amended, of the Company (a copy of which certificate is on file with the Transfer Agent) to which reference is hereby made with the same effect as though set forth in full and to all of which the holder by acceptance hereof assents. This certificate is not valid unless countersigned by the Transfer Agent and registered by the Registrar. Witness the corporate seal of the Company and the signatures of its duly authorized officers. Dated APR 26, 1966

TREASURER

PRESIDENT

BANKERS TRUST COMPANY (NEW YORK) REGISTRAR

MORGAN GUARANTY TRUST COMPANY OF NEW YORK TRANSFER AGENT

Top: From 1906 to 1928, William T. Grant used the private trading of common and preferred shares of W.T. Grant Company stock to fund the company's founding and expansion. Pictured is a 1923 quarterly preferred share dividend notice card for the sixty-store general merchandise retailer. *Author's collection.*

Bottom: The fast growth of the Delaware-incorporated W.T. Grant Company saw common and preferred shares publicly listed on the New York Stock Exchange under Grants' "WGY" ticker symbol from 1928 to 1975. This 1966 Grants stock certificate bears the signatures of Treasurer Richard W. Mayer and President Louis C. Lustenberger. *Author's collection.*

Left: While still serving as chairman of the board until his ninetieth birthday in 1966, W.T. Grant Company namesake founder William T. Grant, seen here in an undated self-portrait, retired from day-to-day operations in 1924 at age forty-eight to take up new pursuits as a world traveler, philosopher, speaker, writer, artist, photographer and philanthropist. *William T. Grant Foundation.*

Below: William T. Grant sent Christmas cards bearing his artworks to the W.T. Grant Company's growing ranks of employees for many decades. Pictured is the cover of a 1954 holiday greeting card bearing his WTG artist's signature. *Author's collection.*

The W.T. Grant Company dabbled in the new advertising medium of commercial network radio, with Grants' "Mr. Magic Buyer" logo inspiring the 1929 creation of the instrumental "March of the Magic Buyers," broadcast over CBS-affiliated New England stations in Boston and Providence, Rhode Island. *Author's collection.*

Top: From 1914 well into the 1930s, "Mr. Magic Buyer" was the William T. Grant–inspired caricature trademark of the W.T. Grant Company. Featuring prominently in advertising and on Grants-branded products, Mr. Magic Buyer also was featured in collectible corporate tchotchke including the convention button, paper weight, cuff links and tie pin seen here. *Author's collection.*

Bottom: Christmas was a special time for children at the W.T. Grant Company, fondly remembered for its massive holiday Toy Town departments and special guest appearances by Santa Claus. Children visiting Santa received a variety of free gifts over the decades, including Christmas-themed pulp comic books featuring a variety of proprietary Grants characters, including magical jack-in-the-box Jo-Joy (1945-53). "Jo-Joy and His Magic Spring" was published in 1945. *Author's collection.*

With a well-deserved reputation as "Doll Town, U.S.A.," the W.T. Grant Company offered several Grants-exclusive lines of dolls. Starting with Suzy (*second from left*), extensions of the line included Suzy's teenage sister, Suzette (*right*), and Bob, Suzette's teen boyfriend. Following the March 1959 debut of Mattel's hugely popular Barbie fashion doll, Grants in 1962 would roll out its own $1.97 fashion doll, Miss Suzette (*left*). *Author's collection.*

Looking to more efficiently supply its fast-growing growing roster of stores and better serve its customers, the W.T. Grant Company in the 1960s formed its in-house Grantfleet trucking system, supplying more than 1,100 Grants, Grant City and Diskay Discount Mart stores from a nationwide network of five major regional warehouse distribution centers in California, Indiana, New Jersey, North Carolina and Georgia. Enduring Grantfleet collectibles, as seen here, include uniform badges and patches, as well as toy Grants semis in several sizes. *Author's collection.*

Left: From 1908 to 1976, food service operations were a widely popular—and highly profitable—part of the W.T. Grant Company's retailing operations. The September 1935 publication of *The Grant Luncheonette Girl* sought to outline company-wide waitress standards for the newly national retailer. *Author's collection.*

Below: Published in 1935, *The Grant Luncheonette Girl* educated waitresses regarding the W.T. Grant Company's national standards for personal appearance and pleasant customer service. *Author's collection.*

THE GRANT LUNCHEONETTE GIRL

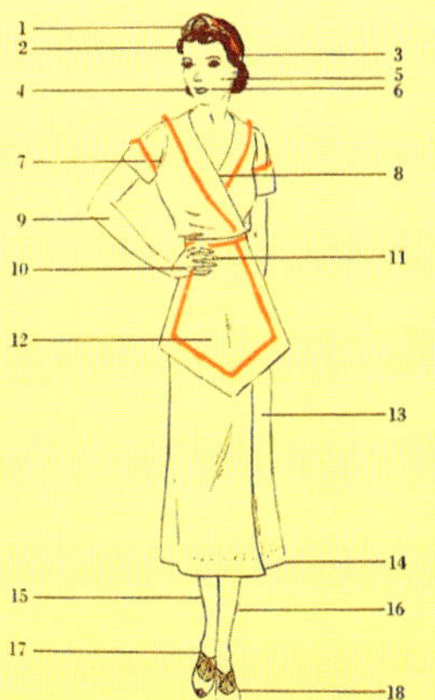

The illustration and information on these two pages are adapted from "BEFORE GOING ON DUTY"—Restaurant Management, 1935.

8

CHECK ON PERSONAL APPEARANCE

Each time before reporting to your department, CHECK YOURSELF ON APPEARANCE to see if you are ready to represent the company.

The numbers on the opposite page, referring to points which should be checked carefully, are explained below:

1. Crisp, clean head-band.
2. Hair neatly dressed.
3. Hair net.
4. Pleasant facial expression and voice.
5. Use cosmetics for naturalness.
6. Clean teeth are beautiful.
7. Guard against body odors.
8. No conspicuous pins or other jewelry.
9. Clean arms.
10. Clean, soft hands.
11. Carefully manicured nails. Avoid extreme manicures.
12. Well-pressed, clean apron.
13. Clean uniform.
14. No slip showing.
15. Stocking seams straight.
16. Clean, run-free stockings.
17. Good rubber heels.
18. Well-polished shoes.

LUNCHEONETTE SERVICE

In addition to careful attention to personal appearance, the Grant Luncheonette Girl insures pleasant service to customers by:

Memorizing daily specials.
Clean counters and dishes.
Pleasant approach.
Promptness in serving.
Courteous treatment.
Careful handling of food and dishes.
"Thank you" at close of each sale.

Details concerning care of counter and dishes, service, and treatment of customers are given in the following pages.

9

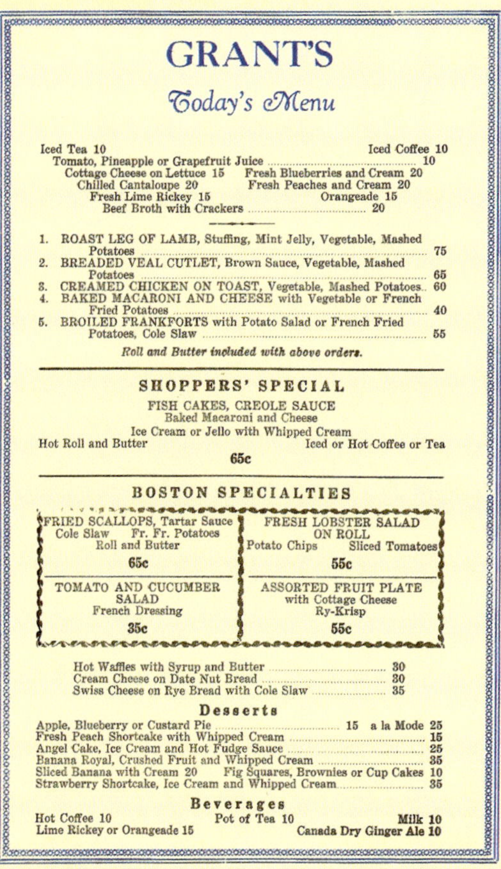

GRANT'S

Today's Menu

Iced Tea 10 — Iced Coffee 10
Tomato, Pineapple or Grapefruit Juice 10
Cottage Cheese on Lettuce 15 — Fresh Blueberries and Cream 20
Chilled Cantaloupe 20 — Fresh Peaches and Cream 20
Fresh Lime Rickey 15 — Orangeade 15
Beef Broth with Crackers 20

1. ROAST LEG OF LAMB, Stuffing, Mint Jelly, Vegetable, Mashed Potatoes 75
2. BREADED VEAL CUTLET, Brown Sauce, Vegetable, Mashed Potatoes 65
3. CREAMED CHICKEN ON TOAST, Vegetable, Mashed Potatoes.. 60
4. BAKED MACARONI AND CHEESE with Vegetable or French Fried Potatoes 40
5. BROILED FRANKFORTS with Potato Salad or French Fried Potatoes, Cole Slaw 55

Roll and Butter included with above orders.

SHOPPERS' SPECIAL

FISH CAKES, CREOLE SAUCE
Baked Macaroni and Cheese
Ice Cream or Jello with Whipped Cream
Hot Roll and Butter — Iced or Hot Coffee or Tea
65c

BOSTON SPECIALTIES

FRIED SCALLOPS, Tartar Sauce Cole Slaw Fr. Fr. Potatoes Roll and Butter 65c	FRESH LOBSTER SALAD ON ROLL Potato Chips Sliced Tomatoes 55c
TOMATO AND CUCUMBER SALAD French Dressing 35c	ASSORTED FRUIT PLATE with Cottage Cheese Ry-Krisp 55c

Hot Waffles with Syrup and Butter 30
Cream Cheese on Date Nut Bread 30
Swiss Cheese on Rye Bread with Cole Slaw 35

Desserts

Apple, Blueberry or Custard Pie .... 15 a la Mode 25
Fresh Peach Shortcake with Whipped Cream 15
Angel Cake, Ice Cream and Hot Fudge Sauce 25
Banana Royal, Crushed Fruit and Whipped Cream 35
Sliced Banana with Cream 20 — Fig Squares, Brownies or Cup Cakes 10
Strawberry Shortcake, Ice Cream and Whipped Cream 35

Beverages

Hot Coffee 10 — Pot of Tea 10 — Milk 10
Lime Rickey or Orangeade 15 — Canada Dry Ginger Ale 10

MASSACHUSETTS OLD AGE TAX 5% Wednesday, August 1, 1951

Left: The restaurant and soda fountain in the W.T. Grant Company's flagship store on Washington Street in downtown Boston featured a wide range of menu specials on August 1, 1951, including fish cakes with Creole sauce, roast leg of lamb, breaded veal cutlet, fried scallops, fresh lobster salad and Grants' famed "frankfort" hot dogs. *Author's collection.*

Below: It was "Grant's for Hospitality" in downtown Boston, where the W.T. Grant Company served hungry shoppers and downtown workers alike with a tempting array of menu options including salads, sandwiches, combination luncheons, malted milks, shakes, ice cream sodas and a variety of desserts including sundaes and fresh strawberry shortcake. *Author's collection.*

In a pleasant and cheerful atmosphere, you are able to enjoy a delicious, wholesome and satisfying repast, served by our friendly and courteous employees.

The W. T. GRANT COMPANY has always endeavored to serve appetizing and healthful food of quality at reasonable prices . . . and we shall continue to welcome suggestions from our patrons that will enable us to serve you better.

"GRANT'S FOR HOSPITALITY!"

GRANT'S

Restaurant and Soda Fountain Menu

Launched in 1959, The Skillet format standardized the W.T. Grant Company's luncheonette operations under a unifying banner at Grants and early Grant City stores in the United States, in addition to Grants' majority-owned Canadian affiliate Zeller's, where Grant's introduced in-store dining in 1960. *Author's collection.*

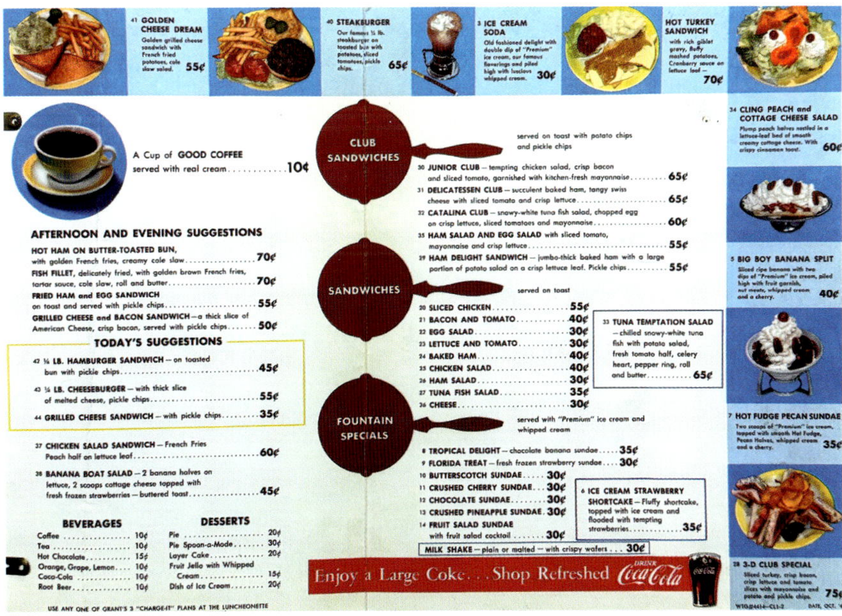

Operating under a quick-service luncheonette format, standard fare at The Skillet included burgers, hot and cold sandwiches, fountain specials, sundaes and Grants' popular, signature "Golden Cheese Dream" grilled cheese sandwiches. Pictured menu was published in October 1960. *Author's collection.*

Above: Vintage collectibles from Grants' The Skillet restaurants include menus, ashtrays, skillet-patterned china and a variety of miscellaneous advertising pieces, including the January–April 1959 Coca-Cola counter sign seen here. *Author's collection.*

Left: In 1964, the W.T. Grant Company began rolling out the Grants Bradford House Town and Country Dining format for its new full-service restaurants in larger Grants and big-box Grant City stores. Bradford House collectibles include this blue-and-white waitress uniform, cutlery pin, uniform patches and name badge. *Author's collection.*

Top: By the late 1960s, Grants Bradford House had supplanted The Skillet as the W.T. Grant Company's new unifying banner across its 840-plus snack bar, coffee shop, restaurant and carryout operations in Grants and Grant City stores nationwide. *Author's collection.*

Bottom: Concurrent with the W.T. Grant Company's 1960s pivot to its big-box Grant City department stores, Grant's food service operations transitioned toward the development of full-service in-store Bradford House restaurants. Pictured menu was published in February 1970. *Author's collection.*

In 1970, the Grants Bradford House menu offered burgers, hot and cold sandwiches, salads, fried chicken, fish and shrimp and signature house specialties including the sloppy joe–styled Wally's Barbecue. A rotating selection of daily dinner specials included roast turkey, breaded veal parmigiana with spaghetti and fried liver, among others. *Author's collection.*

Offering competitive prices, friendly service and three-squares breakfast, lunch and dinner service, the W.T. Grant Company's 840-plus full-service Bradford House restaurants were popular in Grants communities nationwide. Pictured menu was published in September 1975. *Author's collection.*

Featured at top right in this September 1975 Bradford House menu was Grants' $1.49 triple-decker, double-patty Big Boy– and Big Mac–styled "Big Brad" burger. Grants' circa 1964 Bradford Burger was rebranded Big Brad in 1974 as part of a nationwide burger-naming contest. *Author's collection.*

Photographed by his grandfather as his mom looks on, John S. Flack rides a mechanical horse outside the W.T. Grant Company anchor store at Ellisburg Shopping Center in Cherry Hill, New Jersey, in 1966, Grants' sixtieth anniversary year. *Photo by Chester T. Thomas, courtesy of John S. Flack.*

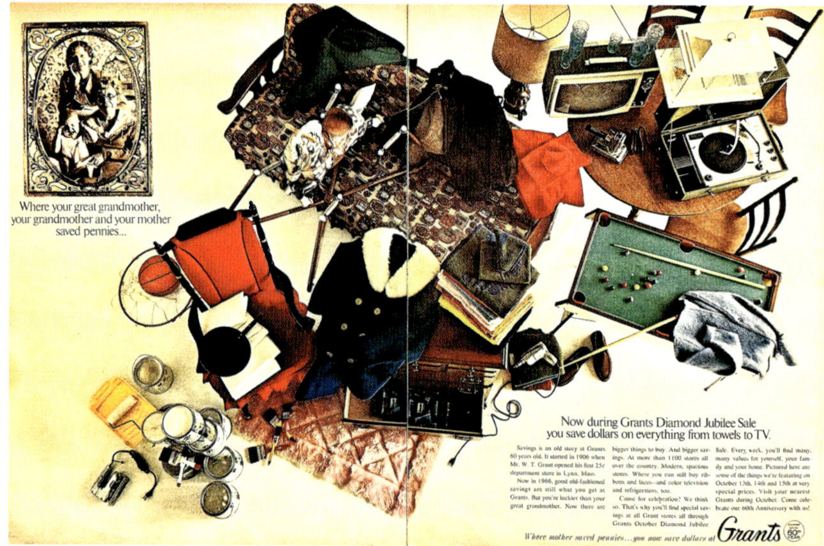

Grants observed its sixtieth anniversary in October 1966 with a gala month-long Diamond Jubilee Sale at its 1,100-plus stores. The sale was advertised nationally in a variety of popular magazines of the day, including biweekly general interest magazine *LOOK* (1937–71). *Author's collection.*

Making a bold architectural statement during its Diamond Jubilee sixtieth anniversary celebrations in 1966, the W.T. Grant Company developed a handful of futuristic prototype "Showcase for Progress" Grant City department stores in the mid- to late 1960s in a handful of select Grants markets. *Author's collection.*

Between 1967 and 1974, the W.T. Grant Company released eight of its popular *A Very Merry Christmas* stereo holiday music albums under the Columbia and RCA labels, featuring the top vocal stars of the day. The series was also marketed in Canada by Grants' majority-owned Zeller's department store chain. *Author's collection.*

The NYSE-traded W.T. Grant Company was at its 1,238-store, forty-six-state peak in the early 1970s, with sales of \$1.85 billion, Grants stock hitting a \$70⅝ per share high and Grant City stores opening at a breakneck pace. But all was not well financially behind the scenes, and an ignominious end came quickly for industry high-flyer Grants—profits slid precipitously in 1973, a staggering \$177.3 million loss was recorded in 1974, the chain filed for bankruptcy reorganization in 1975 and the company was liquidated in 1976. *Author's collection.*

Above: Typical of big-box Grant City stores nationwide was this San Jose, California location, seen in 1971. Broadening its merchandising lines to include big-ticket items, from 1961 to 1975 the W.T. Grant Company offered its proprietary line of Bradford-branded electronics and major home appliances, including the Bradford washing machines at right foreground. *Alamy.*

Left: Pictured in 2002, an increasingly weathered ghost sign still endured on the W.T. Grant Company's former six-story downtown Cleveland flagship Grants at 234–40 Euclid Avenue. Operated from 1940 to 1975, Grants No. 373 was redeveloped in 2004 into the seventy-three-unit "luxury urban living" W.T. Grant Lofts. *Eric A. Johnson photo.*

Grand Opening!

Meet, eat, and relax in the most pleasant atmosphere...

'THE BRADFORD ROOM'

RESTAURANT

THURSDAY SPECIAL
ALL DAY...
ROAST TOM TURKEY
with all the trimmings
95¢

Delicious foods and refreshments at Grants long-famous low prices

You'll find it everything a restaurant should be—a friendly, comfortable place with attentive service. Portions are generous whether it's a meal or a scoop of ice cream. Come in soon, enjoy our hospitality. Try Grants daily special—the family-style treat that can't be beat!

Served from 4:30 p.m. daily **PRIME RIB of BEEF** 2.95 Complete Dinner	Served from 4:30 p.m. daily **NEW YORK STEAK** 3.25 Complete Dinner ... 12 oz.
Served from 4:30 p.m. daily **BROILED LOBSTER TAIL (2)** $3.00 Complete Dinner	Served from 4:30 p.m. daily **½ PAN FRIED CHICKEN** 1.50 Complete Dinner

W.T. GRANT CO. *Your Friendly Family Store*

100 LIDO FAIRE CENTER Newark Blvd. NEWARK

OPEN DAILY 6 a.m. - 10 p.m. • SUNDAY 9 a.m. - 10 p.m.

Left: Introduced in 1964, the W.T. Grant Company's full-service Bradford House restaurants began to roll out across the country in larger new Grants and Grant City stores, quickly becoming Grants' unifying food service banner. Pictured is a November 1965 ad featuring the grand opening Bradford House specials at the Lido Faire Center Grants in Newark, California. *Author's collection.*

Below: Making a bold architectural statement during its sixtieth anniversary celebrations in 1966, the W.T. Grant Company developed a handful of futuristic prototype "Showcase for Progress" Grant City stores in select Grants markets, including Santa Clara, California, seen here in December 1972. *Richard Longstreth photo.*

The year 1966 would prove noteworthy for the W.T. Grant Company in other ways as well, with Grants cracking the 1,100-store milestone for the first time. The only states outside Grants' expansive 46-state footprint were Wyoming, South Dakota and far-flung Alaska and Hawaii, with Grants' highest concentration of stores being in New York (132), Pennsylvania (120), California (89), Ohio (76), New Jersey (71), Florida (67), Massachusetts (62), Connecticut (43), Texas (34) and Illinois (33).

Posting sales increases in fifty-seven of its sixty years, Grants logged its seventeenth consecutive year of record sales with a final $920,797,000 tally for fiscal 1966, with 781 of Grants' 1,104 stores being contemporary shopping center or freestanding locations.

A major milestone development during the year was Grants' January 1966 formation of the W.T. Grant Credit Corporation, renamed W.T. Grant Financial Corporation in 1968, as a wholly owned subsidiary to purchase and finance Grants' growing ledger of customer installment credit accounts.

Also noteworthy in 1966 were several major changes in Grants' management ranks, the most notable being the June 27, 1966 retirement of W.T. Grant Company founder William T. Grant as director and chairman of the board on the occasion of his ninetieth birthday. Following acceptance of his retirement "with reluctance and regret," the Grants Board of Directors unanimously named Grant as Honorary Chairman

Opposite: With its rising national retailing stature and increasingly upscale aspirations, 1,100-store Grants in March 1966 launched an ambitious multi-year reimaging advertising campaign with Grey Advertising Agency featuring monthly color two-page ad spreads in popular major mass-circulation magazines of the day, including *LOOK*, *Good Housekeeping*, *McCall's*, *Redbook* and *Ebony*. *Author's collection.*

Above: Though retired from day-to-day oversight of the W.T. Grant Company in 1924, namesake founder William T. Grant continued to keep an eye on his growing retail chain, shown here reviewing a Grants sale circular. On his ninetieth birthday in 1966, Grant retired from his chairman of the board roles for both Grants and the William T. Grant Foundation. Grant passed away on August 6, 1972, at ninety-six. *Author's collection.*

of the Board for Life. Grant was succeeded as board chairman by former Grants president and longtime board vice-chairman Edward Staley.

In October 1966, Pacific Coast Properties president and former Grants real estate attorney and negotiator Harry E. Pierson was elected by the board as store expansion vice-president. Pierson would later briefly serve as Grant's tenth president in 1973–74.

And effective February 1, 1967, former Grants sales vice-president James Kendrick was elected to serve as president and CEO of Grants' majority-owned 110-store Canadian retailing affiliate, Zeller's, which had just wrapped up the most successful year in its thirty-four-year history with record sales of $117,150,153 and record earnings of $4,837,816. In 1974–75, Kendrick would serve as Grants' eleventh president.

Continuing to build on the launch of its new Bradford line of major home appliances and electronics, Grants' merchandising emphasis continued its focus on capitalizing on the merchandising strengths of the company's longstanding "Grants-Own Brands" proprietary private label program, which by 1967 accounted for more than half of the company's sales.

Grants marked a major turning point in 1968 as twenty-two-year Grants veteran Richard W. Mayer was elected as the company's ninth president to replace Lustenberger, who retired in February 1968. Mayer had been named treasurer in 1961 and added the title of vice-president in January 1964. In a break with longstanding tradition that would have major impacts on Grants in future years, Mayer was the first non-merchandising executive to head the chain.

During Lustenberger's 1959–68 tenure at the company's helm, first under board chairman and company founder William T. Grant and then under Staley, Grants' successor, W.T. Grant Company sales more than doubled and earnings increased from $9,850,000 to more than $32 million. Under Lustenberger, as part of the company's strategic 1963 competitive pivot to Grants' new freestanding and shopping center anchor Grant City department stores, new full-line, big-box Grant stores tripled in size to 75,700 square feet, and the company's total selling footage more than doubled.

As the first non-merchandising man to head the venerable retail chain, previously serving as Grants' national credit manager, treasurer, financial vice-president and sales vice-president, Mayer's selection as Grants' new president and CEO was indicative of the increasingly central role that financial matters were coming to play in Grants' merchandising operations—financing the company's increasingly aggressive new store development program, stocking Grant's fast-growing fleet of ever-larger stores and

Launching its pioneering credit sales program in 1946 as the W.T. Grant Company expanded the breadth of its merchandise offerings to encompass big-ticket items, including the later addition of deliverable furniture, console stereo and televisions and major home appliances, Credit Sales offices were eventually expanded to encompass all Grants stores. Pictured is the Credit Sales office at the Chalmette, Louisiana Grant City store. *From the* New Orleans Times-Picayune.

financing Grant's bulging ledger of customer accounts receivables from the company's in-house installment credit operation, expanded to include Grants' new, aggressively marketed Grantcard revolving credit card program as Grants increased its merchandising emphasis on the sale of big-ticket items including deliverable furniture and proprietary Bradford-branded major appliances and electronics.

Marking its sixty-second year in grand style, Grants sales in 1968 topped the landmark $1 billion threshold for the first time in company history as Grants generated $1,091,658,008 in sales—an all-time high for the nineteenth consecutive year—as the annual sales volume of the average Grant store reached the $1 million milestone. Net earnings, up 14.9 percent, stood at a record $37,895,304.

The scope of Grants' retail operations by 1968 had grown to encompass 1,092 stores—all equipped with in-store credit offices, more than half equipped with restaurants and a third offering major appliances and outdoor living garden shops. Sixty Grants stores offered automotive service centers.

Supporting Grants' fast-growing store network were five major warehouse distribution centers in California, Indiana, New Jersey, North Carolina and Georgia, as well as six divisional offices in New Jersey, Massachusetts, Pennsylvania, Illinois, Georgia and California and seventeen regional Bradford appliance service centers scattered strategically in major Grants trading markets across the United States.

An active presence in the hundreds of communities it called home across the United States, the W.T. Grant Company sought to be a good corporate citizen. One example is this 1965 Grants-sponsored Cubs youth baseball team in Utica, New York. *Author's collection.*

YOUR CAREER

with the W. T. Grant Company

Store 700—Anaheim, Calif., Anaheim Park Shopping Center.

- On-the-job training for store management
- Rapid advancement because of continual store expansion
- Liberal benefits
- Merit ratings
- Promotion from within
- Diversified responsibilities offering opportunity to demonstrate versatility
- Financial stability with above-average income opportunities

The W. T. Grant Company operates a nation-wide system of retail stores. These stores serve the needs of a vast number of families–selling a wide variety of popular-priced merchandise –men's, women's, and children's apparel...housewares...home furnishings...hardlines...smallwares...major appliances.

The W. T. Grant Company operates over 1,000 stores, located in 45 states, with 5 Regional Offices, and a Home Office in New York City.

Sales volume for 1962 will be over $600,000,000. The Company has had a history of growth and progress for over 50 years, and this tradition is setting the pattern for future development.

Store 135—Nashville, Tenn., a large new downtown store.

How to apply...and how to get more information

1. Visit your Placement Director.

He will give you a booklet "W. T. Grant Company–Your Career" (or suggest writing for one)–as well as give the date when a W. T. Grant representative will visit your campus.

Store 644—Pompton Lakes, N. J., in a new park-and-shop center

2. Call or visit a W. T. Grant Office or Store.

New England Regional Office
W. T. Grant Company
45 Bromfield Street
Boston 8, Mass.

Eastern Regional Office
W. T. Grant Company
1441 Broadway
New York 18, N. Y.

Central Regional Office
W. T. Grant Company
20 N. Wacker Dr.
Chicago 6, Ill.

Southern Regional Office
W. T. Grant Company
3330 Peachtree Road N.E.
Atlanta 5, Georgia

Western Regional Office
W. T. Grant Company
3460 Wilshire Blvd.
Los Angeles 5, Calif.

Store 69—St. Paul, Minn., in a downtown shopping location.

3. Or write to

Employment Manager, W. T. Grant Company, Dept. A
1441 Broadway, New York 18, New York

W. T. GRANT CO.

As the W.T. Grant Company began to expand its nationwide footprint more aggressively in the 1960s and 1970s, recruitment of promising young men and women for the company's Manager in Training Program became a top priority. Here, Grants advertises in the College Placement Council's 1963 College Placement Annual, a directory providing information on employment available with principal companies and governmental agencies in the United States and Canada. *Author's collection.*

Grants' store growth program between 1964 and 1968 had encompassed capital expenditures of $46,381,000 for the opening of 174 new stores and the enlargement of 60 stores. During the preceding ten-year period, more than half of Grants' 1,092 stores had been opened, with the average Grant City opened in 1968 being more than double the size of stores opened just five years prior.

"The stores in the 1968 program have started out well and contributed to the sales and earnings increase," noted Staley and Mayer to Grants' 17,958 common and 659 preferred shareholders. "For 1969, we plan to continue our aggressive store expansion program. The Grant organization is well prepared to maintain its strong competitive standing in the retail field and will be in position to take advantage of every opportunity."

Closing out the 1960s, Grants appeared to be headed to even greater heights in the 1970s and beyond as it turned in its eighth consecutive year of record sales and earnings in 1969.

Grants' annual sales over the decade had more than doubled from $513,000,000 to $1.2 billion, while annual profits increased fourfold from $9,200,000 to $41,800,000. Grants stock dividends, meanwhile, increased 133 percent as Grants hiked its annual stock dividend four times between 1964 and 1969 from $0.60 per share to $1.40 per share.

Already the nation's seventh-largest non-food retailer and the country's third-largest big-box discount chain after Woolworth (Woolco) and Kresge (Kmart), Grants had experienced a comprehensive transformation of its retail operations over the course of the 1960s, including the 1962 launch of its Diskay Discount Marts subsidiary and, most notably, the 1963 launch of its Grant City full-line department store concept.

Also of note during the decade was Grants' acquisition of its longtime mobile photography studio vendor, North Carolina–based Jones & Presnell Studios Inc. Founded in 1956 by business partners Tom Jones and Carroll Presnell, Jones & Presnell was a pioneer operator of portable photography shops and baby picture services nationally under its trademarked Lil' Darlin' Pin-Ups banner in a variety of chain retail stores.

At the time of its acquisition as a wholly owned subsidiary, Grants was by far Jones & Presell's largest customer, generating more than 60 percent of its business from Grants and Grant City stores, in addition to serving select department stores operated by national chains like Sears and Montgomery Ward and regionals like Portland, Oregon–based Sprouse-Reitz; Petersburg, Virginia–based Rucker-Rosenstoc; and Charlotte, North Carolina–based Belk among others.

Over the course of the 1960s, Grants stores made a significant transformation in scope, size and substance as the company pivoted from operating traditional variety stores and larger junior department stores offering a limited assortment of merchandise, mainly in soft lines, to an exclusive focus on the fast track opening of full-line, big-box, one-stop-shopping Grant City department stores.

As the decade drew to a close, Grant City stores opened during 1969 were more than three times as large as their 1960 Grants counterparts, with Grant City stores of the late 1960s and early 1970s typically developed in three stock sizes depending on the community—50,000, 120,000 and 180,000 square feet—and offering a wide array of general merchandise lines, including deliverable furniture and major appliances, as well as a variety of value-added services including beauty salons, automotive service centers, home decorating centers, garden centers and full-service Bradford House restaurants.

During the 1960s, the Grants chain had increased from 864 stores in forty-three states to 1,095 stores in forty-six states during the 1960s, even after the closing of 309 smaller, older Grants stores. Indeed, a remarkable 70 percent of Grants' 1,095 stores had either been opened or substantially enlarged over the preceding ten years.

Employment at Grants over the decade rose from thirty-nine thousand to sixty-three thousand employees, with Grants stockholders in 1969 approving a new Employees' Stock Purchase Plan as a continuation of similar plans in place since 1950, allowing Grants employees the opportunity to purchase the company's NYSE-listed "WGY" common stock at market prices on a deferred payment basis.

Reflective of Grants' accelerated store development program under new company president Richard Mayer, Grants in 1969 "completed the most ambitious capital program to date" in its history according to Mayer and Staley, with the opening of 4 million square feet of space in fifty-two new stores and three enlarged stores, in addition to the opening of a state-of-the-art 309,000-square-foot automated warehouse distribution center in Camarillo, California.

The Camarillo warehouse distribution center would serve as a prototype for even larger distribution centers set to come online in the coming years as Grants heavily invested in support facilities to service its growing network of larger Grant City stores.

An offshoot of Grants' search for ever-greater supply chain efficiencies was the related 1960s establishment of an in-house nationwide Grantfleet trucking division providing a critical merchandise transportation link between Grants' regional distribution centers and its network of 1,095 Grants, Grant City and Diskay stores.

Much of the merchandise passing through company distribution centers and moved by Grantfleet trucks included Grants' own proprietary house brands—Grants, Pennleigh, Bradford, I'sis, Grant Master and Grant Maid among them—which had come to account for nearly 60 percent of Grants' $1.2 billion in sales.

As it looked ahead to 1970 and beyond, Grants' ambitious plans for the accelerated development of its growing roster of Grant City stores saw the company grooming 1,814 promising young men and women for store management, buying and executive positions, a policy in keeping with founder William T. Grant's longstanding developmental emphasis on promotion from within.

But dark clouds were already gathering on the horizon.

ALL SALES FINAL

Grants' Great Crash and Burn

As the golden years of traditional urban variety store chains and America's downtowns drew to a close, with the concurrent usurping rise of outlying urban and suburban one-stop shopping centers and the nation's early big-box discount department stores, America's old-line general merchandise retailers—the W.T. Grant Company among them—faced increasingly stiff competitive headwinds and myriad challenges heading into the 1970s.

Still, at first glance for the casual observer, the future looked bright for fast-growing Grants. Given its enviable financial track record and ascendant stature as one of the America's leading retailers, it appeared that Grants' progress would continue rocketing upward.

Accurately foreseeing the future of the big-box store concept, Grants executives went all-in on the company's big-box Grant City department stores following their 1963 debut, opening Grants' final variety-formatted store in 1969. By October 1974, fully half of Grants' nationwide chain of 1,172 stores were full-line, one-stop Grant City department stores ranging from 50,000 to 180,000 square feet—and some even larger.

Still plying the middle-of-the-road niche that had made the company such a longstanding success, Grants positioned its new Grant City stores between the rising cadre of big-box discount department stores like Kmart, Woolco and Target and the traditional mainstream department stores like Sears, JCPenney and Montgomery Ward.

In the late 1960s and early 1970s, the W.T. Grant Company broke ground on hundreds of big-box Grant City department stores at a blistering pace across the country. Here, Grants president Richard Mayer (left, 1968–73) breaks ground with St. Bernard Parish Police Jury vice-president Henry L. Schindler in July 1970 for Grants' East Gate Mall Grant City, 8601 West Judge Perez Drive, Chalmette, Louisiana. Operated from 1973 to 1975 as Grants No. 910, Grant City was succeeded by Kmart No. 3387 from 1976 to 1999. *P.A. Hughes photo, from the* New Orleans Times-Picayune.

Illustrative of the breakneck pace of Grants' expansion under the successive presidencies of Lustenberger and Mayer, the five-year period from 1966 to 1970 had encompassed $62,936,000 in capital expenditures for the development of 233 new stores and the enlargement of 46 existing Grants stores, nearly all Grant City developments.

Setting new annual corporate records for sales and store counts, Grants' coast-to-coast roster of 1,116 family stores generated more than $1.25 billion in sales in 1970 as the company celebrated its sixty-fourth anniversary as one of America's fastest-growing retail chains, ranking as nation's seventh-largest non-food retailer behind Sears, JCPenney, Kresge (Kmart), Montgomery Ward, Woolworth (Woolco) and Cincinnati-based Federated Department Stores, a nationwide conglomeration of legacy local and regional department store chains. Factoring in supermarket chains A&P, Safeway, Kroger, ACME, Jewel, Lucky, Food Fair and Winn-Dixie, the W.T. Grant Company ranked as the nation's fifteenth-largest retailer overall.

Grants' "WGY" stock, listed on the New York Stock Exchange since 1928 and selling in excess of $50 per share with a $1.50 annual dividend, was among the darlings of Wall Street as a reliable blue chip dividend aristocrat, hitting an all-time high of $70⅝ in 1971. Designated as an NYSE "Heirloom Stock," Grants shares were one of just eighty-nine stocks that had paid uninterrupted dividends for fifty or more consecutive years, with Grants being in even rarer company as one of only two retailers that had paid consistent dividends during that same span.

Indeed, since its 1906 founding, Grants had never tallied a losing year or failed to pay a common or preferred stock dividend, even through two world wars and four economic recessions, including the protracted 1929–39 Great Depression. And with the exception of just three years—1932, 1938 and 1949—sales at Grants had hit new records annually.

Heading into the 1970s, investments by $1.8 billion Grants in developing its Grant City format stores had been ambitious under Mayer's leadership, exceeding that of $5.5 billion JCPenney and keeping pace with that of $3.9 billion S.S. Kresge and its fast-growing big-box Kmart discount department store division.

Grant's 1970 capital program, the largest square footage addition in store facilities in company history, totaled more than 5,400,000 gross square feet of new store space, over one-third more than the previous record program undertaken in 1969.

Grants' new store development program continued apace heading into the new decade, the company opening 65 new stores and enlarging eight

As economic growth stagnated in the northeastern and Midwest "Rust Belt" states, the W.T. Grant Company invested heavily in the fast-growing southern and western United States. Shown is the August 1973 grand opening turnout for Grants' sprawling new metro New Orleans Grant City store, No. 910, at 8601 West Judge Perez Drive, Chalmette, Louisiana. *Lee Delaune photo, from the* New Orleans Times-Picayune.

existing stores in 1970 as part of a $15,995,000 capital expenditures budget for the year, bringing Grants' store footprint to 1,116 stores.

Said Grants' 1970 annual report, "What the customer…appreciates is that there's a new Grants store in town, a store KNOWN FOR VALUES… Bright, colorful, cheery—and convenient. That defines the modern Grant store.…We continue to be receptive to changes which enable us to meet customer needs, What we will not change is the basic concept of serving the majority of the people by offering outstanding merchandise in popular priced lines. This has been our goal since our inception sixty-five years ago, and we are certain that this same goal will continue to stand us well in the future."

To meet the logistical needs of Grants' fast-expanding store base, nearly half of which were now the larger full-line Grant City department stores, 1970 saw the completion of more than 1,250,000 square feet of distribution

By the 1970s, the W.T. Grant Company's Grant City big-box discount department stores were taking on more of a traditional department store feel with wider aisles and more engaging merchandise displays. Pictured prior to its February 1974 grand opening debut is the metro New Orleans Grant City at 3324 Williams Boulevard in Kenner, Louisiana. *Jim Pitts photo, from the* New Orleans Times-Picayune.

facilities, including the opening of a "new type facility" in Jersey City, New Jersey, and the replacement of existing older Grants distribution facilities in Edison, New Jersey, and New Haven, Indiana.

Despite the many milestones, some cracks were beginning to form in the foundation underpinning Grants. Earnings for 1970 totaled $39,577,087, 4 percent under 1969's record earnings of $41,809,000. While fourth-quarter earnings set a record for Grants, earnings in the first three quarters showed a decline.

"In relation to our sales and profit objectives, this performance was not up to expectations," noted Staley and Mayer in Grants' 1970 annual report. "We believe that with our organization of loyal, well-trained employees, plus good financial stability, the Company can successfully meet the challenges of 1971. On the longer term, we are confident that the 1970s will be a decade of growth for the Grant Company."

Unfortunately, it was not to be. While Grants logged new sales records and continued the breakneck expansion of its store base in 1971 and 1972, with Grants ultimately reaching a 1,238-store, $1.85 billion peak, the tide was beginning to turn dramatically for Grants.

Troubling signs for Grants continued in 1971. While sales were up 13.9 percent, profits were down 12.5 percent to $35,212,082, marking a second straight year of decline.

Calling Grants' 1971 profit "disappointing," Staley and Mayer predicted better years ahead, pointing to the gross store square footage opened by Grants over the previous five years—2,146,000 square feet in 1967, 3,205,000 square feet in 1968, 3,950,000 square feet in 1969, 5,360,000 square feet in 1970 and 7,283,000 square feet in 1971, the latter encompassing $26,476,000 in capital expenditures—the largest one-year expansion program in company history with eighty-three new Grants stores and five enlargements of existing stores:

> *Why the acceleration? Because throughout America the tempo of growth and change is on the upbeat. We find more customers seeking the convenience of one-stop shopping and the adequate parking available in growing suburban communities. We note shopping lists liberally sprinkled with items which, only a few short years ago, were frequently beyond the reach of the average family budget. The trends all point toward an opportunity to service the need of today's customer and gain a foothold on tomorrow. Our strategy is clear cut—to establish more Grant stores, and larger Grant stores, which feature the expanded lines of merchandise customers are seeking: merchandise they know will, as always, offer quality at value prices. For at Grants, value and progress go hand-in-hand.*

Between 1965 and 1971, Grants opened new store space greater than the space available in ten Empire State Buildings.

"By successfully opening over 7 million gross square feet of new stores space in 1971, the Company reached the goal of what we presently consider to be the most desirable program that can be efficiently sustained within the prudent confines of available good store locations, adequate management staff, efficient filtering and merchandising, and available financial resources," Mayer and Staley wrote. "For the foreseeable future, having reached this goal, we will continue this aggressive store opening program. We are confident that this growth pattern presents us with a great opportunity for the future."

In the near term, they predicted a continued downturn in profitability as the company waited for its growing fleet of Grant City stores to establish themselves and grow into profitability.

"A new store, particularly one in a new Grant trading area, requires three to five years to 'mature' to its estimated sales and profit potential. Generally, the larger the individual store, the longer the maturing period. As the Company has progressed through this period of sharp yearly increases in the size of our new store program we have added proportionately more one and two year old units in our total store mix," they noted. "In the near future this situation will reverse and we will have more third, fourth and fifth year units in our mix. We will have more stores that are reaching their sales and profit potential, and less, proportionately, that are just starting their growth cycle.... Even though the Company has experienced a pause in its profit progression, we start the year 1972 with 40% of our total selling area opened within the last five years....We have great confidence concerning Grants' prospects for the 1970s. Our organization is strong, our financial position sound and we feel that the large group of stores that we have opened in recent years will provide a base for increasing sales and profits in the years to come."

To better support its fast-growing national store network, Grants in 1971 replaced its existing distribution facility in Albany, Georgia, with a new 474,000-square-foot facility.

Symbolic of Grants' rising stature among U.S. retailers and the chain's lofty ambitions, Grants in 1972 exited its longtime Midtown Manhattan Home Office at 1441 Broadway and entered a twenty-five-year, $87.5 million aggregate lease of fourteen floors—399,600 square feet of space—in a newly completed fifty-four-story office tower developed by Samuel Minskoff & Sons in the colorful, frenetic heart of Times Square on the corner of Broadway and West 44th Street, 1515 Broadway.

Grants initially took occupancy of nine floors, with five reserved to accommodate expected future expansion of Grants' corporate operations as the company continued to expand and grow its retailing operations.

Grants would be the lead tenant in architect Der Scutt's International Modern–styled black glass and limestone skyscraper, built from 1968 to 1972, with Grants paying an extra naming rights fee for the W.T. Grant Building.

Grants' stylized cursive logo, inspired by founder William T. Grant's distinctive signature, was installed on all four sides of the building's spiked crown—fifty-foot-long neon signs in time-honored signature Grants orange.

The company's financial picture brightened somewhat in 1972, as Grants posted a slightly improved $37,787,066 profit on a record $1,644,747,319 in sales from an expanded all-time high roster of 1,238 stores in forty-six states.

Grant stores ranged in size from 20,000 to 180,000 square feet in three store categories—219 "traditional downtown landmark" variety stores in cities like Philadelphia, New Orleans, Pittsburgh, Buffalo, St. Paul, Atlanta,

Above: Mirroring its rising ambitions as one of the nation's fastest-growing retailers, the W.T. Grant Company in June 1972 relocated its corporate headquarters to the nine upper floors of the new fifty-four-story W.T. Grant Building at 1515 Broadway at Times Square in Midtown Manhattan. *From* The Grant Game, *author's collection.*

Opposite: The Grants name was raised high in neon over Times Square with the 1,238-store company's June 1972 move to the new W.T. Grant Building at 1515 Broadway in New York City. Four signs were installed on the building's spiked crown, each measuring fifty feet long and containing more than a quarter mile of glowing orange neon tubing. *From* The Grant Game, *author's collection.*

Houston, Providence, Boston and Hartford; 500 convenience-type local Grants junior department stores in smaller neighborhood shopping centers; and 464 large full-line Grant City big-box department stores ranging in size from 50,000 to 180,000 square feet and "accounting for well over 50% of the Company's sales" as the "rapidly growing arm of the W.T. Grant Company" and the company's main driver of growth.

While the Grant City name had been in use in advertisements since the opening of the first full-line Grant City department store at Clementon, New Jersey, in 1963, the stores themselves had never been branded under the Grant City banner, operating under the historic, time-honored Grants name.

Looking to better differentiate its larger full-line Grant City department stores from its smaller, limited-selection legacy Grants variety and junior department stores, much like Woolworth with Woolco and Kresge with Kmart, in late 1972 the Grant City name was officially selected by company executives to formally distinguish its growing cadre of full-line department stores, which had grown from 102 to 464 Grant City stores between 1967 and 1972.

February 1974 grand opening crowd lines up to enter the W.T. Grant Company's new 89,500-square-foot full-line Grant City department store at 3324 Williams Boulevard, Kenner, Louisiana. One of forty-five Grant City stores opened in 1974, the store bore the company's new Grant City logo signage, standard beginning in 1973 with all new Grant City developments. Existing Grant City stores were rebadged by removing the "S" from "GRANTS" and replacing it with a circular sign reading "City." *C.F. Bennett photo, from the* New Orleans Times-Picayune.

"In the mid-1960s the Company embarked on a program of opening larger shopping center stores which would provide the vast assortment of goods and services required…each store a veritable city of merchandise—a Grant City," read Grants' 1972 annual report.

Beginning in 1973, all new full-line stores began to officially bear cursive Grant City signage, while existing Grants full-line department stores began to be rebadged. "The Grant City designation is without a doubt one of the most exciting developments in our corporate history," noted the February 1973 edition of *The Grant Game*. "It is truly a giant step forward and we hope all Grant people take pride in this progressive move. With all Grant folks working together, Grants and Grant City stores are bound to achieve new heights.…Grant City stores give us yet another reason to predict a 'rosy' future for everyone in the growing Grant family."

A historic, seismic change for the W.T. Grant Company came on August 6, 1972, with the death of company founder and namesake William T. Grant at age ninety-six.

Seen in his last official portrait photo, W.T. Grant Company and William T. Grant Foundation founding namesake William Thomas Grant Jr. passed away at age ninety-six on August 6, 1972. Following his 1966 retirement from both organizations at age ninety, Grant held dual Honorary Chairman of the Board titles. *Author's collection.*

With the meteoric rise of popular catalogue showroom stores heading into the 1970s, Grants joined forces in October 1972 with New York–based jewelry manufacturer and catalogue showroom retailer Jewelcor Inc., announcing plans to open some thirty joint venture "granJewel" retail catalogue showrooms beginning in 1973.

For a major mass merchandise retailer like Grants, the allure of entering the fast-growing field of discount-oriented catalogue showrooms was obvious from a financial standpoint, given the popularity of the rival catalogue stores and the concept's attractive cost-saving, low-overhead business model. Net profits for catalogue showrooms ran to 4 percent net after taxes compared to under 1 percent net profit for most general merchandise discounters.

Operations quickly grew to encompass a chain of fifteen joint-venture granJewel catalogue-showroom-warehouse stores in Pennsylvania, New Jersey, Georgia, Florida, Texas, Arizona and California among other locales, with seven additional granJewel catalogue showroom stores scheduled to open in 1974.

Fledgling granJewel published a 360-page color catalogue and operated showrooms equipped with fifteen-thousand-square-foot in-store warehouses to ensure that its more than seven thousand merchandise items were immediately available for customer pick-up.

But Grants' challenges became increasingly evident in 1973, when peak record sales of $1,849,802,346 from a reduced roster of 1,189 stores struggled to generate a thin trickle of just $10,609,000 in profits, down significantly from $34,630,000 the year prior. Grants posted losses in the first and third quarters and profits in the second and fourth quarters, with the bulk of the company's profits for fiscal 1973 realized in its holiday-driven November–January fourth quarter.

In 1973, Grants opened seventy-seven new stores and enlarged four existing stores representing an additional 5,606,000 square feet of store space, logging $23,537,000 in capital expenses. Additionally, a new

Looking to capitalize on the catalogue showroom store craze sweeping the nation, the W.T. Grant Company partnered in October 1972 with New York–based jewelry manufacturer and catalogue showroom retailer Jewelcor Inc. to open some thirty joint-venture "granJewel" retail catalogue showrooms beginning in 1973. Pictured is a 1974 ad for metro Atlanta granJewel showroom stores in Decatur and Smyrna, Georgia. *Author's collection.*

W.T. Grant Company president Harry E. Pierson, 1973–74. *From* The Grant Game, *author's collection.*

475,000-square-foot distribution center in Windsor Locks, Connecticut, came online in the fall of 1973.

Employment at Grants in 1973 reached a peak of more than 85,000 men and women across the United States working in Grants, Grant City, Diskay and granJewel stores, six regional offices, the New York corporate headquarters in Times Square, six fully automated regional distribution centers and a nationwide network of Bradford Appliance Service Depots, with more than 150 domestic and overseas buying specialists.

In Grants' 1973 annual report, new board chairman Mayer and his successor as president, Harry E. Pierson, previously Grants' director and vice-president of store expansion, explained away the company's declining fortunes largely as a growing pains and "blurred image" anomaly part-and-parcel of the company's aggressive and transformational fast-tracked expansion from its historical roots operating variety and junior department stores to its new face as a full-line department store, citing the massive capital investments required for the support facilities needed to buttress the fast-growing W.T. Grant Company chain.

Other perfect storm factors pinching Grants financially were sharply rising interest costs on the company's ballooning short- and long-term borrowings covering Grants' aggressive expansion program, merchandise to stock the growing cadre of larger Grant City stores and floating Grants' ballooning and increasingly troubled Grantcard customer credit card receivables.

As the U.S. economy went into recession in 1973, spurred in large part by the autumn Arab Oil Embargo, interest rates in the nation reached record levels in the second half of 1973, affecting a substantial part of Grants' borrowings, with the company's total interest costs soaring $30 million over 1972 figures—a number nearly as large as Grants' annual profits in recent years.

Meanwhile, the federal government's implementation of inflation-fighting price controls lowered Grants' selling margins and "seriously impaired" the company's "profit potential" in 1973 according to Mayer and Pierson, who noted the "involuntary action caused a substantial profit decrease."

With Grants' significant downturn in profitability, company directors on February 26, 1974, for the first time in company history, reduced Grants' quarterly dividend, with dividends on Grants' common stock cut from $0.375 to $0.15 per share effective April 1, 1974, to reduce the cash payout and conserve the company's cash resources in the face of a longstanding negative cash flow.

Grants' 30,174 common stock shareholders in 1973 held 13,885,813 shares, of which more than 3 million shares were held by Grants employees through the company's twenty-four-year-old Employee Stock Purchase Plan "to put company ownership with the reach of thousands of Grant employees." Additionally, late company founder William T. Grant's charitable legacy, The Grant Foundation, owned or had a beneficial interest in approximately 2.5 million shares, while various other trusts established by William T. Grant held in aggregate more than 1.3 million shares. Said Pierson and Mayer, "We are proud of this Company ownership in the hands of our Grant people."

Unaffected by the February 26, 1974 board action was the $3.75 per share annual dividend on Grants' preferred stock, held by 511 shareholders.

Looking ahead to 1974, with pared-back plans for the opening of forty-five new Grant City stores and the enlargement of one existing store encompassing an aggregate 3 million square feet of new store footage, Mayer and Pierson struck an optimistic tone with shareholders that better days were ahead for Grants. "We will continue opening full line Grant City stores and will continue to expand our revolving credit charge account plan," they wrote. "Management will continue to take aggressive steps to strengthen its entire operation, whether in limited or full-line Grant City stores. We will continue to change the Company to meet the demands of its customers. In the final analysis, our customers will determine the success of the Company. We feel that customers are aware of the positive changes that are occurring and that, as a result, the acceptance of the Grant City stores—as full line stores—will continue to increase."

But fiscal 1974 would unfold much differently than Pierson and Mayer anticipated, as Grants' longstanding tradition of upward progress, mirroring late founder William T. Grant's ebullient optimism, came to an abrupt and thudding halt.

Breaking an annual sales increase streak dating back to 1950, fiscal 1974 sales for the fifty-two weeks ended January 30, 1975, dipped 4.7 percent to $1,761,952,000 from the prior year's $1.85 billion all-time company record.

Profitability, an annual W.T. Grant Company tradition since the trailblazing opening of Store No. 1 in Lynn, Massachusetts, in 1906, turned into an uncharacteristic tidal wave of red ink in 1974 as Grants' reduced roster of 1,152 stores posted losses in all four quarters and logged a first-ever annual loss, a staggering $177,340,000 tide of red ink equal to $12.74 per share—and that coming after a sizable $117.5 million tax credit. At the time, Grants' loss was the largest in U.S. retailing history.

Associated Press business analyst John Cunniff called news of "financially pressed and endangered" Grants' $177.3 million fiscal 1974 loss "shocking to most Americans." Opined Cunniff, "W.T. Grant is an institution, and don't institutions go on forever?"

Grants executives attributed the company's growing losses to declining sales, sharply rising interest rates on company debt and the significant costs incurred by Grants' elimination of its circa 1946 customer credit coupon book program in favor of the company's ill-fated, trouble-brewing in-house Grantcard revolving charge card.

As the company became increasingly short on liquidity due to its longstanding negative cash flow, many retail industry observers and increasingly wary suppliers accurately predicted that a Grants bankruptcy filing might be in the offing.

Grants stock, which had sold as high as nearly seventy-one dollars per share two years earlier, was selling at just over two dollars per share by late 1974.

As Grants racked up increasingly heavy losses as the year progressed, several major changes were made in company management. The board's June 25, 1974 election of John E. Sundman as financial vice-president was followed by the board's August 4 appointment of longtime Grants veteran James G. Kendrick, president of Grants' profitable 51 percent owned Canadian retail affiliate Zeller's Ltd., to a dual role as Grants' president and board chairman, effective September 3, 1974. "It's quite clear we have a liquidity problem," said Sundman, recruited from Singer Company, of the situation he found at Grants. "Growth for growth's sake was a serious mistake. The manner in which the growth was financed was a mistake. Normally it takes several years for a big store to reach its potential. We've run out of the capital it takes to afford the patience."

Said Grants' in its 1974 annual report of the new management team of Kendrick and Sundman, "The Board charged them with responsibility for developing the operational and financial programs necessary to assure the viability of the Company. Since that time, prompt action has been initiated, with new management in place in finance, merchandising, sales and marketing, inventory control and store management. A growing spirit

As W.T. Grant Company financial vice-president John E. Sundman looks on, new Grants president and board chairman James G. Kendrick comments candidly on the growing financial woes of the retail chain in 1974. Longtime Grants veteran Kendrick previously served as president of Grants' profitable Canadian affiliate Zeller's. *Robert Walker and the* New York Times, *via Redux Pictures.*

of enthusiasm and confidence now characterizes the entire W.T. Grant organization."

Kendrick noted both near and long-term programs had been undertaken by Grants to "overcome the three most serious problems" facing the company—"a serious merchandise imbalance, the severe burden posed by the accelerated store expansion program, and the excessive build-up of credit receivables financed at high interest rates and administered through an exceedingly expensive credit program."

Kendrick laid plans to pare as much as $36 million from Grants' overhead operating costs—cutting three hundred trainees from its store management training program, trimming one thousand employees from Grants' credit operations, dismissing seven thousand store personnel and slowing Grants' breakneck new store development program.

Kendrick also began selectively culling unprofitable stores from Grants' nationwide store roster, both fading legacy Grants variety stores and newer full-line Grant City department stores that had failed to gain traction in the marketplace and mature into profitability.

Under Kendrick, Grants also implemented a variety of new programs to win back customers lost in recent years to poor merchandising, addressing "a serious merchandise imbalance" that had dogged Grants in recent years by implementing "a more satisfactory balance between everyday staple items of merchandise and big-ticket items…emphasizing basic needs family shoppers buy every week" with the most-wanted items, including "a substantial infusion of brand name lines…stocked in depth at highly competitive prices."

Fringe items and lines, meanwhile, were eliminated, reducing the number of SKUs per individual department by 20 to 40 percent.

In the stores, changes in merchandising sought to return Grants to its "Known of Values" roots—late founder William T. Grant's canny penchant for building customer excitement around extraordinary values—with the retro back-to-the-basics placement of "Special Buy" point-of-sale promotional merchandising aisles in all Grant City stores highlighting special purchases.

Among the promotional changes put in place at Grants under Kendrick were modernization and improvements to the company's sales circular and print media promotions, as well as an extensive TV advertising campaign highlighting key promotional items in company-wide sales events. The TV ad campaigns aired in thirty-three major and seven smaller Grants retailing markets collectively representing more than 75 percent of the company's annual sales volume.

Looking to shore up Grants' tenuous finances, the company's bankers agreed to let Grants borrow up to $600 million until June 1975 to replace and augment the company's existing lines of credit—some $500 million in outstanding loans and a new $100 million term loan. As early as August 1974, Grants had run out of cash.

Grants' losses for the year included costs associated with sharply higher interest rates on the company's increased levels of short-term and long-term debt; nearly $162 million in net credit expenses, including $92 million in bad debt write-offs for uncollectible receivables from Grantcard holders; and a $24 million provision for store-closing expenses related to the shuttering of sixty-four Grant City stores with "consistent records of unprofitability."

Grants' quarterly common stock dividend, cut from 37.5 cents per share in 1973 to 15 cents per share in the first and second quarters of fiscal 1974 to conserve cash, was suspended altogether in the third quarter—the first time in the W.T. Grant Company's sixty-nine-year history that it failed to pay a dividend to its stockholders.

Addressing the financial challenges brought on by Grants' ambitious store development program, Kendrick said his plans included a "sharply curtailed" expansion program for the chain, with no more than a dozen new store openings planned in 1975, down from forty-four new store openings in 1974, seventy-seven in 1973, ninety-two in 1972 and eighty-three in 1971. Plans for 1975 also included the closing of approximately sixty existing smaller and older Grants stores at the termination of their leases.

Reflecting "reduced personnel needs over the next several years" with the downsizing of Grants' new store development program, an accelerated store closing program and the scale-back of Grants' operations to a planned 1,074 stores by April 30, 1975, Kendrick pared Grants' foundational and longstanding Store Management Training Program by three hundred employees. Kendrick in 1974 also initiated a major restructuring of Grants' corporate operations, reducing the number of regional offices from six to four.

A major focus area for Kendrick and Sundman beginning in September 1974 was Grants' troubled in-house Grantcard revolving credit card program, tightening the existing liberal terms on which credit had been previously granted to customers and substantially reducing the number of outstanding Grants credit cards.

Noted Kendrick, "Steps were taken…to bring credit receivables under control and to develop a viable credit program for our customers," including a substantial reduction in the number of Grant credit customers through the reissuance of new in-house Grants credit cards, the engagement of outside agencies "to collect seriously delinquent accounts" and the centralization of "credit-granting authority and account supervision" for Grants' credit card program from the store level to "ten strategically-placed locations."

Changes to Grants' credit program under Kendrick and Sundman also included third-party installment account financing to relieve the company of the burden of financing credit receivables for big-ticket items including furniture and major appliances.

And following a test pilot of BankAmericard (VISA) and Master Charge (MasterCard) bank credit cards in its 60-plus California stores, Grants in November and December 1974 rolled out acceptance of the popular nationwide bank credit cards at its 1,189 stores nationwide, becoming the first major national U.S. retailer to implement bank card programs company-wide. But as Grants continued to bleed red ink in 1975, the Grantcard revolving charge card program would be discontinued altogether in October 1975.

The enormity of Grants' $177.3 million loss for fiscal 1974, and the increasingly dire state of the company's finances and thinly stocked retailing operations, spurred Kendrick to announce the closure of additional weak and unprofitable stores that were not meeting Grants' volume and profitability criteria.

In late December 1974, Kendrick announced the closure of twenty-six Grants stores in January 1975 as part of a "capital restructuring program." And on January 3, 1975, Kendrick announced the planned cost-cutting closure of an additional sixty-six stores chain-wide between February and July 1975.

The selective surgical reduction of Grants' nationwide store network, in addition to another 60 store closings announced on January 16, 1975, would be partially offset by the opening of around a dozen Grant City stores already in the latter phases of development, leaving Grants with 1,074 stores in operation in a reduced forty-state trading area by early October 1975, down from 1,238 stores in forty-six states at the company's 1972 peak.

A majority of the store closings involved the shuttering of Grant City stores opened in quick succession over the previous five years. Indeed, 413 Grant City stores had been opened between 1969 and 1974—a sizable number of them were perennially running in the red and failing to generate sufficient sales volume to turn the tide. Said Grants' corporate communications director Henry Foreman of the store closings in early 1975, "We [Grants] are going to be all right. It's just a matter of consolidating with profitable operations."

Stepped up store closings and widespread corporate reorganization and streamlining saw Grants' employment fall from eighty thousand to sixty-nine thousand.

After logging a staggering $177.3 million loss and continued negative cash flow, along with the burden of more than $800 million in cumulative short-term and long-term debt, Grants' losses continued in 1975 despite Kendrick's best turnaround efforts, with Grants increasingly turning to the nation's banking community to "ensure the viability of the Company."

Keeping the goods flowing from some eight thousand increasingly nervous suppliers to Grants' nationwide network of stores was a vital concern for company management in its turnaround efforts, with Grants developing a security lien agreement with its creditors to assuage Grants' suppliers.

In his April 18, 1975 annual report letter to Grants' 36,544 common stockholders, who watched Grants' per-share "WGY" stock price fall from a high of $70⅝ in 1972 to just $1.50 per share, Kendrick was optimistic that the tide was turning for the W.T. Grant Company. "The Company is confident that the programs which it has implemented are correcting its problems and that its recovery will be achieved," Kendrick said. "While management anticipates a loss for both the first and second quarters of 1975, it believes that operations will become profitable in the second half of this fiscal year. Net earnings realized in the third and fourth quarters, however, will not be sufficient to offset the first half loss."

Looking ahead, Kendrick said Grants planned to close an additional 162 marginal stores in 1976, with a goal of cutting back to a nationwide "hard core" of around 900 stores. Indicative of Grants' sagging fortunes, the 300 anticipated store closures in 1975 and 1976 announced by Kendrick represented fully one quarter of Grants' locations nationwide.

After more than sixty-five years of growth and forward progress, mounting financial losses and retrenchment of the chain were an ignominious turn of fate for Grants, long one of the industry's enviable high flyers.

Noted *Washington Post* writer Philip Greer of the turn of events at Grants, "Awash in red ink, living on bank loans, suspected by its competitors and suppliers, the W.T. Grant Co. is scraping to regain its once-lofty place among

After a staggering first-ever loss of $177,340,000 in fiscal 1974, W.T. Grant Company management addressed concerned shareholders at Grants' May 20, 1975 annual meeting. Pictured from left are Board Chairman James G. Kendrick, Board Director Joseph Hinsey, General Counsel and Secretary Robert J. Kelly, President Robert H. Anderson and Financial Vice-President John E. Sundman. *Jack Manning and the* New York Times, *via Redux Pictures.*

mass merchandisers. The rapid-fire expansion of the past five years has been scrapped. Virtually the entire top management has been replaced. Cost-cutting has replaced new stores as the route to prosperity. Although the company insists that rumors of its imminent bankruptcy are off the mark—and trots out its bankers for support—nobody in the headquarters office high above Times Square is smiling.…All in all, things have not been going well for the…chain. The store is still a mystery. The problems are a new experience for Grant."

The announcements of Grants' $177.3 million fiscal 1974 loss and the closure of scores of Grants and Grant City stores across the country were just the tip of the iceberg of bad news for the beleaguered legacy retail chain heading into 1975, as Moody's Investors Service downgraded Grants' debt.

In exchange for financial breathing room from its creditors, Grants committed to cut $100 million in annual costs through a variety of means, including rent reductions and the restructuring of long-term leases; the selective closing of Grant City, Grants and Diskay Discount Mart stores; tighter credit controls on—and the eventual elimination of—Grants' troubled in-house Grantcard credit program; and a variety of personnel cost reductions, including cuts in executive payroll and the furloughing of more than seven thousand store employees.

As part of Grants' cost-cutting initiatives in 1975, Kendrick eliminated Grants' thirteen-year foray into the sale of Bradford-branded major appliances and furniture, whose combined $100 million in annual sales generated a significant $50 to $70 million in annual losses for the company by the time the overhead costs for inventory, trucking, warehousing, personnel and a national network of Bradford appliance service centers were factored in.

Despite Grants' mounting problems in 1975, business in many respects continued as usual for the company. A dozen new Grant City stores were opened across the United States, and a variety of trademarks were registered with the U.S. Trademark Office for the planned future rollout of new proprietary brand names.

At the behest of Grants' bank creditors, Grants' board directors replaced Kendrick with fifty-five-year-old Robert H. Anderson, a thirty-five-year veteran with Chicago-based legacy department store chain Sears, Roebuck & Company, then the nation's largest retailer.

A retailing wunderkind cut of the same cloth as Grants founder William T. Grant, Anderson had a preternatural ability when it came to retailing salesmanship, working his way up Sears' corporate ranks from store salesman to merchandising vice-president before accepting the "substantial challenge" presented by the herculean battle to save the badly faltering W.T. Grant Company. Kendrick was subsequently appointed board chairman and CEO.

Upon his arrival at the Home Office in New York, increasingly known by wags as "Grant's Tomb," Anderson worked at a frenetic pace to save Grants and keep goods flowing to stock its regional warehouses and reduced slate of 1,074 stores. But merchandise shipments were slow in coming or not coming at all, leading to a downward retailing death spiral of empty shelves begetting sliding sales, steeper losses and declining customer traffic.

Wrote Scripps-Howard staff writer Robert Dietsch in the *Pittsburgh Press*, "From the first day on the job…Anderson began working virtually around the clock, seven days a week, striving to stave off bankruptcy. He set up a 'war room,' a windowless cubicle in Grant's mid-Manhattan headquarters, with charts listing 90 reluctant suppliers, in order to concentrate on getting their help. But in the end his efforts at persuasion failed."

Anderson also worked on a near total revamp of Grants' retailing model, which centered on a back-to-basics pivot to the company's foundational merchandising strategy emphasizing its traditional trade and strength in soft goods lines and everyday home goods. Anderson also ditched the company's contemporary "The More for Your Moneysworth Store" marketing slogan in favor of a retro-nostalgic return to Grants' time-honored "Known for Values" slogan, built for decades on a longstanding emphasis on competitive pricing, quality merchandise and attentive customer service.

However, Grants' financial condition continued to erode as 1975 progressed, the company greeting dwindling ranks of customers with increasingly empty shelves. Through its first seven months of fiscal 1975 (February–August), Grants lost $126 million, with projected future losses of $23.3 million in September, $24.1 million in October and $125.7 million in its November–January fourth quarter, a staggering estimated $300 million loss for the year. Grants was hemorrhaging red ink—and badly.

Wrote a Home Office employee to a retired longtime Grants colleague in a 1975 letter, "Things here are so hectic at Grants these days. Every day I tell myself that it can't get any worse—but it can, and it does.…As you must have read in the newspaper, we've been closing stores and cutting down on personnel.…I'm not unduly optimistic or pessimistic—probably just fatalistic. A lot of good people are working very hard at it, and…perhaps we can turn it around. As long as I can, I think I'll stay and do what I can to help."

Having accumulated more than $288 million in losses over the previous eighteen months and burning through cash at an ever accelerating rate as it posted ongoing losses in excess of $5 million per week, the W.T. Grant Company reached its tipping point in late September 1975 as Grants' $1.03 billion in debt liabilities outstripped its stated $1.016 billion in book value assets.

In a desperate last-ditch effort in mid-September 1975, Grants, hat in hand, wrote letters to its 750 plus landlords across the country seeking 25 percent rent reductions for at least a two-year period to pare leasing costs for its stores. Fewer than 10 percent of landlords agreed to the cuts.

Rocking the nation's retailing and financial sectors, Grant officials announced on September 29, 1975, that the venerable sixty-nine-year-old retailer—encompassing 1,070 stores in forty states and sixty-two thousand employees—was running "a negative net worth" and in the process of informing its twenty-seven creditor banks of its current financial condition. In a word, Grants was insolvent. The announcement exacerbated the company's woes in adequately stocking its stores, as train and truck shipments of merchandise to Grants were halted.

At Grants' request, the Securities and Exchange Commission announced a ten-day suspension of trading in Grant securities "pending dissemination of news concerning W.T. Grant's financial condition and efforts to renegotiate financing agreements," with trading in the company's "WGY" stock suspended on the New York Stock Exchange for the first time since its 1928 listing.

Collectively, Wall Street, the nation's retail industry and Grants' employees and suppliers waited for the proverbial shoe to drop. It soon did.

Friday, October 3, 1975, the sixty-ninth anniversary of the company's 1906 founding, would prove to be among the most pivotal days in the long history of the W.T. Grant Company as the venerable industry high-flyer retailer crashed and burned with the filing of a voluntary Chapter 11 bankruptcy reorganization petition before Federal Bankruptcy Judge John Jerome Galgay in the U.S. District Court for the Southern District of New York at the federal courthouse at Foley Square in Lower Manhattan.

Appointed to the Federal Bankruptcy Court in July 1973, Galgay would preside over some of the largest corporate bankruptcy cases of the era, including those of Grants, East Coast supermarket chain Food Fair and national package delivery service REA Express (Railway Express Agency).

In filing for Chapter 11 bankruptcy reorganization, at the time the largest retailing bankruptcy in U.S. history, it was hoped by company executives that

Grants would gain sufficient interim breathing room to continue retailing operations as company executives crafted plans to reorganize Grants' finances, repay its outstanding debts and pave the way for the creation of a reorganized, streamlined and profitable Grants.

In making its filing, Grants management said that the company was unable to meet timely payments on its debts, although it was noted that Grants had enough cash on hand to continue operations until the end of its 1975 fiscal year on January 29, 1976. Said Anderson, "In the judgement of the management and board of directors, these proceedings are in the best interest of Grants, its employees, stockholders, vendors, and creditors."

Of its pared network of 1,070 stores, company operations were relatively evenly split between 537 heritage Grants variety and junior department stores and 533 of contemporary full-line Grant City big-box department stores.

Anderson told the court that the bankruptcy reorganization filing was "necessary to get the badly needed time" for reorganizing Grants' retailing operations and replenishing its depleted stocks of merchandise, noting that 99 percent of vendor shipments stopped after the company's September 29, 1975 announcement that it was running a "negative net worth" and incurring losses for the year far larger than anticipated.

"I'm very hopeful that we will get the kind of breathing space and the flow of goods we need for November and December," Anderson said, noting that a good Christmas selling season was critical to the company's reorganization efforts.

Grants' twenty-seven creditor banks, on the hook for $640 million in short- and long-term loans to the company, agreed to support Grants in its bankruptcy reorganization efforts under Galgay's supervision, although additional capital would not be forthcoming given their already hefty exposure. As it was, many Grants lenders announced loan loss write-offs. Morgan Guarantee, Grants' lead lender, wrote off $35 million of its $97 million in loans to Grants immediately after the bankruptcy filing. Citicorp Inc., parent of First National City Bank of New York, followed suit, writing off $35 million of its loans as well.

But the ripples from Grants' bankruptcy filing extended beyond the banking community into the larger business community. Some $70 million was collectively owed to Grants' cadre of eight-thousand-plus merchandise suppliers, while an additional $2 million was owed to hundreds of newspapers across the United States for display advertising placements.

Entering its milestone seventieth anniversary year, the W.T. Grant Company's New Grants reboot made its official debut on January 30, 1976, concurrent with the start of the company's 1976 fiscal year. While sales for New Grants ran well above company projections and the chain's performance under its old operating model, creditors on February 11, 1976, successfully lobbied for the company's court-ordered liquidation, saying that consultants estimated Grants would need an additional $150 million to $160 million cash infusion going forward, with hazy projections for success. *Author's collection.*

Noted Anderson in the court filing, "For the past several months Grant has been severely handicapped by its deteriorating financial position and the resulting lack of vendor confidence. Consequently, we have been forced to divert a substantial portion of our energies from our business. The legal proceedings give us the badly needed time to concentrate on reorganizing our operations so that we can effectively sell the merchandise of our vendors to meet the shopping needs of our customers and to build a new, profitable W.T. Grant Company."

Following the January 29, 1976 end of company's 1975 fiscal year, as part of Grants' reorganization Anderson hoped to launch a "new, profitable W.T. Grant Company" concept that would come to be dubbed "New Grants."

In a *Chicago Tribune* article, Anderson told reporter William Gruber that he looked forward to returning to his wheelhouse comfort zone as a salesman and merchandiser following the bankruptcy reorganization filing: "In the four months I've been here I've had to spend an awful lot of time on things other than what a merchant should be doing. Hopefully I will soon be able to start using my experience at Sears to help build a brand new Grants."

Observed the Associated Press of Grants' woes:

> *Problems for W.T. Grant began with a late 1960s urge to become too big, too fast…A prosperous, growing variety chain since its founding in 1906, top management decided about five years ago to attempt to take on Sears, Roebuck and J.C. Penney's by building "Grant City" outlets across the country. Grant's had to borrow huge sums to finance the expansion. Then in 1973 came a ruinous rise in interest rates. The expansion program that proved to be Grant's downfall was not hatched overnight. Edward Staley, chairman at the time, looked toward the suburbs and by 1960 he had doubled the number of Grants outlets. By 1965, 83 percent of the company's profits came from those new stores. Then Grants found itself caught in a crossfire between growing new discount chains and regional shopping center-based chains. And, as sales and profits began to slip in the early 1970s, Grant continued the expansion program, opening or enlarging 439 stores.*

Indeed, Grants' image with consumers got increasingly hazy in the 1960s and 1970s with the debut and large-scale rollout of its ascendant Grant City stores, which lacked the consumer recognition, service reputation and established track record of the traditional full-line department stores on one end of the retailing spectrum. On the other end, Grants was typically undercut on pricing by as much as 10 percent by a plethora of local, regional and major national one-stop discount department store chains, including S.S. Kresge's rising star, Kmart.

One Wall Street analyst criticized the company's execution of its Grant City concept: "I don't think they [Grants] ever decided what they wanted to be. They look like discount stores but their prices aren't discounted. They're selling house brands, but who's going to put down $400 for a color television named Bradford? Sears can sell house brands because it has a reputation for service, but Grants doesn't. It just leaves the customer confused."

At base, Grants was an operational mess on many fronts. Observed Scripps-Howard staff writer Robert Dietsch in the *Pittsburgh Press*:

> *At the peak of its success, Grant operated almost 1,200 stores in 40 states....Between 1963 and 1973, the chain opened 612 stores and expanded 91 others. Founder Grant retired in 1966, aged 90, and died in 1972. About the time of Grant's retirement the company reached some major decisions. It stepped up suburban expansion, often without adequately surveying the market potential for new locations. It added major appliances and furniture to its merchandise and it went after credit business in a big way, which led some to later to claim it had become a finance company instead of a retail outlet....And that's when things began to slip. The company had to borrow millions to finance its credit business and attention to the store operations fell off. Consequently sales slipped badly. Early in 1974 profits turned lower, collections of credit accounts were off and the balance sheet clearly showed trouble. Suppliers became worried. And then it was alleged that some of Grant's executives had accepted kickbacks from real estate landlords and a shakeup in management was carried out in June 1974. In that shakeup, Robert W. Mayer, who had succeeded Staley as chairman as the giant started to crumble, was asked to resign and Staley left too. James G. Kendrick, who had a solid background of merchandising experience but who had been shunted off to head a Canadian subsidiary, was brought back to head the company and immediately performed massive surgery on staff and unprofitable stores. More than 11,000 employees were fired and 125 stores were closed. Kendrick...and John E. Sundman, financial vice president, sought to de-emphasize credit and return to the traditional business of soft goods and accessories....As losses mounted, directors and creditors brought in...Sears, Roebuck executive Robert K. Anderson as president.*

Galgay affixed his signature approving acceptance of Grants' Chapter 11 bankruptcy reorganization request, it being noted in the filing that the company was one of the largest employers in many of its trading areas including Maine, where the W.T. Grant Company ranked as the state's fifth-largest employer. Florida was home to 80 of Grants' 1,070 stores, while 119 stores were tightly clustered in five New England states, including 60 in Massachusetts.

Grants officials on October 9, 1975, announced the closure of 201 Grants and Grant City stores, including almost all of its stores west of the Mississippi River save for 11 locations—9 in Louisiana and 2 in Missouri. Grant officials said the store closings—107 on or before November 30 and the remaining 94 in late December after the Christmas shopping season—would leave Grants with 873 stores in a reduced twenty-eight-state footprint as part of efforts to "concentrate…store locations where it [Grants] is best known and receives the strongest consumer support."

Unaffected by the closures, at least initially, were the company's joint-venture granJewel catalogue outlet stores, including western granJewels in Texas, Arizona and California.

Anderson, who had just been given the additional duties of chief executive officer on October 9, 1975, said the board's decision to consolidate Grants' footprint of operations to the East, South and Midwest was made in the belief that it would be easier to restore Grants' operations to health in regions where the company name was well known and Grants had built up a strong and loyal customer base over nearly seventy years.

But in the announcement of the store closings, Grants corporate spokesman Jack Edgerton indicated a strong likelihood that more Grants store closings could be in the offing within the next seven to ten days. As Grants' bankruptcy case unfolded, it became increasingly clear that deep expense reductions were needed to bring the beleaguered company's sales and costs back into balance.

On October 12, 1975, Grants pulled the plug on its troubled Grantcard revolving charge card program, which had proven to be a severe financial strain on company resources.

For the 873 Grants and Grant City stores that had survived the company's first round of bankruptcy reorganization cuts, the reprieve would prove short-lived. On October 17, 1975, Grants announced the closure of an additional 100 stores in ten states by late December, leaving Grants with 773 stores in "market areas where we have experienced profitability and a high level of customer acceptance."

Within days of the decision, it was noted in the national press that Anderson was also cleaning house in the executive ranks at Grants' Times Square Home Office in Midtown Manhattan, where Grants' once sizable corporate operations were getting massively pared as part of ongoing corporate cost-cutting—right-sizing corporate operations to meet the needs of an increasingly diminished chain and also allowing Anderson to put together his own hand-picked management team as he took a more dominant role in the company's bankruptcy reorganization and the creation of the company's forward-looking "New Grants" concept.

Already, the week prior, longtime Grants executive Pierson had resigned. Two of Grants' highest-paid officers, board chairman Kendrick and Sundman, soon departed as well, making a virtual clean sweep of Grants' executive ranks.

Given the low returns on its in-house store liquidation efforts earlier in the year, Grants and its creditors turned to a professional liquidator to maximize returns. On October 28, 1975, Grants received court approval from Galgay to hire a professional liquidator—Sam Nassi of Tarzana, California—to oversee going-out-of-business asset sales at the 301 Grants and Grant City stores that had been targeted for closure.

Earning a well-deserved reputation as a "corporate mortician" and feted as the "world's greatest liquidator," Nassi ironically started his liquidation career winding down the operation of his own failed thirty-seven-store White Front retail chain.

Other liquidators approved by the bankruptcy court, like Los Angeles–based David Weisz Company, would hold regional auctions across the country to sell off Grants' store and warehouse fixtures, specialized auto center and restaurant equipment and leftover warehoused bulk merchandise.

Shortly thereafter, on October 31, 1975, Grants announced a third wave of mass store closures, its largest to date, culminating in the closing of 280 Grants and Grant City stores in eighteen states, paring the chain to 493 stores in fourteen states. The closings included all 239 stores in Alabama, Florida, Georgia, Illinois, Indiana, Kentucky, Louisiana, Michigan, Mississippi, Missouri, North Carolina, South Carolina, Tennessee and Wisconsin, in addition to 45 additional stores in New Jersey, Ohio, Pennsylvania and West Virginia.

In announcing the third wave of store closings, Anderson said he felt that the company had "essentially" concluded its store liquidation plans. "By closing these additional stores, W.T. Grant Company restructures its store operations to a market primarily east of Cleveland, Ohio and north of Baltimore,

Bankruptcy-spurred November 1975 store closing ad for the variety-styled W.T. Grant Company store anchoring Rapids Plaza in 89,144-resident Racine, Wisconsin. *Author's collection.*

Maryland," Anderson explained. "Management's thorough analysis of this market clearly identifies the region as having the greatest customer acceptance for the Grant Company, both historically and currently."

With the latest round of closings, now encompassing a cumulative 581 affected stores, the W.T. Grant Company had come full circle back to its roots as a northeastern regional retailer, although Grants maintained a small 17-store northeast Ohio presence.

As the 581 Grants and Grant City stores began to go dark, various retailers expressed interest in picking up turnkey leases or subleases for select stores across the country, including department stores Kmart, Woolco, JCPenney, Murphy's Mart and Montgomery Ward and discount closeout retailer Big Lots.

Meanwhile, business at Grants' 493 surviving stores carried on as usual—albeit with a sense of great urgency—as Grants' corporate management worked feverishly to properly stock its stores for the important upcoming Christmas shopping season and also lay the foundation for the chain's nascent "New Grants" revival as blue-and-white store banners began announcing "Fresh Merchandise Is Arriving Daily."

Wrote Scripps-Howard staff writer Robert Dietsch in the *Pittsburgh Press*:

> *W.T. Grant Co., a fallen corporate Humpty Dumpty, today is trying to gather up its shattered pieces, overcome massive problems on debt and mismanagement and rise again to its once giant dimensions....But with all its ills, W.T. Grant is not dead....The present 493 stores in 14 states...exude optimism—with an undertone of hope....The company is trying to reestablish itself as the type of business envisioned when William T. Grant founded his first outlet...as a "25-cent store" in contrast to the "5-and-10 cent" stores of F.W. Woolworth and S.S. Kresge. Grant's accent was on women's and men's clothing and accessories....The question now—whether Grant will be able to stave off full bankruptcy—is still open....Grant officials said the fate of the "new" company depends not only on Christmas season sales but on business generated next spring, another major selling time. Both Grant suppliers and the remaining employees said the company's future also depends to a considerable degree on Anderson. From the first day on the job last spring, Anderson began working virtually around the clock, seven days a week.*

In mid-November, Galgay set a December 19, 1975 deadline for Grants to submit a debt repayment plan to its creditors. Galgay appointed Charles G. Rodman, the outgoing president of the Grand Union Company supermarket chain, as a standby trustee in case Grants proved unable to reach an agreement with its creditors and the company moved into liquidation.

Nearing the end of the year, Grants had closed 714 stores in twenty-six states, as well as its regional distribution centers in California, Indiana and Georgia, furloughing fifty thousand employees.

Heading into Grants' make-or-break Christmas shopping season, newspapers in Grants' compacted fourteen-state footprint began running Anderson-signed ads introducing the W.T. Grant Company's fledgling "New Grants" stores.

An ongoing work-in-progress, work continued apace on the corporate, district and store levels in November and December 1975 and January 1976 to lay the groundwork for the planned gala January 30, 1976 launch of "New Grants" concurrent with the start of Grants' seventieth anniversary 1976 fiscal year.

But in an ominous sign for the future viability of New Grants, company executives on December 17, 1975, sought and received Galgay's approval for the January 1976 closure of an additional 134 Grants and Grant City stores, leaving the company with 359 stores employing twenty-four thousand.

Since its October 2, 1975 bankruptcy reorganization filing, the W.T. Grant Company had closed 715 stores, fully two-thirds of its store roster.

It was anticipated by company management that the 359-store New Grants chain would generate $650 million in annual sales and be profitable

Often overlooked in the 1975–76 collapse of the W.T. Grant Company was the human toll on Grants employees. Soon to be out of work in November 1975 was twenty-five-year Grants veteran Byron Ferguson (1923–2011). Over his career, Ferguson managed fourteen different Grants stores in seven states, including this Detroit location. *Photographed for the* New York Times *by Andrew Sacks/SaxPix.com, used with permission.*

by 1977 or 1978. By contrast, Grants at its 1972 height had operated 1,238 stores and logged more than $1.8 billion in sales.

Looking to do an ambitious overhaul of its remaining stores, Grants put considerable amounts of its scarce financial resources into not only restocking its Grants and Grant City stores with a new merchandising and marketing emphasis, but also into the repainting, remodeling, reconfiguring and refreshing of its stores, many of which were compacted into a smaller sales floor footprint to reflect the chain's simplified and streamlined merchandise lines.

In a January 1976 interview with the *New York Times* in advance of the formal debut of New Grants, Anderson noted that Grants' fourteen-state footprint represented the company's "best in marketing areas…which have been our greatest strength."

Anderson said that company executives had "put into the new Grant a discipline based on merchandising according to seasonal needs, something Grant hasn't done before," as it pivoted its target customer market to the age twenty-one to thirty "young marrieds…budget-minded shopper who wants casual and leisure apparel with good values."

And while Grants would not be a discounter like S.S. Kresge's Kmart, Anderson said the downsized streamlining of company operations and the reversal of several costly business policies instituted by past management would allow New Grants to "offer prices well below what the old Grants did."

While several outside factors beyond his control had a material impact on the company's fate, including "the free flow of goods" from wary Grants suppliers and the recessionary national economy, Anderson nevertheless was bullish on the prospects for New Grants. Noted Anderson to the *Times*, "With our leaner, tighter organization and our operation from strength, we feel we can compete with anyone."

Indeed, Grants' fledgling New Grants operations began to stabilize and improve. While a 20 percent sales decline was anticipated in December 1975 in the midst of the negative national headlines surrounding Grants' bankruptcy-driven mass store closings, comparable same store sales for New Grants only declined by a modest 3 percent, while January same store sales showed an increase over year-prior figures. The momentum would continue into early February following the gala formal debut of New Grants, as the company saw strong sales gains in the first two weeks of Grant's new fiscal year.

But additional major changes appeared to be pending for Grants in the retail trade grapevine, which hinted at yet more store closures and the possible closure of Grants' large distribution center in Edison, New Jersey.

With corporate headquarters operations downsized by December 1975 to four and a half floors of the W.T. Grant Building in Times Square as the number of corporate executives were pared to five and the company's once extensive buying operations were streamlined into just two lines, Grants was laying plans to relocate to smaller quarters in Sears' former regional New York office near Penn Station, today's 21 Penn Plaza at 360 West 31st Street in Manhattan's Chelsea neighborhood.

In a confidential bound two-volume January 19, 1976 report on W.T. Grant Company operations, compiled on a four-month blitzkrieg basis, management consulting firm Booz, Allen & Hamilton was cautiously optimistic about the future prospects for New Grants, pared from forty-five major markets nationwide to a hard core of just ten in the Northeast and Mid-Atlantic states that "performed substantially better than the rest of the chain over the past five years" and were ranked as "most favorable" or "fair" future prospects in the report: Maine; Boston; Springfield, Massachusetts; Syracuse and Buffalo, New York; Philadelphia; Pittsburgh/Cleveland; Harrisburg, Pennsylvania; and Baltimore/Washington, D.C.

Annual future sales for New Grants—inclusive of final Grant City stores opened at Watertown, Connecticut; Matawan, New Jersey; and Severna Park, Maryland, on May 1, 1975; Napanoch, New York, on May 15, 1975; St. Johnsbury, Vermont, on August 15, 1975; and Avon, New York, on September 28, 1975—were projected at $659.8 million at an average of $1.8 million in sales per store versus the $864,000 realized previously, with "improved overall" performance as a result of "higher volume, productivity and expense performance levels."

Despite the intensive reorganizational efforts by Kendrick and then Anderson, the road ahead for the W.T. Grant Company in 1976 and beyond was tenuous at best, the surviving 359 New Grants "superior performance" stores combining for a $16.2 million loss in fiscal 1975 according to the report.

Said Booz, Allen & Hamilton in its study cover letter to Anderson, "The New Grant chain has been streamlined dramatically…in terms of its number of its stores, its corporate overhead expense and staff, and its ongoing store expenses. The question of viability now depends upon improved merchandising and higher sales results from the Grant organization's ongoing stores."

Standing near a discarded twenty-foot letter "G," a workman in March 1976 watched the dismantling of the four fifty-foot-long cursive neon Grants signs that once adorned the rooftop crown of the former W.T. Grant Building at 1515 Broadway at Times Square in Midtown Manhattan. *Fred R. Conrad/Redux.*

W.T. Grant Company president Robert H. Anderson enters Federal Court at Foley Square in New York City on February 11, 1976. Despite positive results for the fledgling New Grants rollout kicking off the company's seventieth anniversary year, attorneys for Grants' major bank and trade creditors successfully petitioned for Grants' court-ordered liquidation, saying the prospects for Grants' successful revival were "very, very remote." *Neal Boenzi and the* New York Times, *via Redux Pictures.*

After closing for fiscal year-end inventory on January 29, 1976, New Grants blossomed forth on Friday, January 30, for a gala weekend SuperSale relaunching the company's stores concurrent with the start of Grants' new 1976 fiscal year.

Sales for New Grants ran well above company projections and the chain's performance under its old operating model and were still running ahead of plan nearly two weeks later when, on February 11, 1976, after bowing to pressure from its bank and trade creditors, attorneys for Grants and its major bank and trade creditors presented Galgay with a surprise resolution: declare the W.T. Grant Company as being formally bankrupt and liquidate Grants' remaining operations.

In the resolution, it was agreed by both Grants and its creditors that continued reorganization efforts under Chapter 11 bankruptcy reorganization would be virtually hopeless.

Creditors Committee representative Harvey Miller reported that as of January 29, 1976, Grants' total assets stood at $512.1 million in comparison to $1.1 billion in liabilities, saying consultants estimated that Grants would need an additional $150 to $160 million going forward in support of the company's New Grants reboot. Said Miller, "It is in the best interest of all creditors that W.T. Grant be adjudged bankrupt and that its business be terminated. The possibility of reorganization in light of the tremendous cash needs is very, very remote."

Grants' attorneys said they would not oppose creditor calls for liquidation of the company, with Grant lawyer Leonard Rosen claiming it would take a generation to restore the company. "While the operation is going on, this patient may very well die," Rosen said.

Marvin Jacobs, counsel for the U.S. Securities and Exchange Commission, asked Galgay to hear more evidence. "Only a few days ago W.T. Grant was thought to be a viable operation," Jacobs told Galgay, saying Grants stockholders and other interested parties deserved answers to the question of "what has happened to destroy this viability."

Himself surprised by the resolution, coming just four months into the seventy-year-old retailer's voluntary bankruptcy reorganization, Galgay said he needed to gather more information "as to the viability of W.T. Grant's future," ordering hearings to be held to that effect.

After hearing additional information over the course of two days, Galgay on February 12, 1976, ordered the W.T. Grant Company to liquidate its assets and close its remaining 359 stores within two months, with creditors having first priority on monies raised from the liquidation of Grants' assets. Surplus funds after paying the company's debts, if any, would be divided among Grants' forty thousand shareholders. "I find myself compelled to sign this order," Galgay said.

Asked by Galgay if he thought New Grants would have been viable, Anderson indicated that he thought the company's reorganization plan was solid. "If only the circumstances of the past few days could be altered, we certainly would have a good chance at success," Anderson said, expressing wishes the liquidation request could be rescinded.

But Anderson also conceded that Grants would face a long uphill battle to dig itself out of its deep financial hole and its badly damaged reputation with bankers, vendors and customers, noting that an ongoing lack of sufficient working capital to purchase merchandise to adequately stock stores would hamper Grants' best efforts to rehabilitate its business, with vendors still willing to do business with Grants demanding up-front cash payments for their merchandise.

Observed Anderson of stocking Grants' surviving stores during the company's four-month bankruptcy reorganization, "I was frustrated. A merchant is frustrated if he hasn't got the goods."

Grants padlocked all 359 of its Grants and Grant City stores at closing time on Friday, February 12, 1976, in preparation for going-out-of-business liquidation sales overseen by Nassi.

Ultimately, Grants permanently closed 222 of its 359 stores, consolidating inventory for the company-wide liquidation sales at 137 of its largest, highest volume locations across its fourteen-state trade area. The sales began on March 4, 1976.

With news of Grants' impending liquidation, a number of national, regional and local department store chains, closeout retailer Big Lots and various drugstore chains began expressing interest in picking up select stores from Grants' final 359 locations.

Among the major contenders for Grants' final stores were discount department store chains Kmart, Caldor, Two Guys and Murphy's Mart, full-line department store chains JCPenney and Montgomery Ward and

The court-ordered liquidation of the W.T. Grant Company's fledgling 359-store New Grants reboot drew huge bargain-hunting crowds to going-out-of-business sales conducted by California-based Sam Nassi Company. Liquidation sales, as seen here at the Grant City in New Dorp, Staten Island, New York, began on March 4, 1976, with Grants' last handful of stores closing on April 4, 1976, ending the company's storied seventy-year run. *Tony Carannante photo. © 1976 Staten Island Advance. All rights reserved.*

The padlocked doors of the bankruptcy-shuttered former metro New Orleans Grant City at Chalmette, Louisiana, in March 1976. Financially troubled Grants' retrenchment, bankruptcy and subsequent liquidation put more than 1,200 vacant stores on the real estate market nationwide as the country fell into recession. *Lionel M Cottier Jr. photo, from the* New Orleans Times-Picayune.

F.W. Woolworth Company, operator of Woolworth's variety stores and full-line Woolco department stores.

As part of the bankruptcy adjudication of Grants' remaining assets, including the operations of the company's decentralized nationwide network of ten regional Grants Credit Centers, Galgay approved the sale of Grants' outstanding consumer credit accounts receivables to thirty-four-year-old Minneapolis businessman Irwin L. "Irv the Liquidator" Jacobs for just $44 million, plus 5 percent of his first-year collections.

Jacobs put one hundred of his employees to work on collecting Grants' outstanding customer accounts receivable, paying off the $44 million purchase price in just seventy-five days and turning a tidy $9 million first-year profit on the deal. Calling the purchase of Grants' accounts receivable a "mother lode" deal, Jacobs collected on his investment in Grants consumer credit accounts for a decade.

Other asset dispositions approved by Galgay in the months ahead included the sale of Grants' various subsidiary businesses—the joint venture granJewel catalogue stores, pivoted to being a wholly owned Grants subsidiary following Grants' bankruptcy filing, to former partner Jewelcor; the $4.5 million sale of portrait studio operator Jones & Presnell Studios to a newly created Employee Stock Ownership Plan (ESOP) venture; and the $32.6 million sale of Grants' controlling majority 51 percent stake in Canadian general merchandise retailer Zeller's to Field Stores Ltd. of Vancouver, British Columbia.

Ordered to liquidate its operations within sixty days by Galgay on February 12, 1976, Grants' bankruptcy was formally adjudicated by Galgay on April 13, the company's last handful of stores having closed on April 4, 1976, following Nassi's month-long store liquidation sale.

Former Grand Union Company chairman Charles G. Rodman was appointed by Galgay as a Grants trustee to oversee the disposition of the company's remaining fixtures and bulk inventory and also supervise Grants' remaining assets and the accumulation of cash from recent liquidation sales for distribution to Grants' cadre of creditors. Anderson assisted Rodman in his trustee duties through the end of April 1976.

In overseeing the liquidation of the Grant bankruptcy case and winding down the W.T. Grant Company estate under the Bankruptcy Act in coordination with Rodman, it was Galgay's stated desire to obtain "the best possible realization upon the available assets…without undue waste by needless or fruitless litigation."

The mammoth Grants bankruptcy saga would play out in Federal Bankruptcy Court and U.S. Federal Appeals Court for more than a decade, with the Grants bankruptcy case outliving Galgay, who died at age sixty-six in May 1984. Galgay's successor, Judge Tina L. Brozman, presided over the protracted Grants bankruptcy case into the early 1990s.

REQUIEM

An Icon Vanishes

Like the disturbance created from a stone thrown into a lake, the fallout from Grants' spectacular crash-and-burn demise sent economic ripples across the nation—impacting livelihoods, the real estate market and Grants' thousands of suppliers who scrambled to make up financial losses, and business lost, with Grants.

Given its national stature as America's seventh-largest retailer and one of the nation's leading legacy retail chains—a familiar coast-to-coast fixture of old-line downtown Main Streets and new era suburban shopping centers alike—the rapid decline and sudden demise of the W.T. Grant Company left an indelible mark on the nation, leaving more than eighty thousand jobless as the nation was slipping out of one high-unemployment, high-inflation recession and heading toward another.

With its historically low employee turnover rates, reflective of company founder William T. Grant's longstanding emphasis on positive interpersonal relationships, employee development and generous pay and benefit schedules, the W.T. Grant Company had a decidedly family feel all across its ranks from the front lines of its more than 1,200 "friendly family stores" to the company's Midtown Manhattan Home Office towering over neon-lit Times Square.

As Grants employees and executives scattered to the four winds to seek new job opportunities following the company's bankruptcy and subsequent liquidation, many former Grants employees around the country sought to

Survivors salvage memories from the sunken W.T. Grant Company as former Grants employees gathered for a November 1980 reunion luncheon at Rosoff's restaurant in Manhattan. Reunions like this and periodic newsletters, such as Grants veteran Connie L. Hunt's *Grants Memories*, kept the W.T. Grant Company family connected for decades after the chain's 1976 demise. *Fred R. Conrad and the* New York Times, *via Redux Pictures.*

keep in touch with one another with the formation of informal local and regional Grants social groups, holding periodic reunion gatherings and later also taking to the Internet to reconnect, socialize and reminisce.

In a December 1980 *New York Times* interview, former *Grant Game* editor Caroline Logan talked to writer Isadore Barmash about the importance of the Grants employee reunions, including the fifth annual one that she was attending along with nearly fifty other Grants alumni at Rosoff's, a popular Midtown Manhattan restaurant fixture. "They care about each other; they're all interested in how they made out, and many even helped one another get jobs," Logan said.

Retrenchment of Grants as its fortunes quickly declined, followed by its abbreviated four-and-a-half-month bankruptcy reorganization and subsequent court-ordered liquidation, rapidly placed more than 1,200 vacant Grants and Grant City retail stores—as well as warehouse distribution centers, Bradford appliance service centers, regional offices and corporate headquarters office space—onto an already-challenged national retail and real estate market.

In hundreds of U.S. communities nationwide in the mid- to late 1970s, the sight of shuttered, label-scarred former Grants and Grant City stores quickly became a poignant symbol of the economic malaise of inflation and high unemployment plaguing the nation in the recessionary 1970s.

Some W.T. Grant Company stores, particularly the larger, newer, high-volume Grants and Grant City locations, were quickly picked up by rival department store chains, including Montgomery Ward, JCPenney, S.S. Kresge (Kmart), F.W. Woolworth (Woolco), G.C. Murphy (Murphy's Mart), Caldor, Bradlees, Kings, Two Guys, Hill's, Ames and Strouss, among others.

Among the major beneficiaries of Grants' bankruptcy filing and subsequent liquidation was Troy, Michigan–based S.S. Kresge Company's $6.5 billion Kmart division, then the nation's largest discount department store chain, which quickly snatched up 152 of Grants' larger late model

S.S. Kresge Company's burgeoning big-box Kmart discount department store division was a major beneficiary of the W.T. Grant Company's 1975 bankruptcy and 1976 liquidation, picking up the leases of hundreds of idled Grants and Grant City stores nationwide, including the short-lived 1974–75 Grant City at 3324 Williams Boulevard, Kenner, Louisiana. The Kenner Kmart was Kresge's first in metro New Orleans. *A.P. Vidacovich photo, from the* New Orleans Times-Picayune.

In July 1976, Kmart store manager Bill Snyder (*left*) and S.S. Kresge Company Southern Region president Edward C. Andrews welcome shoppers to the reopened former metro New Orleans Grant City at 3324 Williams Boulevard in Kenner. The store was one of more than two hundred Kmart, Kresge and Jupiter stores comprising the company's growing Southern Division. *A.P. Vidacovich photo, from the* New Orleans Times-Picayune.

Grants and Grant City locations across the nation in 1976. Additionally, Kresge constructed 119 Kmarts during the year, changing its corporate name to Kmart Corporation the following year.

Given Kmart's swift expansion and growing market domination as the Walmart of its era in the mid-1970s, the W.T. Grant Company's sizable idled fleet of large format big-box Grant City stores were particularly attractive turnkey acquisitions, requiring only light remodeling and reconfiguring, and possessing value-added facilities including automotive service centers, outdoor living garden centers and full-service restaurants.

The demise of Grants was a boon for fast-expanding Kmart, particularly in the South and West, where Kresge was a relative latecomer on the retailing scene.

On the nation's Gulf Coast, where Grants had shuttered its stores by late November and December 1975, Kmart's January 1976 takeover of seven shuttered Grant City stores totaling more than 1 million square feet at Gulfport, Ocean Springs, Pascagoula and Yazoo City, Mississippi, and metro New Orleans stores at Chalmette and Algiers, Lousiana, quickly catapulted Kmart from a bit player in the region to the dominant discount retailer on the Gulf Coast.

New York–based dime store giant F.W. Woolworth Company, which entered the "big-box" discount department store arena in 1962 with its newly formed Woolco division, was another significant national player for shuttered larger-format Grants and Grant City stores. Woolworth, which had already been negotiating for the leases of 15 bankruptcy-shuttered Grants stores in nine states when news came of Grants' February 1976 court-ordered liquidation, subsequently expressed an interest in picking up a number of Grants' final 359 northeastern "New Grants" stores.

While some former W.T. Grant Company stores were rebranded under the Woolworths banner, including Grants' circa 1954 downtown Philadelphia flagship at 11th and Market Streets, more than thirty remodeled Grant City stores were reopened under the Woolco nameplate, pushing the Woolco division over the milestone $1 billion annual sales mark as sales at the reopened and refreshed former Grant City stores ran ahead of Woolworth's estimates and their historic sales averages under Grants.

In a particularly ambitious move, Woolworth went all in with establishing a new Woolco trading market on Long Island, New York, where Grants had operated twenty-five stores.

Making a big splash, Woolco simultaneously reopened 5 Long Island Grant City stores totaling 500,000 square feet in East Patchogue, Lake

Ronkonkama, Bridgehampton, Rocky Point and Riverhead under the Woolco banner in Suffolk County at 10:00 a.m. on March 30, 1977. Half of the combined workforce of the five stores comprised former W.T. Grant Company executives, managers and rank-and-file employees. Soon after, additional Long Island Woolco stores were added at former Grant City stores in Nassau County at Jericho and East Meadow, bringing Woolco's store count to 270 locations nationwide in thirty-seven states.

The Long Island Woolco stores, which saw Grant City's in-store Bradford House restaurants reopened under Woolworth's cafeteria-styled Harvest House and full-service Red Grille formats, operated until Woolworth's January 1983 liquidation of its 336-store, $2.1 billion U.S. Woolco division, then the nation's third-largest discount chain behind Kmart and Walmart.

Taking over a smaller number of idled Grants and Grant City stores was Plano, Texas–based JCPenney, which picked up store sites as diverse as those at Southland Plaza in Toledo, Ohio; Colonial Village Mall in Rockford, Illinois; and Franklin Shopping Plaza in Westerly, Rhode Island, the latter still operating as a JCPenney.

Chicago-based A. Montgomery Ward & Company, meanwhile, picked up a handful of leases for former Grant City stores as far flung as those at Bedford Mall in Bedford, New Hampshire, and Denbigh Village Mall in Newport News, Virginia, among other locales.

And in Western Pennsylvania, once home to twenty Pittsburgh District Grants and Grant City stores, the W.T. Grant Company's showplace $3 million downtown Pittsburgh flagship, a four-story, ninety-thousand-square-foot Mellen Square anchor at Smithfield and Oliver Avenues from 1955 to 1976, went markedly upscale in 1977 with a flashy new mirrored façade as the relocated home of Saks Fifth Avenue in the city. Enjoying a long run, the downtown Pittsburgh Saks store closed in March 2012.

The liquidation of Grants also provided opportunities for smaller independent regional retailers like Dayton, Ohio–based department store chain Elder-Beerman, which picked up vacated Ohio Grants City stores at Sunset Shopping Center in Piqua and Skyway Plaza in Fairborn as its fifteenth and sixteenth stores. The shuttered Grant City outlets, which were remodeled and restocked, reopened in May 1976.

In Wisconsin, the variety-styled Grants west of Milwaukee in upscale suburban Brookfield, an anchor of the Ruby Isle Shopping Center from 1963 to 1975, was succeeded by Lake Zurich, Illinois–based Schultz Brothers Company, a seventy-six-store midwestern regional variety store chain with operations in Wisconsin, Illinois, Minnesota, Iowa and Indiana.

The Grant City at Sherman Plaza in state capital Madison, meanwhile, was reopened under the Prange-Way banner by Sheboygan, Wisconsin–based H.C. Prange Company, which operated a regional twenty-five-store chain of Prange's department stores, Prange-Way discount department stores and "id" specialty shops in Wisconsin, Illinois and Michigan.

Turning lemons into lemonade, Grants' demise also provided entrepreneurial opportunities for several veteran former Grants employees who maintained tribute vestiges of the W.T. Grant Company after its April 1976 liquidation demise.

In Brunswick, Maine, two generations of the Fenwick family, including career New England Division Grants manager Johnson Fenwick, preserved the local Grant City as the renamed Grand City from 1976 to 2008, first at Hannaford Plaza and later on Maine Street in downtown Brunswick as Grand City V&S Variety.

In Panama City, Florida, meanwhile, thirty-year Grants store manager J.R. "Bob" Robbins, former manager of the Grant City at Panama Plaza, reopened the shuttered store's Bradford House Restaurant in January 1976 as Bob's Bradford House Family Restaurant in collaboration with business partner and restaurant manager Nick Schiavone, employing all of the Bradford House's familiar former staff—Sara Papa, Ruby Futrel, Patty Cox, Marie Pendarvis, Paulette Lancaster, Twila Perkins, Doug Foster, Kay Shaw, Gwen Morgan, Eloise Surrette, Diane Goodman, Charles McCall and Rachel Corbin.

While similar to the Bradford House operated by Grants, Bob's Bradford House offered an enhanced and more localized menu featuring "Bob's Southern Fried Chicken" and homemade cornbread among other southern specialties.

With the reception of Bob's Bradford House going far beyond Robbins's expectations, a second location, managed by family restaurant veteran Earl Lancaster, was added on Highway 98 in the Holloway House Motel at Panama City Beach in April 1976. A third Bay County Bob's Bradford House was opened in May 1976 in the Callaway-Parker area at the Parker Shopping Center, led by manager David French and head waitress Charlene McCall. Robbins added Bob's Family Steak House in Panama City to his Bay County restaurant holdings in May 1977.

Another entrepreneurial venture in Florida was Mr. M's Bradford House in the Golden Triangle Shopping Center at Mount Dora.

Also reopened by another Grants entrepreneur was the popular Bradford House Restaurant at the former North Hanover Mall Grants in North

Hanover, Pennsylvania, the renamed Hanover Bradford House enjoying a solid run from 1976 into the mid-1980s.

Other Grants stores found new retail uses under a variety of store banners. In Boston's "Downtown Crossing" district in 1976, Grants' longtime flagship store on Washington Street was transformed by New York City–based Barnes & Noble Booksellers into its second store. Today the nation's largest bookseller with approximately six hundred stores in all fifty states, Barnes & Noble anchored the former downtown Boston Grants for more than thirty years before closing the location. The former Grants building, which dates to 1881, has since been redeveloped into mixed-use retailing and office space.

Additionally, several smaller former Grants locations found new use as pharmacies under the Walgreens and CVS banners, while closeout retailer Big Lots also picked up a number of former Grants locations.

Several former downtown Grants stores found creative new adaptive reuses, including conversions to bars and nightclubs, professional offices and urban residential developments among other uses.

At 9th and Peach Streets in downtown Erie, Pennsylvania, the vacant 81,450-square-foot former Grants, architecturally distinguished by its towering clock pylon, eventually became the new headquarters building for the Greater Erie Community Action Committee (GECAC) and would also once serve as a remote downtown studio site for NBC affiliate WICU-TV 12.

In northeast Ohio along downtown Cleveland's historic and prestigious Euclid Avenue retailing and entertainment district, just steps off Public Square, the W.T. Grant Company's former six-story flagship department store at 248 Euclid Avenue was redeveloped in 2004 into the seventy-three-unit "luxury urban living" W.T. Grant Lofts, offering a mix of trendy studios, apartments and town homes conveniently close to Playhouse Square, Progressive Field and the Quicken Loans Arena.

And out east in downtown Pawtucket, Rhode Island, Grants' former eighteen-thousand-square-foot circa 1934 store at 250 Main Street was redeveloped in 2006 by architect-planner Michael Lonzo and graphic designer J. Hogue into The Grant, a seventeen-unit mixed-use business incubator for design and arts-related businesses.

But where some Grants and Grant City stores were quickly reopened under new banners, other shuttered locations were slower to see new life, languishing in part because of their sheer size. In Milwaukee, where the W.T. Grant Company developed two massive 120,000-square-foot full-line Grant City department stores in 1967 and 1968, the boarded-up stores stood

Because of their sheer size, many shuttered former big-box Grant City stores were slow to see new life. The 120,000-square-foot, label-scarred Grant City at Milwaukee's Mill Road Shopping Center was just coming back to life in the early 1980s as seen here, ultimately subdivided to house five tenants. While redeveloped, the circa 1968 former Grant City never regained its former high-traffic vitality. *Allen Y. Scott photo, from the* Milwaukee Journal Sentinel.

vacant until the early 1980s, with the northwest side Grant City anchoring the Mill Road Shopping Center eventually subdivided to house multiple retailers. The southwest side Grant City at the Spring Mall Shopping Center in suburban Greendale would eventually be subdivided and repurposed for use by Milwaukee-based supermarket chain Pick 'n Save and national off-price retailer T.J. Maxx.

Grants' idled fleet of legacy downtown department stores often languished on the depressed national real estate market for years—even decades—before finding new uses as the nation's downtowns slowly revitalized, while some of Grants' older, larger downtown flagships, having outlived their usefulness and failing to find adaptive reuses, were eventually razed for new development.

In Buffalo, New York, Grants' circa 1939 Early Streamline Moderne–styled "Store of Tomorrow" flagship at 544 Main Street at Huron, designed by famed Chicago architect Alfred S. Alschuler and legendary Streamline-influenced industrial designer Raymond Loewy, was demolished in 1980 and replaced in 1983 by the nine-story Bank of America Building, 10–12 Fountain Plaza.

Making way for the future development of the $50 million mixed-use Galleries of Syracuse shopping mall, library and office building complex, Grants' long-vacant six-story Streamline Moderne 1947 flagship at 425–427

South Salina Street in downtown Syracuse, New York, was imploded in 5.5 seconds along with the neighboring Daniel Building on October 13, 1985, the controlled explosion raising a dust cloud twenty stories high.

In St. Paul, Minnesota, Grants' vacant circa 1955 downtown flagship at East 9th and Cedar Streets was razed in 1979 to pave the way for the 1980 development of Town Square, a three-building complex featuring twenty-seven- and twenty-five-story office towers and a sixteen-story hotel.

And Grants' long-underutilized Streamline Moderne–styled flagship at Franklin and Cass Streets in downtown Tampa, Florida, colloquially known by Tampa residents as the "Grant Block," was demolished in late 2015 and early 2016 to pave the way for the $100 million development of Nine15, a twenty-three-story, 362-unit urban living apartment tower opened in 2017 at Grants' longtime namesake address, 915 North Franklin Street.

REMEMBERING GRANTS

The Albert J. Duclos Story

Out of the thousands of store managers who worked for the venerable W.T. Grant Company department store chain across the span of its storied but abruptly truncated seventy-year history, perhaps none was more serendipitously famous than Fall River, Massachusetts native Albert J. Duclos, who headed Grants No. 1192 at Westerly, Rhode Island, from 1971 to 1976.

As Grants filed for Chapter 11 bankruptcy reorganization in October 1975 and ultimately met its ignominious end just months later in a February 1976 court-ordered liquidation, Duclos put a human face on the W.T. Grant Company's unfortunate demise in a chance six-page April 1976 *Fortune* magazine exposé by then associate editor Rush Loving Jr.—"W.T. Grant's Last Days—As Seen from Store 1192."

I first read it when I was a teenager in Racine, Wisconsin, attending William Horlick High School, ironically located across Rapids Drive from a boarded-up variety-styled Grants that once anchored Rapids Plaza. I always wondered what happened to Duclos, Loving's *Fortune* article ending on Friday, February 13, with Duclos pensively surveying his fledgling "New Grants" store, darkened and padlocked in advance of its going-out-of-business liquidation sale, somberly noting to Loving that "there wasn't any 1976" for Grants.

Looking to do a journalistic "Paul Harvey" and tell "the *rest* of the story" by bringing Loving's April 1976 *Fortune* story full circle, after a great deal of online research, Duclos was eventually located, eighty-five at the time of our July 2019 interview and living in Burlington, New Jersey, retired from a successful post-Grants retailing career with Target Corporation, the nation's eighth-largest retailer.

Duclos eagerly shared recollections of his nineteen-year career with Grants, as well as the story of his post-Grants career successfully managing a succession of Target stores in Southern California, his voice, like Loving experienced in late 1975 and early 1976, still "edged with the…accents of southeastern Massachusetts."

I then spoke in August 2019 with *Fortune*'s Loving, by then eighty-five and living in Baltimore, where he keeps busy writing books on railroads and World War II, as well as occasional trade journal pieces.

Out of the tens of thousands of stories he's written, Virginia native Loving said that his *Fortune* article on Grants and Duclos was among the three most memorable articles of his long career. "It makes me as sad as it did when I wrote it," Loving said of his April 1976 exposé featuring Duclos and Grants No. 1192, reread by Loving in advance of the interview. "It's certainly one of the saddest pieces I ever did. It was all really dramatic and sad at the same time. I did a lot of pieces that were, to me, memorable, when you invest three months of your time writing a piece for *Fortune*.…This is right up there."

The W.T. Grant Company was no stranger to Loving, at that time in his ninth year with *Fortune*. "From childhood on up I shopped at Grants," Loving recalled. "Woolworth's, Grants and Kresge were my favorite stores. As a child I'd go in with a dime or a quarter and buy a toy car or something. I've got here in my office, my study, a figure of [General] Douglas MacArthur, which came out in '46, that I bought at Grants. That's the kind of stuff as a kid, as a teenager, you'd go to Grants for. As you got older, you'd go buy your socks there. It was a wonderful company."

With Grants' October 1975 bankruptcy filing, Loving sought to put a human face on the poignant saga of the once-proud company's desperate struggle to survive—and found that face in Duclos. "They were in bankruptcy when I started doing research for the piece," Loving recalled. "At *Fortune* we'd spend four to six weeks of research on a piece. I'd read in the [*Wall Street*] *Journal* or the [*New York*] *Times* about the bankruptcy and I had gotten curious about it.…I went to a p.r. man I knew that represented Grants and then he put me together with some of the senior people at Grants. I decided that this was a story for us and so I told them that I wanted to look at a couple of candidates for the piece because I was going to center it on one person, which is what I usually liked to do because, for me, business is people, and that's how you report about it."

W.T. Grant's Last Days —As Seen from Store 1192

Al Duclos worked hard to stave off disaster, and he thought he had victory in sight. Then his hopes were dashed by a decision in New York.

by Rush Loving Jr.

The setting sun behind "Grant's Tomb"—the company's former headquarters in New York City—symbolized the end of a great retail chain. After too rapid an expansion in the roaring Sixties, even new management couldn't fend off bankruptcy. For Albert J. Duclos, manager of Store 1192 in Westerly, Rhode Island, Grant's failure was an intensely personal blow. The $20,000 worth of Grant's stock he had painfully purchased had already lost most of its value, and he saw nineteen years with the company going down the drain.

At 9:30 in the morning last February 10, lawyers for the creditors' committee of W. T. Grant Co. walked into a federal courtroom in New York with a surprising proposal. For months, Grant's had been trying to reorganize under the protection of a bankruptcy court, and the once vast retail chain had shrunk from 1,100 stores to 359, and from 75,000 employees to 30,000. With no warning, the creditors' lawyers declared that the seventy-year-old business should be liquidated at once.

Two days later Federal Bankruptcy Judge John J. Galgay granted the committee's request, and the company's stores were padlocked to await a closeout sale. It was the final chapter in the largest bankruptcy proceeding in the history of retailing—the company's debt totaled more than $800 million.

Fighting for their livelihood

The liquidation of a multimillion-dollar enterprise is a poignant business drama even as it is played out where the public most often views it—at the level of the lawyers, the accountants, and the creditors' committees. But Grant's decline and fall takes on a different, more human perspective when it is perceived at store-level, so to speak, where men and women were fighting for their livelihood as well as the survival of the organization. The view from Store 1192, Grant's branch in Westerly, Rhode Island, also tells a good deal about what went wrong with the company and why it couldn't keep itself off the rocks.

The manager of Store 1192 was Albert J. Duclos (pronounced "du-close"), forty-one, a man whose hazel eyes sparkled with an enthusiasm that seemed almost unquenchable. He is methodical and, surprisingly for one so immersed in detail, articulate as well. His thoughts roll out decisively in a voice edged with the clipped, harsh accents of southeastern Massachusetts. His decisiveness helped to dispense confidence, and some small measure of comfort, among the eighty employees of Store 1192 during Grant's last uncertain hours.

A district leader

Duclos spent nineteen years with Grant's, his entire working career, and over the past ten years he managed six Grant's stores in various New England towns. In that decade his annual income multiplied from $8,000 to $37,000, largely because of bonuses. He was so successful a manager that he led his district in sales and profits for six years.

Duclos took over the Westerly store in 1971. A seacoast town on the Connecticut border, Westerly is a marketing center for 140,000 families. Many shoppers come from across the state line, where the sales tax is a penny higher, and during the summer extra thousands from New York and central New England fill the shingled cottages that line the nearby beaches. Most of these people shop at the Franklin Plaza Shopping Center, a strip of sixteen stores just outside town. The largest of the stores was Grant's.

The year-round residents, many of whom work at the submarine yards of General Dynamics in Groton, Connecticut, shopped in Store 1192 for such staples as work clothes, cosmetics, and housewares. The vacationers, who knew the Grant's name from back home, came for fishing tackle, toothpaste, and similar traveling needs. And both groups patronized the Bradford Room, the store's restaurant. One of the most popular eating establishments in Westerly, the Bradford Room earned 30 cents on the dollar, making it the most profitable department in the store.

During his years in Westerly, Duclos played to this market well. Within two years after his arrival he had increased his store's sales by 19 percent, to more than $2.5 million, while doubling profits to $245,000. This 10 percent return on sales was about twice the average for all America's retailers. Under Duclos, 1192 became Grant's twenty-third most profitable store, and continued to make a little money even after the company had fallen into the red.

Every morning Duclos made the hour-long drive to Westerly from his home in Attleboro, Massachusetts. The commute was inconvenient, but not unusually long for that part of New England, and Duclos and his wife, Val, preferred Attleboro to Westerly as a place to bring up their two daughters. The store was open from 10:00 A.M. until 9:00 P.M., and Duclos was always there an hour or more before opening time. He rarely left before 6:30 or 7:00 P.M.

Cutting his teeth on Kool-Aid

At the store Duclos was used to feeling like the captain of a ship—in charge of just about everything that went on. With the aid of his merchandise manager and two assistant managers, he oversaw all orders for new stock and plotted the mix of goods that Grant's offered Westerly's shoppers. He could raise or lower prices at will to beat the competition, and he had the power to concoct special promotions, even drawing up his own newspaper and radio ads. Once his bosses in New York City tried to keep him from stocking swimming pools, on the ground that pools wouldn't sell in a seaside community. Duclos went ahead anyway and ordered $5,000 worth, selling out in a week. Duclos had been in love with merchandising since the age of eleven, when he set up a Kool-

108 FORTUNE April 1976

FORTUNE April 1976 109

Putting a human face on the dramatic crash-and-burn demise of the W.T. Grant Company, *Fortune* magazine published Associate Editor Rush Loving's compelling April 1976 feature story featuring the front-lines perspective of Grants veteran Albert J. Duclos, the 1971–76 manager of sixty-thousand-square-foot Grants No. 1192 at Franklin Plaza Shopping Center in Westerly, Rhode Island. During his five-year stint in Westerly, Duclos built Store 1192 into Grants' twenty-third-most profitable unit. *From* Fortune *magazine.*

Duclos recalled that a call had been put out by company executives at a meeting of Grants managers, seeking volunteers from among the attendees to potentially participate in a *Fortune* feature story on Grants, with three volunteers stepping forward for consideration. Loving interviewed managers on-site at Grants stores in Long Island and New York, as well as Duclos at Store 1192 in Westerly, Rhode Island, with Loving tapping Duclos for his exposé. "It was exciting for me to be picked to be the one to do it and show off my store," Duclos said. "I felt lucky in a lot of ways."

Recalled Loving, "I wanted to make sure I had a subject that could be useable as a source and also a person who would be quotable and all that… and I settled on Duclos and the store in Westerly. I went up there and spent a good three, four weeks, probably longer, at the store with him and his people and even went home with him one night to see what kind of commute he had and all that. It was a typical thing I always did in a piece. And then I went home and started writing."

Loving subsequently returned to visit Duclos at the Westerly Grants when the court-ordered liquidation was announced just days into the start of Grants' 1976 fiscal year and the successful celebratory "SuperSale" debut of the fledgling "New Grants" chain, with Loving visiting with Duclos in the darkened, shuttered store. Loving returned to visit Duclos again shortly thereafter, when Grants' padlocked Westerly store was reopened for the company's chain-wide liquidation sale.

"It was a pretty complete piece of research, but very sad because this was a great company, as the story reflects," Loving recalled. "I thought that Duclos was more capable of running Grants than this guy [Robert] Anderson that they had brought in at a huge salary….I thought he [Duclos] had more…skills in retailing than the [Grants corporate] people in New York. He really knew what he was doing. He knew how to sell stuff and what kind of [merchandise] mix he needed. He was good."

Wrote Loving in the introduction to his April 1976 *Fortune* story, "The liquidation of a multimillion-dollar enterprise is a poignant business drama even as it is played out where the public most often views it—at the level of the lawyers, the accountants, and the creditors' committees. But Grant's decline and fall takes on a different, more human perspective when it is perceived at store-level, where men and women were fighting for their livelihoods as well as the survival of the organization. The view from Store 1192, Grant's branch in Westerly, Rhode Island, also tells a good deal about what went wrong with the company and why it couldn't keep itself off the rocks."

Describing him as methodical and articulate and possessed with "an enthusiasm that almost seemed unquenchable," Loving said of Duclos's managerial acumen in *Fortune*, "During his years in Westerly, Duclos played to this market well. Within two years after his arrival he had increased his store's sales by 19 percent, to more than $2.5 million, while doubling profits to $245,000. This 10 percent return on sales was about twice the average for all America's retailers. Under Duclos, 1192 became Grant's twenty-third most profitable store, and continued to make a little money even after the company had fallen into the red….His decisiveness helped to dispense confidence, and some small measure of comfort, among the eighty employees of Store 1192 during Grant's last uncertain hours."

Looking back on Grants' 1976 demise with the perspective afforded by forty-three years of reflection, Duclos remained grateful for his nineteen-year tenure with Grants, with the solid foundation his experiences there giving him a lifetime of career success in the retailing industry, including a storied twenty-year run with Target in Southern California that saw Duclos manage Target's first $150 million store. "It [Grants] was a very good experience for me," Duclos said. "I did very well with Grants. It was a heartbreak for it to

His store padlocked for liquidation in February 1976, Grants veteran Albert J. Duclos, the 1971–76 manager of W.T. Grant Company Store No. 1192 in Westerly, surveys his profitable fledgling "New Grants" store. Less than two weeks into its 1976 fiscal year, creditors pressed for the seventy-year-old retailer's liquidation. *From* Fortune *magazine.*

go out of business. I loved Grants. I loved retailing. I was a natural at it, so to speak. I did very well, thanks to W.T. Grant."

Born and raised in Fall River, Massachusetts, ironically the final resting place and former boyhood hometown of W.T. Grant Company namesake William T. Grant, Duclos, like Grant, was destined for a life in retailing. Cutting his retailing teeth at age eleven selling Kool-Aid outside a neighborhood grocery store in Fall River, Duclos by his teen years was juggling three jobs in addition to his high school academics, augmenting income from a newspaper route with retailing jobs at a supermarket and a department store.

Following graduation from high school, Duclos enlisted in the U.S. Army during the Korean War and served out a two-year stateside tour of duty, training at Fort Dix, New Jersey, and later posted to Fort Bragg, North Carolina, where he served with the 18th Airborne as secretary to the general.

After his tour ended, Duclos set his eyes on Connecticut. "There wasn't much happening in Fall River," Duclos recalled. "Unemployment was high. Jobs were plentiful in Connecticut, so I went to Connecticut and got one of those jobs, working for a jet engine manufacturer."

But as the Korean War wound down and eventually ended, so did the work. "When the war ended, obviously they [the U.S. military] didn't need the jet engines so they laid off a bunch of people, me included," he said. "I liked Connecticut and wanted to stay, so I looked in the paper and saw W.T. Grants was looking for people. I always liked retailing as a kid, so I got a job with W.T. Grants as stock room manager."

Taking the job with Grants' downtown store in Wallingford was a pivotal turning point moment that forever changed Duclos's life and paved the way for a successful lifelong career in retailing. "It was a good place to work." Duclos recalled, "Almost right away, all of a sudden, an opening came up for a store manager and two assistant managers. W.T. Grants, they didn't think anything about moving you. I talked to the store manager and was made the second floor manager."

Initially, Duclos served in the Wallingford Grants as a "*local* assistant manager," which meant he could only serve in the Wallingford store. A man of ambition, Duclos wanted more, setting his sights on becoming a "*company* assistant manager," who were typically promoted from store to store and, eventually, if merited, put on a fast track for becoming store managers. "I started *local* and then I took some tests and became a *company* assistant manager," Duclos noted. "I got married and things were going real good for me."

Then one night, Duclos, living fifteen minutes away in nearby Meriden, received a 2:00 a.m. call from his manager that the Wallingford Grants was on fire. "I got in my car, drove to Wallingford and, sure enough, the thing was in flames. It broke my heart. It was a great little store."

Following the fire, employees of the Wallingford Grants were dispersed to different stores, with Duclos landing an assistant manager gig at a larger one-hundred-employee Grants store in New Haven where he "did everything." "One day I went to the manager and asked him how long it would be before I got my own store," Duclos recalled. "He thought I'd do a great job, but he told me, 'I'll be honest with you. There's no such thing as a twenty-two-year-old manager with a high school diploma. You'd have a better chance of getting your own store if you got a college degree.'"

Working fifty to sixty hours per week at Grants, the store manager juggled Duclos's work schedule to allow him time to take night classes at Quinnipiac University in New Haven. Enrollment at Quinnipiac afforded Duclos the opportunity to get on Grants' managerial track with its successful longstanding Managers in Training Program. Recalled Duclos, "I could say, 'I don't have a degree, but I'm working on it.'"

While predominantly "an older company that wanted older managers," Duclos said that Grants' Managers in Training Program nevertheless was an opportunity for ambitious and driven young college graduates to prove themselves on the competitive, fast-moving playing field of American general merchandise retailing, with Duclos counted among Grants' youngest managers. Said Duclos, "W.T. Grants gave you an opportunity to show what you could do."

Duclos's first store assignment as manager was heading the downtown Grants store in Stamford, Connecticut, where William T. Grant lived seasonally. "It was an old, rundown store downtown, three floors," Duclos recalled of his inauspicious start. "It was quite a little store. We didn't do a lot of business, we didn't do a lot of volume."

And things only got worse for Duclos when Grants subsequently opened a "big, beautiful" brand-new Grants store on Stamford's newly developing fringes. "Now, not only were we competing with the other downtown stores, but with the other W.T. Grants as well," he said.

After a year in Stamford, Duclos was promoted to a higher volume store in Belfast, Maine, and, from there, was transferred to manage a problem situation in St. Albans, Vermont, near the Canadian border, an assignment that Duclos remembers as the "coldest year of my life."

The Grants district manager assured Duclos that the move to St. Albans would be worth it, calling it "an opportunity to make a name for yourself." Sure enough, Duclos quickly became one of the New England District's go-to men for straightening out problem Grants stores and managing problem situations, a legacy that Duclos would later carry with him to Target in Southern California. "I made a name for myself fixing problem stores," he noted.

In 1971, Duclos was approached by a New England District manager offering a plum store assignment running Grants' successful sixty-thousand-square-foot anchor Grant City store in the Franklin Plaza Shopping Center at 17,248-resident Westerly, Rhode Island, a beachside community best known for textiles, granite mining and tourism. "It was a good, profitable store, a large store," Duclos said of Store 1192, which opened in 1965 as a replacement for Grants' older downtown Westerly variety store.

At first, Duclos was reluctant to make the move, having put his problem store back on track and settling into a comfortable life. "As manager of a big downtown store I was a big shot," he explained. "I knew people in town, I had built a house."

After friends from Fall River moved to Attleboro, Massachusetts, and a house came available just two doors down, Duclos make the decision to move to Attleboro and accept the transfer to the Westerly Grants, just a forty-minute commute away on I-95. "It was well worth it," Duclos said of the move to Attleboro and his store at Westerly. "I had friends, a nice neighborhood, the nicest house on the street, and a nice, clean store that was like family."

Taking over a well-run operation from a capable longtime Grants manager, Duclos quickly went to work taking a great Grants store to an even higher level. "I knew how to get sales, I knew what it took," Duclos said. "I had some good people and I was in a good area. Being near New Haven, summer business was really good. We did a big summer business with the summer beach business. I wanted to make it [Store 1192] even better. I started opening on Sundays…and sales went zoom."

Duclos was aided in his success at Westerly by the leeway that Grants gave its local store managers, part of founder William T. Grant's foundational operating philosophy of giving store managers, within reason, the freedom to essentially operate as entrepreneurs. In essence, Grants wasn't so much one large chain store operation as much as it was 1,238 individual stores bearing the singular Grants name, a concept that created a wide if somewhat confusingly haphazard array of Grants shopping experiences from store to store, sometimes even within the same town or market area.

Noted Loving in *Fortune* of Duclos at the helm of Grants' Westerly store, "Duclos was used to feeling like the captain of a ship—in charge of just about everything that went on. With the aid of his merchandising manager and two assistant managers, he oversaw all orders for new stock and plotted the mix of goods that Grant's offered Westerly's shoppers. He could raise or lower prices at will to beat the competition, and he had the power to concoct special promotions, even drawing up his own newspaper and radio ads. Once his bosses in New York City tried to keep him from stocking swimming pools on the grounds that pools wouldn't sell in a seaside community. Duclos went ahead anyway and ordered $5,000 worth, selling out in a week."

"W.T. Grants was different than other stores—the store manager was the chief," Duclos recalled. "W.T. Grants let you run your own store—as long as the numbers were right. They were fair in every way. If you could prove you could do the job, they gave you the opportunity to do it. The longer you stayed with Grants…the better you did."

Under Duclos, Store 1192 at Westerly consistently became the New England District's leading performer at $4.5 million in sales at its peak before Grants' collapse. "Becoming the number one volume store in New England was quite an accomplishment," Duclos said. "I had some good people and

I was in a good, high profile area....I loved the excitement. It was a pretty good job. I made pretty good money. The bonuses were good."

But storm clouds had been gathering on the horizon for the W.T. Grant Company dating back to the late 1960s. While Grants' sales volume grew to $1.85 billion as the company continued its breakneck new store development program, profitability stalled and even eroded. After posting an unusually slim profit in 1973, Grants plunged $177.3 million into the red in fiscal 1974 and losses ran nearly $20 million a month in 1975, when Grants filed for Chapter 11 bankruptcy reorganization. Yet even after Grants ran aground, Store 1192 continued to turn a profit under Duclos's management.

"At that time, it seemed there was no chance of W.T. Grants going bankrupt," Duclos said of fast-growing and historically profitable Grants, which ranked as the nation's seventh-largest general merchandise retailer and the third-largest big-box discount department store chain after F.W. Woolworth (Woolco) and S.S. Kresge (Kmart). "People were getting hints, but it [Grants' October 1975 Chapter 11 bankruptcy reorganization filing] was a shock to a lot of people. I know *I* couldn't believe it. I knew how much my store was making, and I knew a lot of other stores were doing well. It was bad for the employees—and bad for the country as well."

Informing his eighty employees of Grants' bankruptcy filing, and later of its court-ordered liquidation, remain for Duclos "the hardest things I ever did" in more than forty-five years of retailing. And with Grants' court-ordered liquidation, Duclos's life was forever changed. "It hit home—I'm gonna be out of a job in a month," he recalled.

Duclos remained with Grants until the bitter end in March–April 1976, presiding over the going-out-of-business sale at the Westerly Grants conducted by California-based liquidator Sam Nassi Company. As the New England District's highest-volume store, leftover merchandise from completed liquidation sales at other Grants stores was trucked to Store 1192 in Westerly, making it among the last Grants stores to close. "During the going-out-of-business sales, whatever was left went to the larger-volume stores," Duclos recalled. "We received in a lot of merchandise from the other stores."

After the liquidation sales ended and the store's doors were locked to the public for the final time, Duclos and a small crew cleaned and prepped Grants No. 1192 for its next occupant. "We made sure it looked good after closure," Duclos said. "JCPenney was after it and finally got it."

Duclos recalled that "a lot of the key employees" at Grants No. 1192 eventually worked for JCPenney, which extensively remodeled Grants'

Westerly store but, knowing to leave well enough alone, left Grants' popular Bradford House Restaurant untouched. Under Grants, the full-service Bradford House restaurant had earned thirty cents on the dollar, making it the most profitable department in the store. "The restaurant did *a lot* of business," Duclos said, citing a "good food manager," a high-traffic location and a quality quick-service menu for the success of the Bradford House. "JCPenney changed the store, but not the Bradford House."

The Westerly JCPenney remains a fixture of today's eleven-store Franklin Shopping Plaza, 100–126 Franklin Street, today anchored by JCPenney, Aldi, PetSmart and T.J. Maxx.

Having spent nineteen years—most of his adult working career to date—with the W.T. Grant Company, despite the brave face that he put on for his employees at Store 1192, Duclos took Grants' demise hard. "I still had Grants in my heart," Duclos admitted. "I found it *very* difficult to adjust."

The exposure afforded by the *Fortune* article—and its portrayal of Duclos's steady, able leadership at Grants No. 1192 in a time of tremendous turmoil—provided Duclos with a welcome boost as he sought to build a new post-Grants career. "Because I was in the magazine, I got *a lot* of calls…from other retailers," Duclos said. "I was luckier than most.…Once Grants went out, I still wanted to do retailing but try something different."

For Duclos, different meant straying from his northeastern roots and moving to sunny Southern California, where he found work with a California department store chain, working in coastal Torrance in the South Bay region of Los Angeles County. "The company reminded me of Grants," he recalled. "They paid me good money and moved me out there."

Like malaprop-prone baseball great Yogi Berra, within three years Duclos was experiencing "déjà vu all over again" as his new employer shuttered all of its stores, leaving him jobless yet again. "The owner of the company said he could make more money on the real estate than in running the stores," Duclos recalled. "I thought, 'Oh no, not again.' How many times can you do that, you know? I decided to stay in retailing, but try a different kind of retailing."

Duclos then went to work as a district manager for a mall-based high-end women's clothing store chain before Dayton-Hudson Corporation's Target discount department store division came knocking at his door. "Then Target came along—'would you like to come work for Target?'" recalled Duclos, who managed a succession of four Target stores in Southern California across the span of twenty years.

After opening and managing a new Los Angeles–area Target store for a few years and a subsequent transfer assignment to manage a nearby Target store, Duclos was transferred to Torrance to manage his third Target, a "monster" 150,000-square-foot store that included a large furniture and appliance annex in an adjacent former supermarket. Long a trouble-shooter for Grants, Duclos ended his career turning around "one of the biggest problem stores in the country" for Target: its Culver City outlet, which Duclos subsequently transformed into the Target's "number one store" and "the first store in company history to hit $150 million."

"I felt good about that," Duclos said of his turnaround of the Culver City Target.

Now retired and living back on the East Coast, Duclos has had plenty of time to reflect on his career with Grants. For months and even years after Grants' surprising and abrupt demise, a variety of news media outlets and collegiate business textbooks and MBA programs offered up lengthy autopsies of Grants' spectacular and newsworthy crash-and-burn as an oft-parsed textbook case in chain store management gone awry, citing a long list of perfect storm ills that brought down the once high-flying W.T. Grant Company with dizzying speed.

With forty-three years to reflect on his career with Grants and the company's sudden and complete collapse, Duclos offered his own take on the fatal blows that took down his longtime employer, agreeing with some, but not all, of the conjectures brought forward over the years. Grants' "Grantcard" revolving credit card program, and the deleterious financial toll it exacted on company finances, was agreed upon as a contributing factor. Noted Duclos in the 1976 *Fortune* story of Grants' credit cards, "We hated the goddam things."

Explained Loving in *Fortune*, "To bolster…sales, the company had entered the hazardous credit-card business full steam ahead. Clerks were offered $1 bounties for each customer they signed up for a card, and Duclos was ordered to push the credit-card program above anything else. The pressure grew so intense that at one point his district credit manager called hourly asking how many accounts he had opened.…On New York's insistence, only cursory credit checks were conducted.…Meanwhile the new card holders were using their new credit cards to haul away hundreds of dollars worth of washing machines and beds. Duclos and virtually every other manager warned that the cards were brewing trouble, but New York didn't listen. By last year, Grant's credit-card receivables totaled $500 million, and half of that was deemed uncollectible. The day of reckoning finally came early last year when the company plunged into the red—$177 million."

Reflecting on his Grants days, Duclos said that while Store 1192 "didn't have a problem" with credit card delinquencies, he nevertheless still agrees that Grants' overall credit card program was "one of the downfalls" for the company. "The background checks were not as rigorous as they should have been," Duclos said, noting the standing joke was that "if you stood in front of the credit desk long enough they'd give you a credit card."

Another major contributing factor to Grants' downfall in retrospect, Duclos said, was "stagnant" and slow-to-react corporate management at Grants' fifty-four-story Midtown Manhattan Home Office at 1515 Broadway in Times Square, nicknamed "Grant's Tomb," perhaps clairvoyantly so, by many company employees.

"Grants had a lot of old thinking," Duclos observed, saying that Grants management failed to adequately meet and beat the outside-the-box thinking being deployed by competitor S.S. Kresge with the industry-disrupting 1962 rollout of its big-box Kmart discount department store concept in suburban Detroit. "Kmart recognized they needed to be different. Meanwhile, they [Grants executives] were still trying to upgrade the same way with the new competition. You had to change with the times. The thinking at Grants was, 'This is the way we did it and this is they way we should always do it.' Employees put the blame [for Grants' downfall, bankruptcy and liquidation] on top management. They were so stagnant in their thinking."

Another contributing factor to Grants' woes, Duclos said, was Grants' hyper-expansion with its massive full-service Sears-, JCPenney- and Montgomery Ward–wannabe Grant City stores, which left Grants stores of all stripes poorly merchandised and stocked as the pace of expansion outstripped Grant's purchasing, warehousing, distribution and personnel infrastructure resources. "They were opening too many stores, the end result being W.T. Grant stores were not stocked as well as they should have been," Duclos explained, adding that Grants' biggest problem, in a volume-oriented business, was "poor [sales] volume" in many of its 1,200-plus stores.

"We had a lot of stores…and no business," Duclos said, citing his first store in downtown Stamford, Connecticut, as a poster child for his argument, recalling a 1960s stairwell sit-in protest at his store that quickly flopped because there was so little customer traffic at Grants to disrupt.

But where many others cited Grants' expansion into high-priced, low-turnover merchandise like furniture and major appliances as another factor in Grants' demise, Duclos remains less sure of the diagnosis, citing the "pretty darned good" quality of Grants' lines of furniture and proprietary Bradford-branded appliances and the fact that his stores "did a pretty good business" in furniture and major appliances, although he concedes that a lot of the success of those particular departments "depended on the department manager" in each individual store and that there tended to be a "low markup" on furniture and appliances "because of the competition" from other retailers. Furniture and appliances, he added, "took up a lot of space" that could have been used for higher-markup, faster-turnover merchandise.

Ultimately, Loving said, "Grants died from mismanagement." He noted, "Its basic problem was the balance sheet and the fact the old management had stretched things too thin with the credit cards. I think they got too greedy. They decided to get into the credit card business and they should have stayed out of it. They weren't a bank. They should have stopped thinking they were and instead should have stuck with retailing."

But that being said, Loving said that Grants really needed to adequately define its market niche to meet the challenges presented by a rapidly evolving retail scene, particularly with the 1962 advent of big-box discount department store concepts pioneered by S.S. Kresge's Kmart and Dayton-Hudson's Target, which saw huge exponential growth in the 1960s and 1970s.

"They tried to make it [Grants] into another Sears, which I'm not sure needed to be done," Loving said. "It was the Targets and Kmarts of the world that started eroding the market share of Grants....They [Grants] should have expanded into becoming another Target, which was relatively unknown then, but was the wave of the future. They should have recognized it and headed that way instead of trying to fancy themselves up."

In Loving's 1976 *Fortune* exposé, Duclos said that he felt new Grants president Robert H. Anderson, a former merchandising vice-president with Sears, was making a lot of the right moves in his creation of a Northeast regional "New Grants" chain—renewing Grants' focus on its traditional stronghold in soft goods, eliminating the troubled credit card program, closing out Grant's slow-moving, low-markup furniture and major appliance departments and putting a fresh, remodeled face on Grants dwindling fleet of stores.

Ultimately, Anderson—and Grants—ran out of time as the company's creditors pressed for court-ordered liquidation mere days into the successful launch of the higher volume "New Grants" stores. "It [Grants' turnaround] was a long way down the road," Duclos said. "Grants was thinking in—and taking—short steps."

For his part, Loving said he felt that New Grants, with a smaller concentrated store footprint in its legacy northeastern and mid-Atlantic U.S.

home territory and a renewed focus on the company's historical strength in soft goods, would have enjoyed decent odds at success given sufficient time to gain traction. "I think it certainly had a chance," Loving said of New Grants. "It's hard to predict, but I think basically what they were trying to do made sense. Certainly cutting the size of the company, particularly the stores that were not making a lot of money, made a lot of sense."

Said Loving of Grants' 1976 demise, "It shouldn't have happened, it really should *not* have happened."

While he lost some $20,000 painstakingly invested in now-worthless Grants stock and also temporarily lost his livelihood, Duclos said that what remains more than four decades later are the *good* memories of Grants—and how it changed his life. "Grants was a good place to work—you had a lot of opportunities," Duclos said, recalling the friendly, family camaraderie of his Grants store staff and the wide breadth of opportunities and entrepreneurial freedom Grants offered its store managers. "It [Grants] got me to love retailing.…Being retired, with a lot of time on my hands, I think a lot about Grants. It's all good memories. I can't say I wouldn't do it all over again, because I would."

CONTINUING THE LEGACY

The William T. Grant Foundation

While the retailing legacy of W.T. Grant Company founder William T. Grant passed into history with the ignominious April 1976 closure of the last Grants department store, William T. Grant's legacy, particularly his rich philanthropic legacy, has been carried forward by the New York–based William T. Grant Foundation, which supports research targeted at improving the lives of young people in the United States.

The William T. Grant Foundation has its roots in namesake founder Grant's success in launching his W.T. Grant Company department store chain in 1906, quickly turning the twenty-five-cent store retailing niche pioneered by Store No. 1 at Lynn, Massachusetts, into the nation's fastest-growing twenty-five-cent, fifty-cent and one-dollar general merchandise retail chain. Along the way of turning Grants into a major coast-to-coast retailer, Grant made millions but found all of his money meaningless without a larger "real business" vision of a "principle of service" to mankind—his "New Idea" that the "greatest values in life lie not in getting things, but in doing them."

Noted *Forbes* of Grant in June 1927:

> *Bill Grant fought his way to the top. At least, that's what he thought he was doing: and that is how anyone, until very recent times, must have interpreted his career. Written from that angle, the story of William T. Grant, head of the great chain of the W.T. Grant Co. stores, is inspiring enough to suit the most ambitious dealer in American business romance. There is nothing lacking. Early poverty, handicaps, discouragements—*

> *they are all there. Also indomitable will, patience, stick-to-itiveness and an inexhaustible capacity for hard work. Then there comes success, deserved success, success beyond the wildest flights of his youth-time imagination—with millions, dazzling millions, as the climax. Only, that isn't the climax. This is Anno Domini 1927 and there are bigger stories than that to tell. If you happen to be a close friend of William T. Grant, he may tell you one. He may tell you that millions, by themselves, are futile. He may tell you that time is too precious to spend in mere money-making. He may tell you that he has quit the game and has gone into real business instead. And he may tell you, although his millions bored him, that this real business is giving him the time of his life.*

Explained Grant to *Forbes* writer Charles W. Wood, "I was just thinking about business. I was thinking of what this thing we call business actually is. I went into it to make money for W.T. Grant. I got the money, but the money gave me no satisfaction. I did get many things out of business as I went along, and I have many worthwhile experiences. Nevertheless, this money ideal blinded me. Until I got rid of the money ideal—and that was an experience of only a year or so ago—I never realized how much real fun there is in life."

Through the gift of W.T. Grant Company stock serving as principal, with stock earnings funding philanthropic grants, William T. Grant's "New Idea" dream of service to mankind, particularly in improving the lives of young people, would eventually manifest itself in the November 18, 1936 creation of his philanthropic The Grant Foundation, today's William T. Grant Foundation.

For many years housed in the W.T. Grant Company's Midtown Manhattan Home Office corporate headquarters at 1441 Broadway in New York City, the Delaware-incorporated Grant Foundation was initially launched with three board trustees, with Grant as president, W.T. Grant Company research director C. Frederick Hansen as vice-president and William T. Grant's personal secretary, Adele W. Morrison, as secretary and treasurer. Hansen retired from the foundation board in 1947. A longtime foundation fixture, Morrison would serve The Grant Foundation as secretary from 1936 to 1967 and as associate director from 1967 to 1969.

Noting that "charitable work designed to alleviate helpless poverty, sickness and distress gets popular attention," Grant looked in a different direction, envisioning a foundation that would "assist research, education, and training through the sciences which have their focus in the study of man."

Retired from day-to-day operations of the W.T. Grant Company in 1924 at forty-eight as a self-made rags-to-riches millionaire merchant, William T. Grant in November 1936 launched his philanthropic Grant Foundation, today's William T. Grant Foundation, with the gift of Grants stock serving as principal and stock earnings funding philanthropic grants. *William T. Grant Foundation Collection, Rockefeller Archive Center.*

In his Horatio Alger rags-to-riches rise from relative poverty to entrepreneurial success as a self-made Renaissance man and multimillionaire, Grant had been a keen observer of those around him, particularly those in his employ with the W.T. Grant Company. Recruiting and training personnel for his growing chain of stores, Grant became aware of and increasingly concerned with the state of mental health of American children and young adults, wondering why so many promising young people often floundered and failed to lead rewarding lives.

"My thoughts and ambitions are to aid the greatest possible number of people, regardless of race or creed, to overcome destructive prejudices and to cooperate constructively in working for the common good," Grant noted. "The object is enrichment of life, with a primary interest in people and in their adjustment to the world in which they live.…If something could be done on the level of supplying the individual with the help he needs in pursuing a more satisfactory life, a real contribution could be made and the larger problems would be a long way to solution."

Having researched the accomplishments of the most successful foundations of the era, Grant was convinced that a foundation could be an instrument of social progress. Surveying the scope of foundation work at the time, Grant, ever the trailblazer, saw the emerging realm of sociology as a field ripe for exploration, putting the financial resources of his fledging The Grant Foundation behind the effort.

Noted the foundation's inaugural 1936–37 annual report, "Appropriations chiefly will be made in lines which supplement each other in the field outlined by Mr. Grant, with the purpose of building a cumulative body of knowledge which will have comprehensive social value."

Said Grant of the founding of The Grant Foundation, "What I have in mind is to assist, by some means, in helping people or people to live more contentedly and peacefully, well in body and mind. The well-being of people depends in large part on the discovery and comprehension of the fundamental principles of human relations which contributes to the welfare

The Grant Foundation Board of Directors convenes a 1954 meeting in the foundation's original home alongside the W.T. Grant Company in Grants' corporate headquarters Home Office at 1441 Broadway, Times Square, in Midtown Manhattan. *William T. Grant Foundation Collection, Rockefeller Archive Center.*

of all. The individual needs the understanding of these principles to get on with his fellowman in friendliness and peace."

Inaugural grant awards by The Grant Foundation totaled $70,000—$60,000 to Harvard University to kick off the seminal Grant Study in Social Adjustments; $5,000 to the American Friends Service Committee for the Penn-Craft Project in Fayette County, Pennsylvania; and $5,000 in support of the Assembly Hall Fund at the Friends School in Ram Allah, Palestine.

Some grant awards by The Grant Foundation catered to founder William T. Grant's special personal interests. In memory of his late brother, Dr. Elihu Grant (1873–1942), an ordained Methodist minister and professor of biblical literature at Smith College (1907–1917) and professor of biblical studies at Haverford College (1917–1938), The Grant Foundation financially supported Mrs. Elihu Grant's 1944 establishment of the Elihu Grant Memorial Scholarship Fund at Haverford to provide scholarship aid for graduate and undergraduate students in humanistic studies, primarily those specializing in biblical literature.

The Grant Foundation in its first eleven years through 1947 awarded more than $1 million in grants, chief among them a major grant supporting the landmark 1938–47 Grant Study of Adult Development at Harvard University, a groundbreaking human development study that has now formally and informally followed the lives of study subjects for more than seventy-five years.

The Grant Study, an investigation of normal behavior characteristics of reasonably successful young men in collaboration with Harvard University Heath Service director Dr. Arlie V. Bock, was an ambitious, trailblazing early effort to combine the disciplines of medicine, psychiatry, psychology, anthropology and social services in a study of normalcy.

The seminal Grant Study of Adult Development spawned several smaller-scale simultaneous studies for interested outside organizations with a leadership identification and leadership development focus, including the Boy Scouts of America, the W.T. Grant Company and, during World War II, the Navy Department's Bureau of Naval Personnel.

A follow-up study of the charter participants in the Grant Study of Adult Development at Harvard was conducted in 1957–77. The research team, led by Harvard psychiatrist Dr. George Valliant from 1972 to 2004, continued

The Grant Foundation in its first eleven years through 1947 awarded more than $1 million in grants, chief among them a major grant supporting the landmark 1938–47 Grant Study of Adult Development at Harvard University, a groundbreaking human development study combining the disciplines of medicine, psychiatry, psychology, anthropology and social services. *William T. Grant Foundation Collection, Rockefeller Archive Center.*

to follow the participants well into old age. Dr. Valliant's last book, *Triumphs of Experience*, showed that caring and trusting relationships were more important than socioeconomic accomplishments for happiness in old age. Today, the study is led by another Harvard professor, Dr. Robert Waldinger, who recently received funding from the National Institute on Aging to study the offspring of participants in the original Grant Study.

Over the years, the size of the foundation's board of trustees was expanded to include, among others, trusted "Grant Men" including Grants board director Howland S. Davis (1938–64), W.T. Grant Company president and board director Raymond H. Fogler (1942–78) and Grants president and board chairman Edward Staley (1954–74), with the first non-Grants board directors appointed to the expanding foundation board in 1947—Morris Hadley (Milbank, Tweed, Hope & Hadley), Milton H. Glover (Hartford National Bank), Cleveland E. Dodge (Phelps Dodge Corporation) and R. McAllister Lloyd (Teachers Insurance and Annuity Association). Today, the William T. Grant Foundation is overseen by a thirteen-member board of trustees.

Serving under board chairman William T. Grant as day-to-day executive directors of The Grant Foundation were Perrin C. "Perry" Galpin (1948–55) and John Byler (1955–65).

By the late 1940s, The Grant Foundation had become a major supporter of the African American community through its longtime support of the United Negro College Fund and National Medical Fellowships for minority medical students.

Well into the 1940s, The Grant Foundation did not "seek to define its activities precisely" but rather was "engaged in the general field of human relations and more particularly with projects involving youth," including support of the national Boy Scouts and Girl Scouts organizations.

"The Foundation will attempt, within the scope of its resources, to assist research, education, and training through the sciences which have their focus in the study of man," it was noted in the foundation's 1947–48 annual report. "The Foundation is interested in the problems of normal people. In general it has supported projects that involve the preventive rather than the remedial aspects of social problems. The Foundation is currently concerned with methods and means by which individuals may reach maturity, may be aided to handle their problems, may exercise their capacities, and so adjust to the world in which they live."

"Undertaking an appraisal of its areas of operation" in 1951–52, The Grant Foundation sought "to discover promising approaches which may be

Well into the 1940s, the Grant Foundation did not "seek to define its activities precisely," but rather was "engaged in the general field of human relations and more particularly with projects involving youth," including support of the national Boy Scouts and Girl Scouts organizations. *William T. Grant Foundation Collection, Rockefeller Archive Center.*

made to advance mental health through a concentration upon those factors which most directly relate to the growth of emotionally stable children."

As a result of those efforts, The Grant Foundation in the 1950s began to focus its philanthropic efforts on awarding grants in support of child-rearing studies, parent education and child mental health. Leading recipients of funding from The Grant Foundation included Dr. Benjamin Spock's child-

The Grant Foundation began to focus its philanthropic efforts in support of child-rearing studies, parent education and child mental health in the 1950s. Dr. Anna Freud's work at the well-baby clinic and nursery school at the Hamstead Clinic in London, England, was among the Grant Foundation's funding recipients. *William T. Grant Foundation Collection, Rockefeller Archive Center.*

rearing studies at Case Western Reserve University in Cleveland, Ohio; the child mental health and development research into parent-infant attachment and early social-emotional development being conducted by psychologists John Bowlby, Margaret Mahler and Mary Ainsworth; and Dr. Anna Freud's work at the well-baby clinic and nursery school at the Hamstead Clinic in London, England.

As the W.T. Grant Company rapidly grew into a major nationwide general merchandise retailer, with a corresponding need for more space at its Midtown Manhattan Home Office at 1441 Broadway, the growing Grant Foundation in March 1955 relocated from its longtime home in the W.T. Grant Building to new quarters at 130 West 59th Street in New York.

As women increasingly shifted into the workplace, the foundation's research grant awards in the 1960s reflected changing trends in society with an emphasis on supporting research into daycare, preschool education and the U.S. government's "War on Poverty." As part of its interest in daycare, in 1969, The Grant Foundation provided grant support of the first industry-sponsored daycare facility at KLH Corporation in Cambridge, Massachusetts.

Moved to new Midtown Manhattan quarters at 130 West 59th Street in March 1955, Board Chairman William T. Grant meets with The Grant Foundation secretary and treasurer Adele W. Morrison. Formerly Grant's personal secretary, Morrison was a longtime foundation fixture, serving the Grant Foundation from 1936 to 1969, including a 1967–69 tenure as associate director. *William T. Grant Foundation Collection, Rockefeller Archive Center.*

The 1960s also represented a time of major change for The Grant Foundation, as founder William T. Grant, upon his ninetieth birthday in 1966, simultaneously retired from his dual longtime roles as president of The Grant Foundation and board chairman of the W.T. Grant Company. Grant, who was bestowed with honorary emeritus titles at both organizations for his dedicated longtime service, passed away in 1972 at age ninety-six.

Grant was succeeded by Douglas D. Bond, MD, as chairman of The Grant Foundation.

In the years following Grant's retirement, The Grant Foundation began to distance itself from the W.T. Grant Company in a variety of ways. Following a 1967 revision of the foundation's bylaws, only two directors or officers of the W.T. Grant Company were allowed to serve as trustees, down from the four allowed previously. Continuing on the foundation's board were longtime directors Fogler and Staley. Staley resigned from the board in May 1974 after twenty years of service. Appointed to the board in 1942, Fogler, the foundation's last Grants-affiliated board member, retired in June 1978 and was subsequently elected an honorary trustee.

Presciently in hindsight, given the W.T. Grant Company's spectacular crash-and-burn with its massive $177 million 1974 loss, historic 1975 bankruptcy reorganization filing and 1976 court-ordered liquidation, The Grant Foundation began to financially distance itself from a near total financial reliance on Grants equities in the late 1960s, a move spurred in part by the asset diversification requirements for charitable foundations included in the federal Tax Reform Law of 1969. As it was, foundation board chairman R. McAllister Lloyd had already long advocated for the foundation to move its endowment portfolio away from a heavy reliance on W.T. Grant Company stock.

Since its 1936 founding, the foundation's principal endowment fund was invested in a combined 1.3 million common and preferred shares of the W.T. Grant Company, with annual dividend income in support of foundation grant awards rising from $10,000 in 1937 to $4 million by 1970.

In 1969, foundation trustees adopted and began implementing a plan to diversify The Grant Foundation's investments through the sale and reinvestment of its existing stake in Grants common and preferred shares, which at their peak represented 12 percent of the company's outstanding shares. Between 1969 and 1972, the foundation sold nearly 900,000 of its 1.3 million shares of Grants stock.

And in a 1970 shift in focus, the William T. Grant Foundation ended its Grant Charitable Trust program, established in 1956 to award needs-based four-year William T. Grant Scholarships in support of the college or university studies of eligible Grants employees and the children of active or retired Grants employees nationwide, with applicant testing services provided by Educational Testing Service of Princeton, New Jersey. Using test results, scholastic standing and personal history information, the Grant Charitable Trust provided scholarship awards ranging from $200 to $2,500 annually, subject to appropriate scholastic standing and predicated on continued financial need. A total of 364 scholarships were funded by The Grant Foundation between 1956 and 1970, when the final slate of four-year scholarship recipients were announced.

As it entered the 1970s, The Grant Foundation began shifting its grant award investments toward social services, education, child mental health, social policy and advocacy efforts on behalf of disadvantaged children and

In the 1970s, the Grant Foundation began providing grant funding to Dame Jane Morris Goodall (pictured in the field in Kenya), David Hamburg and Harry Harlow for their primate studies, believed to be relevant to human psychology and social behavior. After sixty years studying their social and family interactions, English primatologist, anthropologist and ethologist Goodall (1934–) is considered the world's foremost expert on wild chimpanzees. *William T. Grant Foundation Collection, Rockefeller Archive Center.*

youth, including the foundation's instrumental role in the creation of the Children's Defense Fund.

In the 1970s, The Grant Foundation also began providing grant funding to Jane Goodall, David Hamburg and Harry Harlow for their primate studies, believed to be relevant to human psychology and social behavior.

Following William T. Grant's death at age ninety-six on August 6, 1972, Grant Foundation Board Chairman R. McAllister Lloyd paid a special five-page tribute to Grant in the foundation's 1972 annual report:

> *Although expressing his own interests and preferences from time to time, Mr. Grant nonetheless made it clear from the start that the board of directors would have broad powers of discretion over what fields of endeavor the foundation would support, and recognized that it would want to change its emphasis from time to time, as new knowledge was gained and as new*

opportunities and new problems arose. Mr. Grant expressed the hope that the foundation would assist in developing "a cumulative body of knowledge which will have comprehensive social value." At the same time, he made it clear that he was equally concerned to have such information put to the test in guiding young people to happy and productive lives, as well as to assist in establishing new programs of training and education which would be of assistance in that endeavor....The trustees and officers of the foundation are mindful of the basic intent Mr. Grant had in establishing the foundation. Although the program has changed, and will continue to change, from time to time, in response to ever-changing social needs, we all share a deep sense of responsibility to continue the board and well-conceived program of its founder.

The next several years proved to be a financially tumultuous time for The Grant Foundation with the ensuing decline and fall of the W.T. Grant Company. The immediate net effect of Grants' bankruptcy was a 50 percent reduction in income available for grant awards.

While the foundation had begun a diversification of its investment portfolio in the late 1960s, 400,000 shares of Grants stock still held by The Grant Foundation were left worthless and written off, with a resulting drop in the foundation's assets from $73 million to $48 million before recovering in the late 1970s and 1980s. A beneficiary trust comprising 864,000 shares of Grants stock, bequeathed to the foundation following William T. Grant's 1972 death and slated to be disbursed to The Grant Foundation over a period of years beginning in 1977, were also rendered worthless by Grants' 1975 bankruptcy and 1976 liquidation.

Litigation against The Grant Foundation beginning in 1976, related to its endowment diversification initiative out of a sole reliance on Grants equities, was successfully resolved in the foundation's favor in 1980, bringing a troubled decade to a close.

Philip Sapir, former assistant dean at the Albert Einstein College of Medicine, succeeded Bond in 1976, with The Grant Foundation renamed the William T. Grant Foundation in January 1977.

Closing out the decade, the foundation in 1979 moved to new quarters at 919 3rd Avenue. Relocated to 515 Madison Avenue in 1987, the William T. Grant Foundation moved to the eighteenth floor of the G.E. Building, 517 Lexington Avenue, in 1997. In 2018, the William T. Grant Foundation moved to new leased quarters encompassing the entire forty-third floor at One Grand Central Place, 60 East 42nd Street in New York.

In 1986, the William T. Grant Foundation formed its Commission on Work, Family and Citizenship to undertake an ambitious multi-year research project focusing on the plight of the 50 percent of U.S. children not attending college. The project culminated in the November 1988 publication of *The Forgotten Half: Pathways to Success for America's Youth and Young Families. William T. Grant Foundation.*

In 1981, Robert Haggerty, MD, began a twelve-year tenure as president of the William T. Grant Foundation, with the foundation's focus shifting to studies of older school-age children and the 1982 establishment of the foundation's Faculty Scholars Program, today's William T. Grant Scholars, in response to major federal funding cuts to social science research.

Taking a page from the foundation's landmark Grant Study, the William T. Grant Foundation embarked on an ambitious new research initiative in 1986 with the creation of the Commission on Youth and America's Future, which studied the plight of the 50 percent of U.S. children not attending college. The work of the commission, which included First Lady Hillary Rodham Clinton of Arkansas, came to fruition with the publication of *The Forgotten Half: Pathways to Success for America's Youth and Young Families*. Building on the work begun with *The Forgotten Half*, the foundation continued its focus on America's underserved children and youth.

In commemoration of the William T. Grant Foundation's fiftieth anniversary in 1986, Yale University doctoral student Emily Cahan was commissioned to write a comprehensive history of the foundation—*The First Fifty Years: 1936–1986*—in collaboration with Professor William Kessen. In the foundation's 1986 annual report, President Robert J. Haggerty noted that the history "documents a remarkable consistency of purpose" in the foundation's mission to "further understanding of human behavior through research," while maintaining the flexibility to support special projects as the needs arose.

In 1991, Haggerty was succeeded by psychiatrist Beatrix Hamburg, MD, as the foundation's first female president. The first African American woman to attend the Yale School of Medicine, Hamburg was distinguished in the field of psychiatry for advancing the fields of

Membership of the 1986–88 William T. Grant Foundation Commission on Work, Family and Citizenship included First Lady of Arkansas Hillary Rodham Clinton (*right*), seen here with Karen Hein, MD, a leading physician and health policy expert who would serve as president of the William T. Grant Foundation from 1988 to 2003. *William T. Grant Foundation.*

youth and adolescent psychiatry. Under Hamburg, the foundation's focus increasingly shifted toward the prevention of youth violence and addressing minority youth issues.

In 1998, Hamburg was succeeded by leading physician and health policy expert Karen Hein, MD, who put an emphasis on grant support of positive youth development initiatives and "helping the nation value young people as a resource."

In the new millennium, the William T. Grant Foundation launched two significant initiatives—improving the quality of after-school programs and understanding and improving youth social settings.

Hein was succeeded internally in 2003 with the appointment of Robert C. Granger, EdD, the William T. Grant Foundation's senior vice-president for programming and an expert in evaluating policies and programs affecting children and youth.

In 2004, the William T. Grant Foundation launched its Distinguished Fellows program, and in 2006 it launched its Youth Service Improvement Grants program to help New York City community-based organizations strengthen their youth-oriented programs. In 2009, the William T. Grant Foundation launched a new funding interest with its Understanding the Acquisition, Interpretation and Use of Research Evidence in Policy and Practice, in response to concerns that, too often, research findings are not used to improve the lives of young people, the ultimate aim of the foundation. Later, in 2015, the foundation announced a new phase of this initiative, calling for research that identifies, creates and tests strategies to improve the use of research evidence in ways that benefit youth.

Granger was succeeded in 2013 by University of Wisconsin–Madison sociology professor Adam Gamoran, PhD, a renowned scholar of educational inequality. Soon after, in 2014, the foundation launched its newest research interest—programs, policies and practices that reduce inequalities in the academic, behavioral, social and economic outcomes of young people. Also launched under Gamoran's leadership was the Institutional Challenge Grant, which challenges universities to form partnerships with public agencies or nonprofit organizations, jointly develop and execute research to reduce inequality in youth outcomes, build the capacity of the agency to use evidence in its decision-making and shape the incentive structure in the university to reward partnership-oriented, engaged scholarship.

Gamoran explained:

> *Making research evidence useful is a major goal for the William T. Grant Foundation. Shortly after I arrived, my colleagues and I launched a new effort to support research on reducing inequality in youth outcomes. Many social scientists have excelled at showing the extent and sources of inequality and documenting its terrible consequences, but studies that identify ways to reduce inequality are all too rare in our field. I am convinced we can do more. Social science can make unique contributions by motivating approaches to reducing inequality, identifying the mechanisms through which programs work, or fail to work, to reduce inequality, and providing evidence of the effectiveness of specific efforts to reduce inequality. And making these contributions will be just the start. Most of us have the idea that our job*

The William T. Grant Foundation Board of Directors, pictured on October 24, 2023, at the foundation's One Grand Central Place headquarters in New York City. Shown from left are Kenji Hakuta, Greg Duncan, Mark Soler, Russell P. Pennoyer, Elizabeth Birr Moje, President Adam Gamoran, Andrés Alonso, Estelle B. Richman, Scott Evans and Hirokazu Yoshikawa. *William T. Grant Foundation.*

> *is to produce credible findings, write them up, and assume that the findings will be useful to practitioners or policymakers. It turns out, that's not enough to get our research findings used for decisions....As grantees of the William T. Grant Foundation's use of research evidence portfolio have shown, more important than the quality of evidence is the quality of relations between producers and consumers of evidence, and the intermediaries who knit them together. Research-practice partnerships are one way to build relationships between producers and consumers of evidence, and we are seeing those mergers all across the country.*

More than eighty years after the founding of the William T. Grant Foundation, and more than fifty years after founder William T. Grant's death, the ebullient can-do spirit and single-minded vision of the affectionately remembered "Uncle Billie" lives on at the foundation's new Midtown Manhattan headquarters.

"William T. Grant was a visionary businessman who believed, back in 1936 when he started the foundation, that social science research was the key to learning how young people could grow up to live happy and productive lives," Gamoran noted. "In fact, he observed at the time that 'economics is being well covered by various organizations, but there remains a vast field in sociology for foundation activity.' Today, we fund research in sociology, economics, psychology, and other fields, all aimed at improving the lives of young people."

ABOUT THE AUTHOR

A native of Milwaukee now living in Rockford, Illinois, award-winning Midwest journalist Eric A. Johnson has earned forty-five writing, photography and community service awards from a variety of organizations over his career, including those awarded by Wisconsin Newspaper Association and the National Newspaper Association. An alumnus of Marquette University in Milwaukee, he is the author of three other Arcadia Publishing books: *Rockford: 1900–World War I* (2003), *Rockford: 1920 and Beyond* (2004) and *Ashtabula Firefighting* (2006). A retired sixteen-year second-generation Wisconsin volunteer firefighter, serving in a variety of roles including fire prevention officer, public information officer, assistant fire chief and fire chief with the Boulder Junction Volunteer Fire Department, Johnson was awarded Emergency Responder of the Year honors by the Wisconsin legislature in 2021. A longtime local historian and lifelong fan of the W.T. Grant Company, Johnson teamed with downtown Rockford businessmen Jerry Kortman and Doc Slafkoski in the early 1990s to successfully lobby the City of Rockford Historic Preservation Commission to bestow protective landmark status to downtown Rockford's long-vacant circa 1931 Art Deco W.T. Grant Building, saving it from impending demolition and paving the way for its subsequent preservation and restoration as a revitalized and vibrant downtown anchor space. For more Grants images and history, readers are invited to view Johnson's "Known for Values: Remembering the W.T. Grant Company" page on Facebook.

Visit us at
www.historypress.com